Retiring to

Spain

Guy Hobbs

Published by Vacation Work,
9 Park End Street, Oxford
www.vacationwork.co.uk

RETIRING TO SPAIN
by Guy Hobbs

First edition 2006

Copyright © Vacation Work 2006

ISBN 13: 978-1-85458-361-1
ISBN 10: 1-85458-361-1

Publicity by Charles Cutting

Cover design by mccdesign

Typeset by Vacation Work

Cover photograph: fountain in the Plaza Mayor, Merida

Printed and bound in Italy by Legoprint SpA, Trento

Contents

PART 1 – BEFORE YOU GO

Setting the Scene

Basics

PART II – A NEW HOME IN SPAIN

Where to Retire

Your New Home in Spain

Housing Finance

PART III – A NEW LIFE IN SPAIN

Adapting to Your New Life

Quality of Life

Personal Finance

Healthcare

Crime, Security and the Police

Returning Home

Case Histories

MAPS

ACKNOWLEDGEMENTS

The author would like to thank everybody who helped with this book, especially Joanne and David Kitching and all at the Gandia Area Social Club for welcoming me into their fold and providing accommodation, entertainment and interviews.

In addition, this book could not have been written without the assistance, expertise, hospitality, time and patience of the following individuals and organisations: Ashley Clark of *Needanadviser.com* for his guidance on all financial matters, Charles Svoboda, president of *Abusos Urbanisticos No* (www.abusos-no.org) for checking and adding to the section on the LUV in the Valencia region, Mrs Audrey Zortea for her hospitality, Patricia Webb and all at the *Age Concern España* office in Torrevieja, IMSERSO (*Instituto de Mayores y Servicios Sociales*), Maurice Hamlin of www.practicalspain. com, The Spanish Embassy in London, Mary Anderton and all at the U3A in Calpe for inviting me along to their AGM, TurEspaña – the Spanish National Tourist Office, Virginia Yanez Gonzalez, Phil Pembroke for his knowledge of angling in Spain, John Butler for his ornithological insights, and finally Clodagh and Dick Handscombe for information on gardening and rambling in Spain. Dan Boothby's *Buying a House in Spain* has proved an invaluable source for the chapter on buying, renting and restoring property.

Special thanks also to all those who have enriched these pages with their personal experiences and anecdotes: Andrew and Margaret Slepyan, Anthony Pieter van Antwerpen, David and Joanne Kitching, David and Liz Austen, Danny Dana, Graham Smith, Ian Adams, Jane Martin, Lindy Walsh, Mac and Meryl Macdonald, Margaret Jones, Margaret Hales, Michael and Vivian Harvey, Raymond Fletcher, Sam Jones and Valerie Mash.

FOREWORD

The first edition of *Retiring to Spain* comes hot on the heels of news that by 2020, one in five older people will be living outside the UK. This is at least partly because notions of retirement have changed. Without exception, the retirees interviewed during the course of writing this book agreed that they didn't see their retirement as time for a well earned rest after years of toil, but as a new beginning; a time to finally enjoy all of the things that they didn't have time for during their working lives.

By far the most popular location for retirement is Spain (Over 77,000 British people are drawing their pension in Spain, second only to Australia and Ireland). This is hardly a surprise. As the UK's most popular holiday destination, the country holds special memories for many of us: blissful weather, stunning beaches, and cheap food and wine, but in recent years we have also come to realise that Spain is so much more than a resort destination. Spain offers savage landscapes of such startling diversity that the budding rambler, cyclist or wildlife enthusiast will never tire of their appeal. The cities of Spain are also being recognised as some of the hippest in Europe, and culture lovers can while away hours of their retirement marvelling at the elegant architecture of Barcelona, the galleries of Madrid, Bilbao's Guggenheim, and the ravishingly romantic squares of Seville. Ever since being released from the shackles of dictatorship over thirty years ago, the Spanish have adopted an attitude of living for every single moment. Nowhere in Europe will you find so many festivities, enjoyed by a fiery, passionate people who like nothing more than to take to the streets in the spirit of celebration. Whatever else it may be, retirement in Spain will certainly not be dull.

Whilst the idea of retiring to Spain may have been an impossibility for previous generations, it is now an increasingly viable option. For a start, there are regular flights from the UK to all of Spain's thirty international airports and with so many budget carriers in operation these days, the cost of returning home for visits is negligible. Secondly, house prices, although having risen non-stop in Spain for the last twenty years, are still lower than in the UK, and the proceeds from selling your UK property will hopefully allow you to buy a beautiful Spanish home, and leave you enough left over to supplement your retirement income. As the cost of living is at least 20% cheaper than in the UK, that income should also go a lot further, leaving you with greater reserves to spend on enjoying yourself. Finally, with around half a million British people already living in Spain, the transition should be fairly simple. Even if your Spanish is not quite up to scratch, the presence of so many of your compatriots will help ease you into a new culture; a culture with a gentler pace of life, lower crime rates and a sense of community spirit that harks back to a Britain of several decades ago.

Of course it won't all be plain sailing. The language barrier may prove a problem, and you should certainly be prepared to jump through numerous bureaucratic hoops in order to become a resident property owner in Spain, but the consensus amongst the hundreds of thousands of Brits already there is that it is worth it. With this book as a guide, a little pioneering spirit and boundless enthusiasm, it won't be long before you're sitting in the evening sunshine, with the scent of orange blossom heavy in the air and a glass of Rioja in your hand, wondering why you didn't think of retiring to Spain sooner.

Guy Hobbs
Oxford
May 2006

TELEPHONE NUMBERS

Please note that the telephone numbers in this book are written as needed to call that number from inside the same country. Spanish numbers are easily distinguished from UK numbers. They are made up of 9 digits (eg.965-241309). All Spanish landline numbers begin with a 9, and all mobile numbers begin with a 6. To call these numbers from outside the country you will need to know the relevant access code.

To call Spain from the UK: Dial 00 34 and the number given in this book.

To call the UK from Spain: Dial 00 44 and the number given in this book minus the first 0.

Part one

Before
You Go

Setting the Scene
Basics

Setting the Scene

CHAPTER SUMMARY

○ Almost a million Britons already draw their pension abroad, and many more have retired early to the sunshine. People no longer dread reaching retirement age, but look forward to a new life-stage free of the shackles of the 9-to-5 day.

○ The Spanish themselves put quality of life first and those who can afford it are retiring early to enjoy their independence and pursue their leisure interests.

○ Retiring to Spain is a well-trodden path for the British. They are lured by sunshine and cheap beer, but stay for deeper qualities such as the savage landscape, glorious architecture, the customs, the food and the people.

○ For now retirement is well funded, but the country's ageing population puts the future of the Spanish pension into question.

○ Many consider Spain's attraction to lie in the more traditional, gentler way of life, where there is less violent crime and a greater sense of community.

○ Many foreigners choose to become part of an expatriate community. If that doesn't appeal, the country is 2½ times the size of the UK, and there is plenty of space to find your own perfect hideaway.

○ In the last three decades Spain has undergone an enormous economic transformation. Spaniards today are around 75% richer than they were 30 years ago.

○ Family is of the utmost importance to Spaniards and it is common for three or four generations to live together.

○ The Spanish have an unmatched zest for socialising. They love a good party and the number of fiestas has increased every year since the end of the Franco regime.

THE NEW 'OLD': CHANGING ATTITUDES TO RETIREMENT

At the start of the twenty-first century we are in the midst of a major social transformation. The post-war notion of retirement as a time to put your slippers on and settle in front of the telly with a nice cup of tea is fast becoming obsolete. The very word 'retirement', not to mention the images of encroaching decrepitude that it conjures, no longer fits the reality of how people are living their lives post full-time employment. Today's retirees are often younger, fitter and wealthier than their forebears and together they are reshaping the very meaning of 'old age' and 'retirement'.

Many social commentators suggest that these changes are being wrought by the baby boomer generation. Born between 1945 and 1965, they are a force to be reckoned with, making up almost a third of the UK population and responsible for nearly 80% of all financial wealth. The baby boomers grew up in an era of postwar optimism and new social freedoms, and as such, have always represented a force for social change. Indeed, they have spent a lifetime reconstructing social norms. In 2006 the first wave of this generation is approaching retirement age, and with such political and financial clout their approach to growing old is profoundly different. As *The Times* recently put it: *'the pioneers of the consumer society are unlikely to settle for an electric fire and a can of soup'*.

One of the main reasons that the concept of retirement is changing is that people are living far longer. Life expectancy in the twentieth century rose by 20 years due to better healthcare and greater health awareness. Around 18 million people in the UK are over 60. This is creating something of a crisis in the British economy and if the government had its way, then we would all work until we dropped, easing the pressure on the already over-burdened state pension fund. The new generation of retirees however, are not prepared to do this. Not only are people living longer, they are also leaving the workforce younger. Many are giving up work in their early fifties when they are still fit and active, in order to enjoy a new stage in life – not their 'retirement', according to the American website www.2young2retire.com, but their 'renaissance'.

A recent report by *Demos*, a democracy think tank, claims that the baby boomers are intent on having their time again; of creating a new life phase in which they can revisit their own desire for personal fulfilment, free

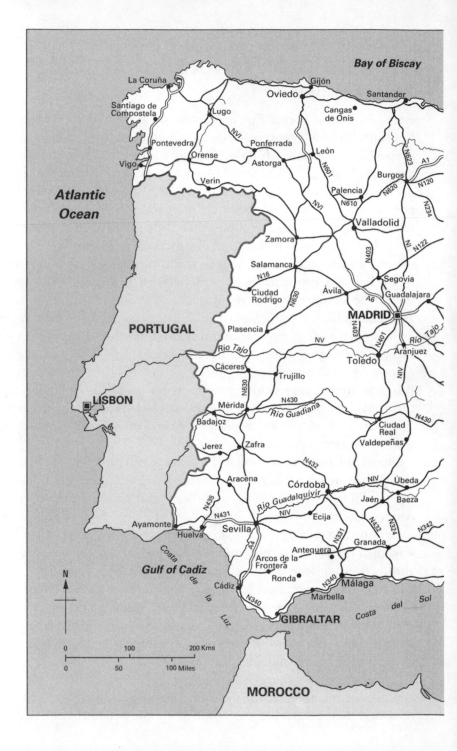

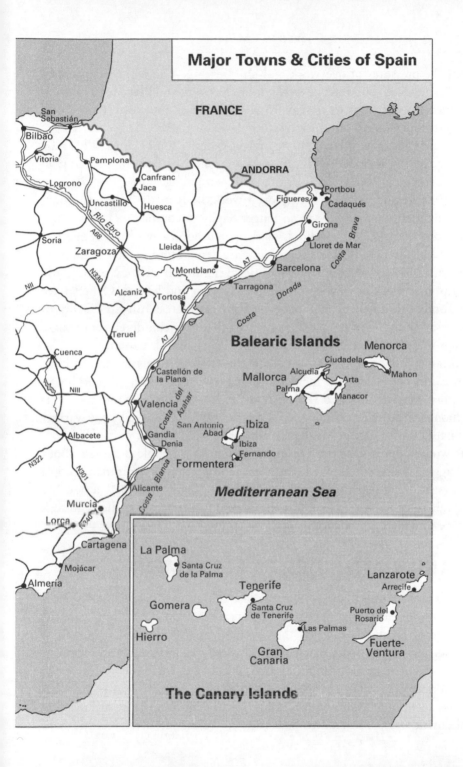

Major Towns & Cities of Spain

FRANCE

ANDORRA

San Sebastián
Bilbao
Vitoria
Pamplona
Logrono
Canfranc
Jaca
Uncastillo
Huesca
Soria
Zaragoza
Lleida
Figueres
Portbou
Cadaqués
Girona
Lloret de Mar
Barcelona

Río Ebro
A68
N330
NII

Montblanc
Tarragona
Costa Brava
Costa Dorada

Alcaniz
Tortosa
Teruel
Cuenca
NIII
A7

Castellón de
la Plana

Balearic Islands

Menorca
Ciudadela
Mahon
Arta
Manacor

Mallorca
Alcudia
Palma

Costa del Azahar

Valencia
Albacete
N322
N301
Gandia
Denia

San Antonio
Abad
Ibiza
Ibiza
Fernando
Formentera

Costa Blanca

Alicante
Murcia
Lorca
N340
Cartagena
Mojácar
Almeria

Mediterranean Sea

La Palma
Santa Cruz
de la Palma

Tenerife
Santa Cruz
de Tenerife

Gomera

Hierro

Las Palmas

Gran
Canaria

Lanzarote
Arrecife

Puerto del
Rosario

Fuerte-
Ventura

The Canary Islands

from the pressures of overwork and childrearing. The report identifies a new 'experience economy' of travel, food, learning and lifestyle. The baby boomers do not want to retreat from the world as the word 'retirement' suggests, but to head out into it with renewed vigour.

The new retirement is all about finding a better life balance. This may not necessarily include giving up work – around half of the people who leave permanent 'career' jobs before state pension age move initially into part-time, temporary or self-employed work, be it in the UK or abroad. It would seem that people are no longer happy to compartmentalise their lives into linear stages – school, work, parenthood – with retirement at the end of the line. Retirees these days are demanding greater flexibility; preferring to see life as a never-ending cycle, in which they can choose to dip in and out of periods of work, education and leisure. Others have the funds behind them to pursue a hobby or interest full-time. And an increasing number of people have realised that they can do either of these things in a climate far removed from the dreary British winter.

Almost a million Britons already draw their state pensions abroad, and this figure does not include the many more who have retired early. According to a report from Alliance and Leicester, one in five older people (an extra four million) will be living outside the UK by the year 2020, lured by the warmer climate, a slower pace of life, health advantages and a lower cost of living.

It would appear that the prevailing gloom that people once felt about the ageing process is slowly being replaced by a sunny optimism. People no longer dread reaching retirement age, but eagerly anticipate a new life stage, in which, released from the shackles of full-time work, they can seek out new cultural experiences.

SPANISH ATTITUDES TO RETIREMENT

Spain's rapid modernisation over the last thirty years has led to an enormous amount of social change in all areas of Spanish life, not least the attitude of Spaniards towards their retirement. Many social commentators suggest that as Spain catches up politically, economically and socially, after years of repression under Franco, it becomes increasingly European in outlook. Hence the changes in attitudes to retirement in the UK, discussed above, are becoming increasingly prevalent in Spain. Until recently retirement was considered to be a time for relaxation after years of hard

work in the factories, or tilling the land. Retirees lived with the families of their offspring, and were looked after and cared for in the home. These days retirement has become a time of far greater independence. Spanish pensioners are healthier and more active than ever before.

Spain is one of the healthiest places in the world to live. Spanish women are the longest living group of people in Europe, living to an average age of 83.7, three years longer than women in the UK. Spanish men on the other hand can expect to live to 77.2 years. A recent report by the pharmaceutical company *Pfizer* suggests that Spain's excellent health care system, and a diet with lots of olive oil and red wine are responsible for the longevity of its people. Considering that women in Spain can retire and receive a pension at 60, and men at 65, retirees anticipate a long and active retirement and look forward to a far better quality of life once they have dispensed with full-time work.

For most retirees family ties remain an overwhelming priority. As more women enter the workplace, there are more and more families where both parents work. This has led to a new social phenomenon that the Spanish media has christened *'abuelos canguros'* (baby-sitter grandparents). Retirees that are far fitter and healthier than their own parents were at a similar age relish the chance to help bring up the children and have become indispensable to working parents.

Nevertheless, it is now far less common for the elder generation to live with their children (although it is still the case for the very frail or infirm as retirement homes are expensive and still something of a rarity in Spain). For many of today's retirees, those who began work in Franco's Spain, retirement has become their first opportunity to really enjoy the new liberal Spain; their first opportunity to travel and leave the towns and cities where they have spent their entire adult lives.

Those who can afford it are buying up houses in the countryside and on the costas and spending their time pursuing leisure interests such as walking and swimming. The Spanish government has recognised this desire to travel and in the last few years has set up the *'Viajes del IMSERSO'* for those with lower financial reserves. The Institute of Migration and Social Services in Spain established these subsidised trips for people of the *tercera edad* (third age) in 2000 and they have become an enormous success. These trips only run in the winter and have helped to revolutionise the tourism sector. Coastal towns such as Benidorm are taken over by Spanish (as well as British, German and Dutch) pensioners almost immediately after the hoardes of sun-seeking tourists have left.

Retirement is well funded in Spain, to the extent that private pension schemes were virtually unheard of until recent years. The state pension that an individual receives is equal to the minimum wage related to their occupational category and so is sufficient for most to live on. Equally impressive is that healthcare and prescription medicine in Spain are free for pensioners. However, Spain's ageing population means that a growing number of retirees are being supported by fewer and fewer workers. The future of the Spanish pension is therefore in jeopardy and by 2015, when there will be over 7.5 million pensioners, the state pension may run into problems. The government is therefore encouraging the establishment of private and company pension funds, and – as in the UK – it is likely that future governments will attempt to raise the age of retirement.

REASONS TO RETIRE TO SPAIN

Recent research by Parador Properties attempting to unravel the mystery of why British retirees are escaping to Spain in record numbers came up with three main answers. First and foremost people are attracted by the climate; secondly they are looking for the opportunity to spend more time outdoors and generally be more active; and finally they are lured by the cheaper cost of living. Overwhelmingly then, people are seeking a better quality of life from their move to Spain but whilst it may be these more superficial factors which lure people to Spain, it is the deeper qualities of the Spanish way of life and culture which captivates them and prevents them from returning home.

Climate. Spain's climate is certainly a draw, especially for those coming from the more dreary and drizzly climes of northern Europe. In fact Spain's climate varies dramatically, but it is possible to enjoy sunshine all year round, especially on the southern Mediterranean coast and in the Canary Islands. The Costa del Sol offers expatriates 3,000 sun hours each year, an enormous benefit for those who enjoy being able to spend time outside. Clearly not all of Spain offers such a climate, and those who choose to move to Galicia or anywhere along the Costa Verde in the north, will discover a climate not dissimilar to that of Ireland. It is for this reason that the majority of expats choose to retire to the south.

Spain's climate not only gives you a feeling of smug satisfaction when you listen to the British weather forecast, but it also allows for a completely different lifestyle as expat Valerie Mash explains:

The best thing about my life here is that I am always outside and not stuck indoors as I was in the UK. I spend many pleasurable hours on my roof terrace just enjoying the sunshine, or cooking and eating dinner. I swim in the sea, I walk in the mountains. It's bliss. I never watch television any more – in fact I threw my aerial away!

Health Advantages – Keeping Fit and Active. Retirees cite the health advantages of living in Spain, which come from the mild climate and the ability to spend more time being active. This is not just a myth: the Spanish have one of the highest life expectancies in Europe. Indeed the World Health Organisation recently claimed that the Valencian coastline is one of the healthiest places to live on earth due to its climate, recreational facilities and relaxed way of life. Dietary factors in Spain lead to a far lower number of cases of heart disease, as does the relaxed way of life and reduced stress levels. Those who are healthy and active upon arrival in Spain can therefore hope to remain so for longer. Even those who arrive in Spain with minor health issues, find the climate and way of life beneficial and many retirees claim to find relief from arthritic or rheumatic ailments within a few weeks. Certainly those living in the south of Spain will find that there is a much lower incidence of the colds and flu that affect UK residents during the cold damp winters.

The ability to be mobile, to take leisurely walks in the fresh air and warm sunshine also has obvious health benefits and statistics do show that older people stay healthy for longer in Spain's stress-free climate. Karen O'Reilly in her sociological study, *The British on the Costa del Sol* (Routledge, 2000) sees an enormous contrast between the elderly in Britain, where grey skies can sap their motivation to go out for walks, play bowls, swim, or simply chat with friends in a nearby café or bar:

It often struck me how different the elderly migrants in Spain looked compared with elderly people in Britain. They wore bright colours, suntans, shorts and T-shirts, lots of jewellery, and smiles. They looked fit and healthy…The migrants were aware of a feeling of freedom from restriction on dress and behaviour. I overheard Joan, a Resident in her fifties, tell her new migrant friend, 'You can wear what you like, no-one takes any notice really. I couldn't dress like this back home, not at my age!

Cost of Living. The lower cost of living is also important. Crucially it is the things that make life more enjoyable that are considerably cheaper: wine, beer, cigarettes, eating out, leisure activities. The warm climate also reduces the excessive heating bills that we are forced to pay in the UK. However, many of life's necessities are not that much cheaper and certainly prices are catching up. For example house prices in Spain have been rising steadily for years now, becoming restrictively expensive in the bigger cities. Estimates suggest that overall, the cost of living is around 20% lower than in the UK.

Ease of Travel. Clearly the country's increasing accessibility is a major factor. Getting to and from Spain has never been easier (see *Getting There and Away*), with an ever-increasing number of no-frills carriers offering more and more regular flights to numerous destinations in Spain. Any worries that you may have had about losing touch with family and friends can be forgotten. For expat Ian Adams, who still has family in the UK, this was a decisive factor: *'The beauty of Spain for me is that it is so accessible. I know that if anything happens at home then I can get a flight back in two hours, and I won't even have to worry about the cost'.*

British Communities. There are two broad types of British retiree. The first group wants to retire to an area where there are already other Brits and they have a ready-make social circle; where they do not necessarily need to learn the language, and can find English-speaking shops and services. The other group consider themselves to be true hispanophiles and scorn the ghetto expats, who they see as having brought Blackpool to the Med. Whereas the hispanophiles can be found assimilating into Spanish life all over the country, the former group tends to be based on the costas. For many, the presence of so many Brits makes the transition to life in Spain that much easier and offers the chance to become part of a new community. For retirees who want to remain active this can be an enormous advantage, as British journalist Bettina Brown, who lived and worked just outside Marbella for seventeen years, found. She writes:

There are clubs for just about everything you can think of: bridge, chess, amateur dramatics, while classical music and the sporting facilities are excellent. There are so many charities which need helpers that those who are not sporty, loathe bridge and have few hobbies still have an opportunity to socialise and to make friends. There is no need to be lonely.

Way of Life. For the hispanophiles, the presence of so many British, Dutch and German communities represents a corruption of the uniquely Spanish way of life that they have come to enjoy. Fortunately Spain is two and a half times the size of the UK and has only two thirds of the population, so there are vast areas of unspoilt beauty away from the noisy and hectic coastal resorts. Many people consider the attraction of Spain to lie in its more traditional, gentler way of life. Emigrants rave about Spanish characteristics such as the lack of violent crime, feeling safe in the streets, the respect that young people show for the elderly, the love of children that the Spanish display and the sense of community. Many foreigners, such as Jane Martin who lives in Valencia, are lucky enough to be accepted into this community and find the warmth of the Spanish people remarkable:

My husband and I are the only foreigners in our block of 50 flats but they make us feel so welcome. Recently, after a spell of illness, I received a gift - a hamper of food and wine from the family across the hall. When we knocked on the door to say thank you for being such lovely neighbours, he looked aghast and said – 'Neighbours? We are not neighbours, we are family'. It is a truly wonderful community and we have made many lasting friendships.

There is undeniably a slower pace of life in Spain. The country has modernised incredibly quickly over the last few decades, yet somehow much of the country has retained strong rural and agricultural roots and the air of a simpler more relaxed way of life.

Even those who live within expat communities find themselves becoming more laid back, as expat Margaret Jones describes:

In England we are governed by the clock, but everybody has so much more time here. Trying to organise coffee with a friend back home requires getting the diaries out. But here, if you're out taking a stroll and bump into a friend, it naturally follows that you go for a drink or even lunch.

PROS & CONS

Pros

B Easy access thanks to the cheap flight revolution. This means you can afford to travel back to the UK frequently, or quickly in the case of an emergency, and you can encourage friends and family to visit.

B Land and property are cheaper than in the UK, as is the general cost of living. Your private funds or your pension will go much further. Those with a UK property can sell it and use the proceeds to upgrade to a luxury villa and fund their retirement.

B Spain is two and a half times the size of the UK, so you are bound to find your perfect home, be it a timbledown finca in the mountains, a spacious apartment in the city, or a luxury villa with sea views.

B The Spanish lifestyle is much more relaxed and geared towards outside activities.

B A superb variety of cuisine and wine, available at a fraction of the cost you would pay in the UK.

B Buying property in Spain is a well-trodden path for the British, so it is easy to find good legal and financial advice, in English, from professionals with many years of experience.

B The bureaucratic procedures relating to foreigners from the EU living in Spain have been simplified in recent years.

Cons

B Retiring to Spain means making new friends and creating a new social life for yourself, which may be difficult if your Spanish is not up to much or if you choose to live away from the costas.

B Spanish bureaucracy is cumbersome and can be extremely frustrating. Those without sufficient Spanish skills may need to employ the services of a *gestor*, or administrative assistant.

B Property prices in the most popular areas (i.e. the costas and the bigger cities) have risen rapidly in recent years and are now on a par with UK property prices.

B Some of the cheaper regions in which to buy property are cheap for a reason: they may be remote and slightly backward and the inhabitants may not be accustomed to foreigners.

B Whilst the public health system in Spain is first class, those retirees who reach old age may find that the infrastructure for caring for the elderly and infirm is in its infancy and the provision of social care can vary enormously from one town to the next.

INTRODUCING SPAIN

The history of Spain is fascinating and it would take more than several retirements' worth of reading to exhaust all its subjects. There are hordes of Spanish history titles and the Spanish Bookshop (www.thespanishbookshop.com), Amazon (www.amazon.co.uk) or local libraries are good places to start. Below is a chronology of some pivotal events in Spanish history, which may help to set the scene of the country you have adopted for retirement.

Key Dates Of Spanish History

219 BC The first Roman troops invade the Iberian Peninsular during the second Punic War against the Carthaginians. The province of Hispania is annexed under Augustus.

206 BC-415 AD *Roman Spain.* Spain becomes the most important centre of the Roman Empire after Italy. However, by the third century Hispania becomes increasingly vulnerable to barbarian invasions from northern Europe and Roman influence begins to collapse.

415 The Visigoths march across the Pyrenees and begin their conquest of the Iberian Peninsular. Visigoth Spain is brought to an end in 711 by the invasion of an Arab-led Muslim army. The Moorish conquest is affected with remarkable speed and the land under their control is dubbed 'Al-Andalus'.

711-1469 *Moorish Spain.* Unlike its predecessors, the Arab-Muslim empire was based on religious zeal. In the tenth century Moorish Spain was at the peak of its power and its capital, Córdoba, was the most prosperous and civilised city in Europe. But by 1031 the region had fragmented into small independent kingdoms (*taifas*) and internal divisions weakened resistance to the Christian kingdoms.

727-1469 *The Reconquista.* Throughout the period of Islamic predominance there were pockets of Christian resistance, particularly in Asturías, Cantabria and the Pyranees, which were eventually to form the springboard for the Christian reconquest. The Reconquista was a unifying religious movement upon which the character of Spain was founded.

1037 León-Castile becomes a kingdom under the rule of Fernando I and is now the strongest of the Christian states. There follows a period of kingdom formation in the north.

c.1043-1099 *El Cid.* Spain's most famous medieval hero - Rodrigo Diaz, better known as 'El Cid' has become a legend of the Spanish *Reconquista*. His Christian exploits were romanticised in chronicles written long after his death. Though he may have been a brilliant general, he was more an opportunist than a chivalrous Christian. He amassed a fortune working as a mercenary fighting Christians and Muslims alike and in 1092 he took advantage of the internal disarray in Valencia to seize the city for himself.

1236 Fernando III of León-Castile takes Córdoba on 29 June.

1248 After a three year siege, Seville also falls to the Christians led by Fernando III, bringing Almohad rule in the region to an end. This is the most decisive victory of the Christian Reconquest.

1348 The *Black Death* enters Spain wiping out entire villages, and cutting Barcelona's population in half.

1469 Isabel of Castile marries her cousin Fernando of Aragón in Valladolid uniting the two largest kingdoms in Spain. Subsequently the composite kingdom would become known as España (Spain).

1478 Isabel I inaugurates the *Spanish Inquisition* with the declared purpose of rooting out heresy within the Catholic Church. The first Inquisitor-General was *Tomás de Torquemada*, and in his hands the Inquisition particularly targeted Jewish and Moorish converts to Christianity. Torquemada was ruthless, using torture to extract confession and burning around 2000 heretics at the stake. Throughout its lifespan the inquisition was used as a means of political repression and an instrument of social control.

1479-1516 *Los Reyes Católicos.* Ferdinand and Isabella shared a visionary sense of purpose that was to eventually forge the Spanish nation-state. They established the basis for religious unification of Spain. Under their reign Muslim rule came to an end and Spain gained a reputation as a bastion of the Christian faith; a reputation that gained strength after the discovery of the Americas and the conversion of the Indians. Spain began to establish itself as an empire.

1492 *Christopher Columbus* (1458-1506) sets sail across the Atlantic inaugurating the European conquest of the New World. Columbus's four voyages were an incredible achievement, but he was tyrannical in his dealings with native Americans and motivated by greed. His discovery sowed the seeds of 300 years of pillage and the murdering of millions of American Indians.

1494 The ***Treaty of Tordesillas*** between Portugal and Spain, divides up the non-European world.

1516 Ferdinand dies and is buried in Granada beside Isabella. The crown passes to Ferdinand's grandson Duke Charles of Burgandy who was also to become Holy Roman Emperor.

1516-1700 ***Habsburg Spain.*** Spain's powerful world empire reached its height and declined under the Habsburgs. Charles (Carlos V) was able to pool the resources of the Holy Roman Empire and invest them in imperial venture; giving rise to the conquest of the new world under *conquistadores* Hernán Cortés and Francisco Pizarro. In the 1560s, plans to consolidate control of the Netherlands gradually led to the **Eighty Years' War**, which consumed much Spanish expenditure.

1588 ***The Armada*** – Philip II, angered by Elizabeth I providing the Dutch rebels with supplies, sends a great fleet to invade England. By commandeering England's ports, he aims to reassert supremacy at sea and lead the English back into the Catholic fold. The ensuing battle is a disaster for the Spanish. Half of the fleet and 15,000 men are lost marking a turning point in Spanish imperial history.

1700 Carlos II dies having nominated Louis XIV's grandson Philip of Anjou as his heir. This begins Spain's era of Bourbon monarchs. Philip V's accession to the Spanish throne brings about the ***War of Spanish Succession*** against Archduke Charles of Austria. Gibraltar is seized by the British during the war and under the Treaty of Utrecht, which ends the war in 1713, Spain loses her territories in Belgium, Luxembourg, Italy and Sardinia.

1759 Carlos III accedes to the throne and embarks on a programme of enlightened despotism. There follows a ***Second Golden Era*** in which the empire once again becomes prosperous.

1804-1805 ***The Napoleonic Wars*** Combined Spanish and French fleets are defeated at the battle of Trafalgar in October 1805.

1808-1814 Popular discontent leads to Carlos IV's abdication. Napoleon Bonaparte installs his brother Joseph on the throne. Spain rises up in popular revolt leading to the ***Peninsular War***. The British and Spanish gradually wear the French down. Fernando VII is restored to the throne in 1814.

1873-1874 ***The First Republic.*** King Amadeo abdicates leading to the creation of a short-lived republic.

1891 Universal male suffrage is granted.

1898 The short-lived **Spanish-American War** leads to Cuba's independence.

1914-1918 Spain remains neutral in the **First World War**, but internally there is great social and industrial unrest.

1923-1930 General Primo de Rivera leads a military coup against the government and forms a dictatorship.

1931 The victory of anti-monarchist parties in municipal elections forces the abdication of Alfonso XIII and the **Second Republic** is proclaimed. Women are granted the vote, freedom of worship is guaranteed and Church and State separate.

1933 José Antonio Primo de Rivera creates the *Falange*, a political party based on Mussolini's Fascists.

1936-1939 *The Spanish Civil War* – An incredibly bloody war between Nationalists and Republicans. Half a million Spaniards lose their lives. The Nationalists, led by Franco, received enormous support from Fascist Italy and Nazi Germany. The Republicans won several battles and held out in Madrid but the Nationalists prevailed. When the International Brigades left the Republican side

and Barcelona fell to the Nationalists, it was clear that the war was over. Madrid fell in early 1939.

1939-1975 *Franco's Dictatorship.* Spain was too weak to do anything but remain neutral in **World War II** but Franco's support for the axis powers left Spain economically and culturally isolated. The extreme hardships of the post-war years came to be known as *Los años de hambre* (the years of hunger). However, economic progress came quickly in the latter stages of the dicatorship and the economy grew annualy at a rate of 7% from 1961-1973. Franco's Spain permitted only one political party, the Falange and censorship was rigidly enforced.

1959 AD ETA (*Euskadi Ta Askatasuna*) is founded by a group of militant Basque nationalists, with the goal of achieving Basque independence. IMF loans are agreed for Spain and as a result tourism takes off. By the mid 1960s Britons, French and Germans have started to acquire retirement homes.

1967 AD The people of Gibraltar vote overwhelmingly to remain under British rule.

1975 Franco dies and Juan Carlos de Borbón is proclaimed king. Spain becomes a constitutional monarchy.

MODERN SPAIN

After Franco's death in 1975, King Juan Carlos transferred power to a democratically elected parliament. In consequence Spain has become what can best be described as a federal-monarchy, which the Spaniards call an *estado de las autonomías*. Over the last thirty years Spain has emerged from dictatorship and international isolation, built a successful economy and established an effective democracy. Few countries could claim to have achieved so much, on so many fronts, in such a short space of time.

The Constitution

In 1978, the Spanish constitution was drawn up, largely at the behest of King Juan Carlos. The most important task of the constitution was to allow the devolution of power to the regions, which entitled them to have their own governments, parliaments, regional assemblies and supreme legal authorities. This radical transition to a democratic and devolved system of government, carried out more slowly in some regions than others, formed the present-day seventeen Autonomous Communities of Spain, each having their own flag, capital city and president. The central parliament, or *Cortes*, retains overall control of such matters as foreign policy and defence. Spain is a mosaic of parliaments and regional identities, and local politics still arouse far more interest from Spaniards than the machinations of politicians at a national level.

Modern Political History

The election of 1996 saw in a government led by the Popular Party of José María Aznar. Aznar was able to turn the PP, which had been suspected by many as being Francoist in its sympathies, into a respectable centre-right organisation. He also presided over eight years of economic growth (at an average of 3.2% per year), sound management of the public purse (no budget deficits like those of France, Germany and Italy), fairly low inflation and a cut in the unemployment rate from 22% to 11%. During the first term, Aznar successfully continued the devolution of power to the autonomous communities.

However, the PP increasingly lost touch with the electorate during their second term. The issue that most alienated the electorate was the decision to support the Iraq invasion. Although Spain's involvement was minimal, the very gesture of sending Spanish troops to Iraq provoked outrage. In poll after poll, 90% of Spaniards opposed the war and Spain's part in it. Nevertheless, by early 2004, the polls suggested that the majority of Spaniards would vote the PP in for a third term, under Aznar's chosen successor Mariano Rajoy. The events of March 2004 were to change all of that.

The Madrid Bombings and the 2004 Elections

March 2004 proved to be one of the most dramatic months of recent Spanish history, sending Spain spiralling into a period of transition and uncertainty. In the early hours of 11 March, a dozen bombs exploded on four Madrid commuter trains, killing 191 people and injuring 1,430. The events of the next few days were to prove the undoing of Prime Minister Aznar and the *Partido Popular*, as he attempted to contain and even turn to his political advantage an overwhelming feeling of horror and outrage surging through the country. The government's behaviour in the period between the bombings of 11 March and the elections on 14 March so infuriated a large group of Spaniards that they voted Socialist in disgust. Nobody could have foreseen such an enormous turnaround of public opinion.

One of Aznar's main achievements had been his hard-line against the Basque terrorist group ETA. Had ETA been responsible for these latest attacks, then this surely would have provided Aznar with a popular mandate to continue his zero-tolerance policies. The PP therefore embarked on a policy of 'superspin', promoting indiscriminately the theory that ETA were behind the blasts and suppressing any evidence suggesting that Al-Qaeda were responsible. When the news was finally revealed, despite government attempts to suppress it, that those connected with the bombings had been arrested and that they had suspected Al-Qaeda links, there were enormous demonstrations outside the PP headquarters in Madrid. People felt that they had been betrayed by a government acting purely in its own interests. Turnout at the elections was huge and the PP were defeated by Zapatero's *Partido Socialista Obrero Español (PSOE)*.

The Current Government and the Future

Zapatero's critics suggest that the events of 11 March have thrust him into a position which his lack of government experience and relative youth make him unworthy of. However, the new government has made a strong start embarking on a series of social reforms, which many argue are long overdue. Spain's premier is keen to prove himself as a liberal moderniser in Europe and in 2005, Spain became the third European country to allow same-sex marriages.

Possibly the biggest issue which Zapatero will have to deal with is that of immigration. Spain has been struggling in recent years to assimilate an increasing number of immigrants, mainly from Africa. In less than ten years Spain has transformed from a largely homogeneous nation into a multicultural one and the infrastructure is struggling to cope. With high unemployment, the job prospects in Spain are not as good as the new arrivals anticipated. In 2005, Zapatero took the first bold step towards dealing with the immigration problem, by offering an amnesty for 700,000 illegal residents who can prove that they have a Spanish employment contract. Many have hailed this a humane, realistic and, in the long-term, economically effective approach to the problem. However, violence and deaths at the borders of Ceuta and Melilla in October 2005 prove that the problem is far from resolved.

The Spain of Zapatero's government is rapidly changing and Zapatero's long-term popularity rests on his ability to adapt to the realities of Spain's new circumstances: a richer country with a demand for highly-skilled and educated workers, immigration on such a vast scale; and an internally strained society, managing the differing ambitions of the Basques, Catalans, Galicians etc. The permanent ceasefire declared by ETA in 2006 suggests that he is having some success. Despite the extraordinary circumstances of the socialists' rise to power, they are by no means incapable of the job in hand and Zapatero, who was chosen as party leader largely because of his reputation as a modernizer, will surely make the most of his chance to help shape the new Spain.

The Spanish Economy

Franco's death in 1975 led to a period of rapid liberalisation of the economy. Spain has transformed itself from a backward, rural country with an agriculturally-based economy, to a nation with a diversified economy made up of strong retail, property, industrial and tourism sectors. As recently as 1964, the United Nations classed Spain as a developing nation, yet today Spain takes its modernity for granted.

Recent economic developments such as the joining of the European Monetary Union in 1998, followed by the adoption of the euro in 2002 have placed Spain in a position of strength in the world markets. Spaniards today are about 75% richer than they were thirty years ago, and have seen their economy grow faster than the European average for nearly ten years.

Population

The current population of Spain is around 40.2 million. However there is a wide disparity in the population density region by region: the Basque country and Madrid province together comprise only 3.02% of the total surface area but house around 16% of the population. This population imbalance and the wide variations in prosperity between regions are the result of decades of internal and external migrations, the former from the rural to the industrialised areas, where the cities continue to expand their populations at the expense of the countryside. The largest conurbations are Madrid (3,092,759), Barcelona (1,582,738), Valencia (780,653) and Seville (709,975).

While the populations of several EU countries, notably Italy, France and Germany, have been falling, the population of Spain has been increasing at one of the fastest rates in Europe. This is surprising as the Spanish birth-rate has fallen dramatically to just 1.25 children per woman of child bearing age (compared to 1.64 in the UK). This is perhaps because Spanish women work longer hours, face mounting childcare costs and delay having children until after their 30th birthday.

Two factors help to explain this apparent contradiction. The first is high life expectancy. Figures from the EU's Eurostat department suggest that Spanish women live to an average age of 83.7 and Spanish men, an average of 77.2 years.

The second factor is high immigration and the numbers of children born to immigrants in Spain. For Spain such high immigration is a new experience, driven both by globalisation and Spain's internal demand for cheap labour. There are over 2.6 million foreigners in Spain, mainly coming from Latin American countries (38.6%), especially the Andean countries; Africa (19.6%); and the EU (22%).

Geography

Spain occupies 85% of the great landmass that forms the south-western extremity of Europe, the Iberian Peninsula, covering a total of 194,885 square miles/504,750 sq. km. Including the Balearic and Canary Islands,

Spain is the third-largest European nation after Ukraine and France, and in its average altitude second only to Switzerland. The Pyrenees form a natural barrier between Spain and France to the northeast while Portugal lies to the west. The province of Galicia in the northwest of the country has an Atlantic coast, and northern Spain is demarcated by the Bay of Biscay. The south and east of the country has Mediterranean frontage, and a mere ten miles (16 km) of sea (known as the Strait of Gibraltar) separates Spain from Africa where Spain holds sovereignty over the two tiny enclaves of Melilla and Ceuta in Morocco. The Balearics, which comprise the four main islands of Mallorca, Ibiza, Menorca and Formentera, lie off Spain's northeast coast and occupy 1,936 sq. miles/5,014 sq. km. The Canary Islands, of which seven are inhabited, are situated about sixty miles (97 km) off the west coast of North Africa and occupy 2,808 square miles/7,273 sq. km.

THE SEVENTEEN AUTONOMOUS REGIONS OF SPAIN AND THEIR PROVINCES

ANDALUCÍA – Almería, Cádiz, Córdoba, Granada, Huelva, Jaén, Málaga and Sevilla (Seville)

ARAGÓN – Huesca, Zaragoza (Saragossa), Teruel

ASTURIAS – Oviedo

CANTABRIA – Santander

CASTILLA-LA MANCHA – Albacete, Cuenca, Ciudad Real, Guadalajara, Toledo

CASTILLA Y LÉON – Avila, Burgos, León, Palencia, Salamanca, Segovia, Soria, Valladolid, Zamora

CATALONIA (CATALUÑA) – Barcelona, Girona, Lléida (Lerida), Tarragona

COMUNIDAD DE MADRID – Madrid

EXTREMADURA – Badajoz, Cáceres

GALICIA – A Coruña, Lugo, Orense, Pontevedra

ISLAS BALEARES (BALEARIC ISLANDS) – Palma

ISLAS CANARIAS (CANARY ISLANDS) – Las Palmas de Gran Canaria, Santa Cruz de Tenerife

LA RIOJA – Logroño

MURCIA – Murcia

NAVARRA (NAVARRE) – Pamplona

PAIS VASCO (BASQUE COUNTRY) – Bilbao, Donostia-San Sebastian, Vizcaya-Gasteiz

VALENCIA – Alicante, Castellon, Valencia

Climate Zones

Spain is a country of climatic extremes. In the north-west of the country (Galicia) the climate is as wet and the landscape as correspondingly ver-dant as parts of Wales or Ireland while in the south much of the province of Almería is so arid that Westerns have been filmed in the scrub there.

AVERAGE MAXIMUM TEMPERATURES				
Area	Jan	Apr	Aug	Nov
Cádiz	15°C	21°C	30°C	20°C
Málaga	17°C	21°C	30°C	20°C
Sevilla	15°C	23°C	36°C	20°C
Murcia	12°C	19°C	29°C	20°C
Alicante	16°C	22°C	32°C	21°C
Valencia	15°C	20°C	29°C	19°C
Barcelona	13°C	18°C	28°C	16°C
Santander	12°C	15°C	22°C	15°C
Pontevendra	14°C	18°C	26°C	16°C
Madrid	9°C	18°C	30°C	13°C
Mallorca	14°C	19°C	29°C	18°C
Gran Canaria	21°C	23°C	31°C	24°C

The town of Seville in Andalucía has the highest temperatures in Spain and regularly reaches 34°C/94°F between July and September. By con-trast, Santander, in Cantabria in the north of Spain, has a climate similar to that of England. Inhabitants of the vast area of central Spain known as the *meseta* (tableland) are baked by the sun in summer and endure freezing temperatures in winter. The capital Madrid, located slap bang in the cen-tre of Spain, has the lowest winter temperatures in the country and those looking to buy property there should be prepared for the colder conditions that prevail due to the altitude of the city.

Along the Mediterranean coast the climate is far less variable than in the *meseta*, but the *costas* to the northeast of the country may be subject to cold winds, which in the winter bring snow to the Pyrenees and the *meseta*. The mountainous sierra ranges of the Mediterranean hinterland protect the *costas* from extremes of climate and funnel warm air to them in the summer.

The offshore provinces of Spain – the Balearics and the Canaries – have their own weather patterns. The Balearic Islands usually have warm comfortable summers, tempestuous autumns and colder winters, while the Canaries, situated off the coast of Africa, are in fact nearer to the equator than the Bahamas and their winter climate is correspondingly warm and welcoming to those in search of winter sun.

CULTURE SHOCK

Anyone moving to Spain will have the opportunity of immersing themselves in a culture and way of life that is amongst the liveliest and most colourful in Europe. Many foreigners however, choose to live in Spain because they like the climate and the kind of lifestyle that they have experienced whilst on holiday there, and not necessarily because they like the Spanish and their customs. Whilst an extreme culture shock can be avoided by moving to the areas of expat predominance where social distractions are geared to British and other national tastes, those who venture away from the *costas* may experience certain feelings of isolation and uncertainty as they begin the process of acclimatisation. It will be worth it in the end. Nobody who moves to a new country can expect to be immediately accepted by the locals, or to immediately fit into their new way of life – there is of course a whole system of etiquette and behaviour that one will need to learn about in order to successfully settle in. Some of these cultural differences are outlined below.

National Character

- Traditionally Spaniards have a reputation for self-reliance and self-centredness; for being smouldering and quarrelsome by turns; for being macho, (petulant for women), proud and flamboyant, and on occasions capricious.
- Among younger Spaniards, an increasing prevalence of a more liberal tolerance of those with a different way of life is noticeable.
- Spaniards are far more tactile than northern Europeans; men embrace their male friends, as well as patting them on the back. Male and female acquaintances kiss each other on the cheek, both cheeks in Madrid and northwards, one cheek in the south.
- Much is made of the *mañana* attitude, largely as a source of frustration to the irate foreigner desperately trying to get things done. In fact the Spanish

are largely misunderstood. Whilst the British put great stock in the phrase *why put off until tomorrow what can be done today,* the Spanish prefer to put off life's irritations until such a time when there is nothing better to do. It is a case wanting to enjoy *now* and there is a sense of fatalism to the Spanish zest for enjoyment, a result of so many years of repression.

o Towards foreigners, Spaniards tend to be open and genuinely helpful. They are as warm and friendly, and show less formality, than the Italians or Portuguese.

o As in the other Mediterranean countries, even today, it is regarded as an honour to be invited to a Spaniard's home as he or she tends only to ask close friends.

'Los Por Favores' – The Spanish and their Pleases and Thank Yous

One cultural difference which the British find difficult to get to grips with is the abrupt nature of Spanish interaction. The Spanish are not in the habit of saying 'sorry' (*lo siento*) or 'please' and 'thank you' anywhere near as much the Brits, and find it amusing how polite the British are. Expat David Kitching explains: '*When the Spanish go into a bar and ask for a beer, it is very unusual for them to say please – they will just say 'una cerveza'. Equally, when they answer the phone they will say 'Digame' (Speak to me). The British, who are so accustomed to being polite, find this a little rude, but it is simply the way the Spanish are. The Spanish on the other hand are so bewildered by the Brits saying please and thank you all the time that in the area around Gandia, where we live, I have heard the Spanish refer to the Brits as 'Los Por Favores'!*

The Family

o Family is of the utmost importance to Spaniards. It is not unusual for three, sometimes four generations to live together.

o The elderly are revered and cared for in the home and the Spaniards are very indulgent towards their children. On fiesta nights children accompany their parents to restaurants and bars, and stay up with them until the small hours.

o Young people do not usually leave home until they get married and are not really expected to contribute financially, or even help around the house.

o Spaniards fear the disintegration of the close family unit due to social change. Children are leaving home to attend universities further afield, girls have far more options post-school, people are marrying later or not at all and having fewer children, and divorce is becoming more common. People are also beginning to accept the necessity for residential homes as the ageing population increases.

Attitudes to Women

○ Machismo is a social attitude that has been in steady demise for some years now. The diminishing influence of the Catholic Church and hence an increasingly liberal attitude to issues such as divorce, contraception and abortion have also helped women to gain a more equal footing in Spanish society.

○ There are more women than ever before in the workplace, in politics, and in the academic world. Women bullfighters have begun to make an appearance and female troops joined their male counterparts in Iraq in 2003. Women are regarded with respect in the workplace.

○ Spain's determination to cast aside the stigma of such patriarchal social mores has recently been enshrined in law. In April 2005, an amendment to the civil marriage contract obliged men to play a greater role in the housework and in the raising of children.

The Siesta

○ In these days of air-conditioning and global markets, the siesta is not as prevalent as it used to be. Many hard-pressed executives, shift workers and busy mothers no longer have time for this once essential afternoon nap. Most Spaniards now work what is a comparatively relaxed 9am-6pm or 7pm day with one or two hours for lunch.

Lust for Life

○ The Spanish have an unmatched zest for socialising and nightlife and tend to go out much later and return much earlier in the morning. The climate is one cause of this custom, hence the fact that northerners burn less midnight oil than southerners.

○ The Spanish love a good party and the number of fiestas and ferias has increased every year since the end of the Franco regime, which did its best to stamp them out. In the mind of a Spaniard the next celebrations may never come, so why not enjoy this one to the full?

○ Spaniards never refer to the end of the evening, nobody will ever suggest the last drink, rather *la penúltima,* and often the evening doesn't end until it is suddenly time to shower and go to work again.

Basics

CHAPTER SUMMARY

- ○ Cost of living analyses indicate that Spain is around 20% cheaper than the UK, but it would be a mistake to assume that you will be far better off there. It all depends on your lifestyle.
  - ○ Crucially it is the things that make life more enjoyable that are much more affordable in Spain – eating out, alcohol, leisure pursuits and so on.
- ○ Retiring to Spain full-time may not be for everyone, and there are numerous alternatives such as extended renting and homeswaps.
- ○ The best way to avoid a costly abortive move to Spain is to have a trial period. This will iron out any concerns and give you the opportunity to get to know the area.
- ○ It is advisable to make some headway learning the language before you leave. Spanish is a beautiful language and speaking it will open doors to new friendships and opportunities.
- ○ Those who retire to Spain and live off a pension or their savings must apply for official residence status (a *residencia*). You will need to provide evidence that you have sufficient funds to support yourself.
- ○ Getting to and from Spain has never been easier. There are over forty no-frills carriers serving an ever-increasing number of Spanish airports.
- ○ Before you depart the UK permanently you should arrange to have your UK pension paid into your bank account in Spain.
- ○ If you are taking cats and dogs to Spain they must be micro-chipped and vaccinated under the Pet Travel Scheme.
- ○ The cost of transporting your belongings from the UK to Spain is likely to come to around £3,000 to £4,000, and the whole process will take a couple of weeks.

THINGS TO CONSIDER

Is it Affordable?

Those who can afford retirement in the UK will certainly be able to afford it in Spain. The economic pundits tell us that the cost of living in Spain is around 20% cheaper in Spain than in Britain. However, the gap is certainly closing and it would be a mistake to assume that you will be far better off if you live in Spain – it depends entirely on your lifestyle and how much you spend on goods and services to create and maintain it, how regularly you want to make trips back to the UK, whether your pension and any other income amounts to a secure, regular long-term income.

Nevertheless, many expats, including Sam Jones, a retiree in the Alicante region, find that their retirement income goes far further than it did in the UK: *'Life here is so much more affordable. My wife and I love to go out for meals, or for a drink, and now this is something that we can afford to do every day. In England, despite being 67, I still had to work in order to make ends meet, but here my company pension covers everything.'*

One factor that people fail to consider is the fluctuation of the exchange rate. The majority of migrants have enough funds to cover living expenses, but there are many who rely largely on their UK state pension, and are therefore dependent on the strength of the British pound. Whenever the exchange rate drops significantly for any length of time, Age Concern España reports that it receives a flurry of enquiries, from people who have suddenly found themselves in difficult circumstances. If you intend to rely heavily on your state pension, it is a good idea to get a forecast of exactly how much you will receive (see below).

UK Retirement Pension Forecast

Those who have not yet reached retirement age, but plan to start receiving their UK state pension in Spain should continue to pay national insurance contributions in the UK in order to qualify for a state pension once they reach 65. You should also request a Retirement Pension Forecast. This tells you the amount of state pension you have already earned and the amount you can expect to receive upon reaching pension age. This will help you to plan your finances for the future. To receive a forecast, obtain form BR19 from your local social security office or contact the Retirement Pension Forecasting and Advice Unit: ☎0845-3000 168.

Cost of Living in Spain Compared to the UK

NB The figures quoted below were gathered in 2005 (Source: EIU Worldwide Cost of Living) and refer to costs in the larger cities. In rural areas the cost of living is considerably cheaper.

Alcohol. As much as 50% cheaper than in the UK. Local wines, beers and spirits are of extremely good value and quality.

Product	Spain price (€)	UK price (£)	Spain price in £ sterling equivalent
Table wine (750 ml)	4.90	4.99	3.48
Beer – known brand (330 ml)	0.56	0.92	0.40
Scotch (6 yrs old – 700 ml)	9.79	12.34	6.96

Books and Newspapers. Generally about the same price.

Product	Spain price (€)	UK price (£)	Spain price in £ sterling equivalent
Daily local newspaper	1.00	0.60	0.71
Imported daily newspaper	2.00	1.20	1.42
International weekly news magazine (*Time*)	3.95	2.60	2.77
Paperback novel	9.25	6.99	6.57

Cars. New cars are about the same price, although running costs are generally cheaper. Insurance and repairs may be more in the cities. Second-hand cars however are much more expensive in Spain than in the UK.

Product	Spain price (€)	UK price (£)	Spain price in £ sterling equivalent
New low priced car (900-1299 cc)	11,480	8,995	8,156
Unleaded petrol (1 litre)	0.93	0.80	0.66
Annual road tax	83.56	160	59.38
Low price insurance premium in the city	1,182	005.66	840
Cost of a tune up	207	150	203.92

Cigarettes and tobacco. Considerably cheaper in Spain. Smoking is much more prevalent in Spain than in the UK and is not so highly taxed.

Product	Spain price (€)	UK price (£)	Spain price in £ sterling equivalent
Cigarettes – Marlboro (20)	2.60	5.20	1.85
Cigarettes – local brand (20)	1.80	4.77	1.28
Pipe tobacco (50 g)	3.45	9.21	2.45

Electronics. Generally electronic goods are slightly more expensive in Spain as the majority have to be imported. Bringing them from home however may not save money as they may not work on a Spanish power supply and it will be difficult to find parts when they break down.

Product	Spain price (€)	UK price (£)	Spain price in £ sterling equivalent
Personal Computer	1,450	941	1,031
Colour Television (66 cm)	745.90	498.98	530.37

Food. Supermarket products cost about the same as in the UK (see below) but there are many indoor and open-air markets that offer very good value for fresh produce. Buying local brands of products rather than those you are used to in the UK will also dramatically reduce your food bills.

Product	Spain price (€)	UK price (£)	Spain price in £ sterling equivalent
Pasteurised Milk (1 litre)	0.76	0.49	0.53
Eggs (12)	1.81	1.02	1.29
Orange Juice (1 litre)	0.68	1.22	0.48
Butter (500g)	3.62	1.96	2.58
White Bread (1 kg)	3.03	0.55	2.16
Ground Coffee (500 g)	2.40	3.30	1.71
Tea bags (25 bags)	1.80	0.30	1.27
Fresh Chicken (1 kg)	2.95	1.78	2.10
Potatoes (2 kg)	1.61	1.50	1.15
Onions (1kg)	0.68	0.64	0.48

Healthcare. For pensioners who are registered as resident in Spain all visits to the doctor, hospital treatment and prescriptions are free. However, those who have retired early, or who choose not to take out a residencia may not be eligible and should factor in the cost of healthcare. All dentists are private in Spain, and this is an extra cost that should be factored in.

Product	Spain price (€)	UK price (£)	Spain price in £ sterling equivalent
Routine checkup at family doctor	74.95	85	60.04
x-ray at doctor's office or hospital	105.25	45	74.78
Visit to dentist (one x-ray and one filling)	142.50	60	101.25
Aspirins (100 tablets)	13.75	7.13	9.77

Leisure. The Spanish enjoy their leisure time to the full and most activities are extremely cheap. One exception is playing a round of golf, as there are simply not enough courses to keep up with demand from foreign residents as yet. Pensioners receive concessions on many services such as public transport, and entrance to theatres, cinemas and public swimming pools.

Product	Spain price (€)	UK price (£)	Spain price in £ sterling equivalent
Four best seats at the theatre	237	214	168.50
Four best seats at the cinema	23	34	16.50
3-course dinner at a top city restaurant for 4 people	359	288	252
Compact Disc Album	18.10	11.99	12.93
Green fees on a public golf course	82	15.00	58.26

Rents. Much lower than in the UK generally. The figures below compare London with average prices in Madrid and Barcelona. Rents are considerably cheaper outside of the two major cities.

Product	Spain price (€)	UK price (£)	Spain price in £ sterling equivalent
Furnished moderate 1-bedroom apartment (pcm)	815	700	579
Furnished moderate 3-bedroom house	2195	2137.50	1433.50

Utilities. Electricity is considerably more expensive in Spain and most people tend to use gas as much as possible. The figures given below are based on city prices where people are on mainline gas. However, in most of Spain people use bottled gas, which is very cheap (around €9 per bottle). If you are in the south of Spain remember that your heating bills will be far cheaper than they would be in the UK.

Product	Spain price (€)	UK price (£)	Spain price in £ sterling equivalent
Phone line – average monthly rental	19	10.66	13.50
Phone – average charge per local call from home (3 mins)	0.11	0.14	0.08
Electricity, monthly bill for family of four	185	45	131.20
Gas, monthly bill for family of four	52	39.50	36.95
Water, monthly bill for family of four	40.70	25.83	28.74

Leaving Family and Friends

As well as sufficient funds, you will also need to possess copious amounts of energy and enthusiasm to deal with the move practically and emotionally. Many people cite moving house as one of the most stressful times in their life, but for most the move may be just down the road, or to another town. It does not involve moving to another country, isolating yourself from friends and family and having to assimilate into an alien culture. Problems often arise when children and grandchildren are left behind. For some the homesickness can have a very negative effect on the new life in Spain. You will need contingency plans to stay in touch with and assist close friends, children, grandchildren elderly parents and relatives, and to deal with any emergencies that may arise in the UK. Warm weather and fantastic views may not be sufficient compensation for the life you have left behind. This is one of the reasons why a trial period (see below) is such a good idea.

Looking Ahead

It is also vital to consider whether you will be able to cope with your new life in Spain further down the line. Whilst the Spanish climate and lifestyle may well be beneficial to your general health, and the public health system first-class, it is important to consider the future, and what will happen if you become seriously ill or are no longer able to care for yourself. The family unit is so much tighter in Spain than we are used to in the UK that traditionally there has not been the need for networks of nursing homes, and personal home care services. Whilst social and economic developments in Spain are forcing this situation to gradually change, the infrastructure is still insufficient in all but the most heavily ex-pat concentrated areas.

If you are a couple, you must also consider what will happen if one of you dies or becomes seriously ill. Recent research shows that such events can quickly lead to a crisis amongst expats in Spain as the social support networks often prove inadequate. In the case of bereavement it is vital to consider whether the surviving partner will want to stay on or return to the UK. This ties in with whether or not you sever all links with the UK tax and national insurance system. If you have wholly left the British system and then want to return to it, you may find it financially punitive to do so, unless you have made plans for this contingency.

ALTERNATIVES TO PERMANENT RETIREMENT IN SPAIN

If you have any doubts at all then it may be worth considering one of the alternatives to permanently uprooting your life. Retiring to Spain will not be for everybody and there are a lot of advantages to keeping your UK property and simply taking extended holidays in Spain. Retirees are able to take holidays during low season and school terms when prices are much lower and the resorts are quieter. For years now British tourists-cum-expatriates have been exploiting the availability of cheap air travel to spend the winter months in Spain, thereby avoiding the heating bills and cold weather back home. Over 400,000 Britons spend the winter in Spain each year during the so-called 'swallow season'. Around half of these own a holiday home, but others enjoy extended rentals or take advantage of timeshare and home-exchange deals.

The obvious advantage of the last three of these alternatives is that it relieves you of the worry of having to buy and maintain your own property. Equally advantageous is that if you do not own a Spanish property then you are not tied to one particular area, and can spend your extended holidays discovering new, unspoilt areas of Spain. Some of the main points of these alternatives are discussed below.

Holiday Homes. Many people favour holiday homes over permanent relocation or as a stepping-stone to full retirement. There are around a million British people who own properties in Spain and live there for at least part of the year. An increasingly common trend is for people to buy a holiday home in their mid-forties or early fifties with the intention of eventually settling there permanently. In the meantime they have the chance to take regular inexpensive holidays, to get to know the area and to meet the locals, giving them a far better idea of what permanent residence might be like.

Another advantage of buying a holiday home is that the property can be let out in your absence. Renting out property is a good way of accruing income on your investment or simply helping to repay the monthly mortgage.

Timeshare. The average timeshare costs from £3,000 to £12,000. However, the Timeshare Consumers Association states that for £4,000 you should be able to buy a good quality, two-bedroom timeshare in a decent resort in Spain, during peak season. Unfortunately, the resale value on timeshare is not very high and unless you have bought into a property in a sought-after area you are unlikely to recoup the price that you initially paid.

Timeshares have had a very bad reputation in the past so make sure you do your research before buying, and try not to be taken in by high-pressure sales tactics. EU regulations demand that should you agree to a timeshare purchase you are given a 'cooling off' period, usually of fourteen days, allowing you to pull out of a contract before any monies are paid. Remember that contracts must be printed in the mother tongue of the prospective purchaser and should give the identity and address of the sellers, all the costs involved, the location and description of the property, and the number of weeks a year you can use it. It is important to be fully informed of management fees payable on a property as these can add considerably to the initial outlay. For further advice contact the Timeshare Consumers Association (☎01909-591100; 24hr advice line: 0901-607 0077; www.timeshare.org.uk).

Extended Rentals. Many companies offer out of season lets at a cheaper rate. Such lets are often impractical for those seeking to remain in one area for some time as the rental period is only as long as the low, winter season. However, for many retirees this is ideal. They can escape the gloomy British winter, and return just in time for Spring.

- Holiday rentals are charged by the week and longer rentals are regarded as any period longer than a month. Some rental companies only rent up to a maximum of three months, others will consider a year.
- A short term rental contract is known as *Por Temporada* and covers anything up to six months.
- Major tour operators like *Thomson* (www.thomson-holidays.com) and *First Choice* (www.firstchoice.co.uk) offer many such longer-term stays, and in particular cater for older people.

Useful Contacts

Casa Paraíso: ☎616-374973/0870-128 9000; www.rent-in-spain.com.

Holiday-Rentals.com Ltd: ☎020-8743 5577; www.holiday-rentals.com.

Interhome Ltd: ☎020-8891 1294; www.interhome.co.uk.

Villa Spain: ☎01273-623723; www.villaspain.co.uk. Selection of privately owned villas and apartments for rent on the Costa Blanca from Calpe to Moraira.

Villas Spain Rentals: ☎02920-215568 www.villas-spain-rentals.com.

Home Exchanges

Home exchanges began in the late 1950s as a way of holidaying economically, and recently they have seen something of a revival, largely due to the internet. Exchange websites now offer instant communication, virtual tours and thousands of homes worldwide.

- Most agencies charge an annual fee of around €50-€130 which covers the cost of promoting your home.
- Most house insurance policies cover home exchanges.
- Usually both parties continue to pay their own utility bills, community charges and mortgage repayments etc.
- House swapping gives you the chance to get to know the area and help you decide if you would like to buy your own property there.

> **Exchange Agencies**
> **Homelink International (Spain):** ☎935-894809;www.spainlink.net.
> **Homelink International (UK):** ☎01962-886882; www.homelink.org.uk.
> **Intervac Home Exchange:** ☎01249-461101; www.intervac.co.uk.
> **Club Intervacaciones:** www.intervacacionesclub.com.

A TRIAL PERIOD

There will always be people who decide on the spur of the moment to retire to Spain. The temptation just to up-sticks and go is huge, especially when confronted by the grey drizzle and dark evenings of British winter after returning from a blissful two-week holiday there. However, such a life-changing decision should never be taken lightly and many people who rush into retirement abroad find that the grass is not necessarily greener. As mentioned above many people miss their family and friends, feel isolated by the cultural differences or simply find economic inactivity interminably boring. Even if you know the area well, your romanticised notion of retirement to Spain may not quite meet the reality. This was the experience of Graham Smith upon moving to the Costa del Sol: '*We had travelled to Benalmádena for 16 years before we retired here and we liked it and knew the people. Even so, after 6 months I found that I was absolutely bored to tears*'. Graham and his wife alleviated their boredom by buying and running a small bar for expats, but many return home.

The simple way to avoid an abortive move to Spain is to have a trial period. By approaching the move in a methodical way, all the disadvantages and advantages can be weighed up having been experienced at first hand. It could even be a way of easing yourself into retiring to Spain. A trial period can take the form of several 'reconnaissance trips' staying in different regions for more than the usual holiday length of one to three weeks. Ideally you should plan to stay for several months continuously by renting either in one location or several different ones. It is also essential to spend a winter in the place where you intend to retire to as many areas undergo a complete change of character in the 'off-season' months; coastal towns may become deserted, and inland destinations become liable to lengthy periods of bone-numbing cold. You also need to see if you can survive with minimal Spanish skills, or better still you can use the reconnaissance period to brush up and improve your Spanish so that you are ready to handle dealing with everyday bureaucratic and financial matters in a foreign language.

LEARNING THE LANGUAGE

These days Spanish is an international language. After Chinese and English, it is the most prevalent language on earth, spoken by about 320 million people, and as the primary tongue in 20 countries, mainly in Latin America. Despite the enormous importance of Castilian Spanish worldwide, it is only spoken as a first language by 74% of the country. Three of the Autonomous Communities also have their own languages, Catalonia, Galicia and the Basque Country. However, a knowledge of literary Spanish (Castilian) is much more useful than a knowledge of Catalan, Basque or Galego since all Spaniards understand Castilian but very few outside their communities can communicate in the regional languages.

It is strongly advised that anyone planning to move to Spain try to make some headway learning the language before leaving home. According to Dutchman Anthony Pieter van Antwerpen, who teaches Spanish to expats in Calpe:

Castilian Spanish is one of the easiest languages to learn at a basic level, especially if the student has a prior knowledge of any of the Romance languages. Without exception my students find that the Spanish really appreciate it if you make the effort to speak to learn their language, and they will never laugh if you make a mistake. My advice is just to throw yourself into it. Speaking Spanish opens so many doors and enriches your experience here.

Tips for Learning Spanish

○ **Enrol in a Spanish Course.** Evening language classes offered by local authorities and colleges usually follow the academic year and are aimed at hobby learners or those wishing to obtain a GCSE or A level. Intensive one-on-one Spanish courses offered privately are more expensive (£15-£20 per hour). Once in Spain the cheapest option in the major cities is usually the state-run *Escuela Oficial de Idiomas* (www.eoidiomas.com).

○ **Study in Your Own Time.** Self-study allows students to work and absorb material at their own pace. The BBC (☎0870-2415 490; www.bbcshop.com) produces excellent workbooks and audio cassettes at various levels. *Linguaphone* (☎0800-282417; www.linguaphone.co.uk) distributes more elaborate (and more expensive) self-study courses. Studying Spanish online has become remarkably popular in recent years and a quick Google search will come up with a number of options. The BBC offers their own online courses at www.bbc.co.uk/languages/spanish/.

○ **Take a Study Holiday in Spain.** Language courses in Spain are a fantastic way to get a head-start and a taste for the country and its culture. Most are total immersion and offer a programme of social, cultural and sporting activities to supplement academic study. Contact *Spanish Study Holidays* (☎01509-211612; www.spanishstudyholidays.com) or *Cactus Language* (☎0845-130 4775; www.cactuslanguage.com).

○ **Join a Spanish Society.** Find out if any Anglo-Spanish clubs or societies exist in your area, as these will organise various social events and discussion groups and hopefully function to soften the culture shock on arrival in Spain. Check with your local further education institute, university, or local library.

○ **Set up a Language Exchange.** Link up with a native speaker of Spanish living in your local area, possibly by putting an advertisement in a local paper or making contact through a local English language school.

○ **Watch Spanish Films.** Spanish films have received enormous international recognition in recent years, especially the anarchic, urbane comedies of Pedro Almodóvar. Some wonderful South American films have also been produced. You may not understand at first because of the fast gabbling pace and the regional accents, but you will pick up Spanish more quickly if you keep at it.

○ **Listen to Spanish Radio.** Another excellent way to immerse yourself in the Spanish language. Many stations offer continuous news, discussions and phone-ins. You can listen to Spanish radio online. Visit www.madridman.com/multimedia.html for a full list of stations and their websites.

○ **Read Spanish Books.** Reading something light, perhaps even a children's book in Spanish will help enormously with your comprehension. The Spanish Bookshop (www.thespanishbookshop.co.uk) has a wide selection of bestsellers in Spanish.

Useful Organisations

Instituto Cervantes: ☎020-7235 0353; www.cervantes.es. World's largest Spanish teaching organisation run by the Spanish government. UK presence in London, Leeds and Manchester. The London HQ has an information and audiovisual department to which members have full access. Membership fee includes admission to cultural events and exhibitions.

Hispanic and Luso Brazilian Council: ☎020-7235 2303; www.canninghouse. com. Non-profit organisation founded to stimulate understanding between Britain, Spain, Portugal and Latin America. Runs a number of cultural and educational programmes. Also distributes a free list of Spanish conversation classes in and around London.

RESIDENCE REGULATIONS

Those who are retired in Spain and living off a pension, or from their savings, must apply for official resident status. This is a legal requirement and although many expatriates have not gone through the process of receiving their residence card, it is highly recommended that you do so and in fact there are fiscal advantages.

Residence in Spain is not the same as citizenship. Those who wish to become a citizen of their new host country will need to have lived there for ten years first. Residents of Spain with overseas nationality have most of the rights and obligations of a Spanish national in employment, health and other fields; but no right to vote in national elections.

Numero de Indentificación De Extranjeros (NIE)

The first step for anyone moving to Spain is to apply for the foreigner's identification number. If you reside in Spain, or if you own a property and are non-resident then you need an NIE. This is a tax identification number and is obtainable from the *oficina de extranjeros* or police station. An application form can also be downloaded from www.mir.es. The filled out form and a passport are usually sufficient to obtain the NIE, which will be sent to you by post as soon as it has been processed. The NIE does not need to be presented as a document, simply memorised or copied onto a slip of paper which you can carry around with you.

Residence Cards

You are able to apply for a residence card (*tarjeta de residente comunitario*, known simply as the *residencia*) as soon as you arrive in Spain. The process is fairly straightforward, although you cannot expect English or other foreign languages to be spoken by the police and taking along a Spanish-speaking friend or using the services of a *gestor* (see box below) is a good idea. The application form should be submitted to the local provincial police station (*Comisaría de Policia*) or Foreigner's Office (*Oficina de Extranjeros*).

The list of required documents can vary from office to office and from region to region, but some or all of the following documents are often required:

○ Completed application form (*solicitud de tarjeta en regimen comunitario*).
○ A full, valid passport.
○ NIE (see above).
○ Proof of residence such as utility bills, rental contracts etc.
○ Proof of pension.
○ Marriage documents (if applicable).
○ Four passport sized photographs.
○ A standard medical certificate from your doctor.
○ Bank statements showing your regular income.
○ Details of your health insurance (a statement from the insurance company stating that full treatment is covered, or evidence of registration with the Spanish Department of Health/Social Security, the INSS).

> Those who are obliged to apply for a residence card because they are 'inactive', i.e. pensioners and 'persons of independent means' must provide evidence that have sufficient funds to support themselves such as evidence of their pension or an income equal to or above the official minimum wage. One way of proving that you are in receipt of a UK state pension is to arrange for it to be paid into your Spanish bank account, and then display a stamped letter from the bank as proof.

Once you have presented the above documents, the application will be processed and the authorities will contact you when your card is ready. This could take anything up to six months, depending on the region and how busy/efficient the civil servants are. In the meantime you will be issued with a document stating that your application is being processed, which should be sufficient when dealing with official red tape. Upon notification by post, you should return to the police station or *Oficina de Extranjeros* to collect your card and have your fingerprints taken for police records.

Gestores

Many administrative matters, including applying for residence and work permits may be more conveniently tackled by a *gestor*. The peculiar Spanish love of bureaucracy has created the need for an equally peculiar and quintessentially Spanish institution known as the *gestor*. Spanish bureaucracy is so labyrinthine that it is necessary for ordinary people to be guided through it by a special official. If you have fluent Spanish, limitless patience and no time restrictions then you may save some money by wading through the quagmire of red tape yourself. Otherwise, it is recommended that you consult your local *gestoría* (the office of *gestores*). The gestor is less qualified than a full lawyer but also far less expensive. Gestorías are listed in the yellow pages (*las paginas amarillas*).

Empadronamiento (Registration)

Once you have become resident, it is a good idea (though not compulsory) to register with the local *ayuntamiento* (town hall). This process is known as *empadronamiento*. Being included on the *padrón*, the list of inhabitants in the municipality, will allow you to be included on the electoral roll and therefore vote in local and European elections (although not national elections). Registering is a very straightforward process. Simply present your local council with identification and proof that you are living in the area. Because councils receive central government funding based on the number of registered inhabitants, many councils claim that if all foreign residents were registered, local facilities and services would improve enormously.

Embassies And Consulates

Once resident in Spain, as anywhere in the world, it is also advisable to register with your embassy or consulate. This registration enables the authorities to keep emigrants up to date with any information they need as citizens resident overseas and, in the event of an emergency, helps them to trace individuals. Your embassy or consulate can also help with information regarding your status overseas and advise with any diplomatic or passport problems, and offer help in the case of an emergency, e.g. the death of a relative overseas.

British Embassy and Consulates in Spain

Visit http://www.ukinspain.com/english/contact/addresses.asp. or phone ☎917-008200 for a list of contact details and opening hours for the British Embassy in Madrid, or the British Consulate offices in Alicante, Barcelona, Benidorm, Bilbao, Cádiz, Granada, Ibiza, Las Palmas de Gran Canaria, Madrid, Málaga, Menorca, Palma de Mallorca, Santa Cruz de Tenerife, Sevilla and Vigo.

Spanish Embassies and Consulates in the UK and Ireland

Spanish Embassy: 39 Chesham Place, London SW1X 8SB; ☎020-7235 5555; fax 020-7259 5392; e-mail embespuk@mail.mae.es.

Spanish Consulate General: 20 Draycott Place, London SW3 2RZ; ☎020-7589 8989; fax 020-7581 7888; conspalon@mail.mae.es.

Spanish Consulate General: Suite 1A, Brooke House, 70 Spring Gardens, Manchester M2 2BQ; ☎0161-236 1262; fax 0161-228 7467; e-mail conspmanchester@mail.es.

Spanish Consulate General: 63 North Castle Street, Edinburgh EH2 3LJ; ☎0131-220 1843; fax 0131-226 4568; cgspedimburgo@mail.mae.es.

Consular Section: Spanish Embassy, 17 Merlyn Park, Ballsbridge, Dublin 4, Ireland; ☎+353 1-269 1640/2597; fax: +353 1-2691854; e-mail embespies@mail.mae.es.

GETTING THERE AND AWAY

These days getting out to Spain and back could not be easier. The massive demand for air travel by hundreds of thousands of travellers to Spain each year has created a boom-time for airlines offering cheap, no-frills tickets. This stampede of air travellers, lured by the cheap flights, cheap property and guaranteed sun has put an enormous strain on the infrastructure and new runways and airports are constantly in progress. Approximately 10% of the population in the UK fly at least three times a year to the UK's favourite destination, with 3% taking more than six flights per year.

Depending on when you wish to travel, the no-frills airlines are not always the cheapest, and because they have created such fierce competition in the flight market place, some of the mainstream carriers such as BA and Iberia have been forced to drastically reduce their prices. There are now far more reasonably priced alternatives, so always spend time researching the various possibilities before booking a flight. Useful websites that search for the cheapest flights available at any time are www.whichbudget.com, www.skyscanner.net and www.openjet.com.

THE AIRLINES

Please note that airline services can and do change frequently so it is best to check current routes on the internet and to keep an eye on the travel press:

Aerlingus: ☎0845-084 4444; from Ireland: ☎1-886 8844; www.aerlingus.com. Destinations: Alicante, Barcelona, Bilbao, Gran Canaria, Lanzarote, Madrid, Málaga, Seville, Tenerife, Valencia.

Air Scotland: ☎0141-222 2363; fax 0141-222 2362; e-mail cs@air-scotland.com; www.air-scotland.com. Destinations: Alicante, Málaga, Palma (Mallorca).

BMI Baby: ☎0870-264 2229; www.bmibaby.com. Destinations: Alicante, Barcelona, Ibiza, Málaga, Murcia, Palma (Mallorca).

BMI: ☎0870-6070 555; www.flybmi.com. Destinations: Alicante, Madrid, Palma (Mallorca), Tenerife.

British Airways: ☎0870-850 9850; www.ba.com. Destinations: Barcelona, Ibiza, Madrid, Málaga.

Easyjet: www.easyjet.com. Destinations: Alicante, Almería, Barcelona, Bilbao, Ibiza, Madrid, Málaga, Oviedo, Palma (Mallorca), Valencia.

Excel Airways: ☎0870-169 0169; fax 0870-163 3003; e-mail flight.bookings@ excelairways.com; www.excelairways.com. Destinations: Alicante, Almería, Fuerteventura, Gran Canaria, Lanzarote, Madrid, Málaga, Menorca, Murcia, Palma (Mallorca), Tenerife.

Flybe.com: ☎0871 800-0535; www.flybe.com. Destinations: Alicante, Almería, Málaga, Murcia, Palma (Mallorca).

Globespan: ☎0870-5561 522; www.flyglobespan.com. Destinations: Alicante, Barcelona, Gran Canaria, Lanzarote, Madrid, Málaga, Palma (Mallorca), Tenerife.

GB Airways: (formerly Gibraltar Airways, now owned by BA). ☎0870-850 9850; www.gbairways.com. Destinations: Alicante, Almería, Gibraltar, Girona, Gran Canaria, Jerez de la Frontera, Lanzarote, Málaga, Murcia, Palma (Mallorca), Seville, Tenerife, Valencia.

Iberia: ☎0845-850 9000; www.iberia.com. Destinations: Alicante, Barcelona, Madrid, Málaga, Santiago de Compostela

Jet2: ☎0870-737 8282; www.jet2.com. Destinations: Alicante, Barcelona, Málaga, Murcia, Palma (Mallorca), Valencia.

Monarch Scheduled: ☎08700-405040; www.flymonarch.com. Destinations: Alicante, Almería, Barcelona, Gibraltar, Granada, Gran Canaria, Lanzarote, Madrid, Málaga, Menorca, Palma (Mallorca), Tenerife.
MyTravelLite: ☎08701-564564; www.mytravellite.com. Destinations: Alicante, Almería, Barcelona, Gran Canaria, Ibiza, Lanzarote, Málaga, Murcia, Palma (Mallorca), Tenerife.
Ryanair: www.ryanair.com. Destinations: Almería, Girona, Granada, Jerez de la Frontera, Málaga, Murcia, Reus, Santiago de Compostela, Seville, Valencia, Valladolid, Zaragoza.
Thomson Flights: ☎0800-000 747; www.thomsonflights.com. Many destinations.

Charter Tickets

These days there are very few differences between charter and scheduled flights as it is possible to buy flight-only tickets, in many cases all year round. These can be booked direct through companies such as Monarch (www.flymonarch.com) and Excel (www.excelairways.com) or through an agent. The only real difference with flight-only charter tickets is that they are still usually issued for a fixed period, such as 7 days or 14 days. The largest UK purveyor of flight-only charter tickets is Avro (☎0870-458 2841; www.avro.com), offering flights from many UK airports to Alicante, Almería, Fuerteventura, Girona, Gibraltar, Gran Canaria, Ibiza, Lanzarote, Malaga, Menorca, Murcia, Palma and Tenerife.

Websites Selling Flights

www.airflights.co.uk	www.flightline.co.uk
www.avro.co.uk	www.lastminute.com
www.cheapflights.com	www.dialaflight.com
www.opodo.co.uk	www.statravel.co.uk

By Sea

Depending on your budget regarding time and money, travelling by sea to Spain is possible, but tickets are not cheap and travel time can be up to thirty-six hours. *P&O European Ferries* run ferries between Portsmouth and Bilbao twice a week, which take around 36 hours one way. Ferries operated by *Brittany Ferries* run between Plymouth and Santander twice weekly and take around 18 hours. As a rough price guide, a family can travel at peak rates to Spain and back with a car for around £1000. However, prices do fluctuate dramatically depending on the time of year.

Ferries also connect Morrocco with Algeciras, Almería, Málaga, Tarifa and Gibraltar. A car ferry also serves Tenerife and Gran Canaria, leaving Cádiz once a week. The trip takes around 40 hours.

The Balearic Islands can also be reached by ferry services, operated mainly by *Trasmediterranea* from Barcelona, Valencia, Denia and Vilanova I la Geltru near Sitges.

Ferry Services

P&O European Ferries: ☎08705-202020; www.poporlsmouth.com

Brittany Ferries: ☎08703-665333; www.brittany-ferries.co.uk

Transmediterranea Ferries: www.trasmediterranea.es

Balearia: www.balearia.net

Booking Agents: www.directferry.com; www.ferrybooker.com; www.onlineferries.co.uk

---

By Land

Once across the Channel, the fast roads in France can get you to the Spanish border in around 20 hours, but realistically you should reckon on two or three days' travel overland to reach southern Spain. Remember that if you stick to the motorways in France and Spain you will have to pay a hefty amount in tolls (the cost of getting from Calais to the Spanish border alone is around £50). It is therefore better to stick to the main trunk roads and take your time, take in the scenery and acclimatise yourself to the life of 'mañana' waiting ahead of you. For information about current toll rates, the Spanish motorway system and motoring in Spain, visit the Dirección General de Tráfico website (www.dgt.es).

Route Planner Websites

www.spain.info	www.viamichelin.co.uk
www.theaa.com	www.rac.co.uk

With the ease and low cost of flying to Spain from the UK, very few people choose to go all the way by coach or train. However, these options are still available. Eurolines (operated by national express) offer coach services running from London Victoria to numerous destinations in Spain: www.nationalexpress.com. Travelling by train is almost always more expensive than flying and takes around twenty-four hours. The most obvious route is to take the Eurostar from London to Paris Gare du Nord, and then change stations to Paris Austerlitz to get a train to Barcelona or Madrid. Consult www.raileurope.co.uk for further details. Following heavy state investment in the country's infrastructure, Spain's rail network is now very efficient and express high speed Talgo200 services run from Madrid to Malaga, Cadiz, Jerez de la Frontera, Huelva and Algeciras, and Valencia. There are high-speed AVE services linking Madrid to Toledo and to Seville via Cordoba. Further information is available from RENFE (☎902-240202; www.renfe.es).

PREPARATIONS FOR DEPARTURE

If you are planning to move to Spain permanently, then it is a good idea to begin the essential preparations several months in advance. Every aspect of daily life will need to be considered as you decide what should be cancelled in the UK, what should be transferred to Spain and how it should be done. For such an arduous undertaking checklists are virtually essential in order to bring a degree of organisation into the process. How your checklists pan out depends on your personal requirements. The items below are the essential ones.

Banking

Whether you intend to live in Spain permanently or simply spend a lot of time there, it will be necessary to open a Spanish bank account. If you are spending a trial period in Spain or visiting to look at properties you can withdraw money from your UK bank account from a Spanish ATM. However, this can quickly become an unnecessary expense as there are often charges and the exchange rate may not work out favourably. Many people wait until they have moved to Spain before opening an account but estate agents often advise that you open an account when you are looking for a property to buy so that the financial part of the process can take place quickly and smoothly.

In order to open an account before you go it is necessary to visit either the UK (London) office of a major Spanish bank, or visit a British bank that is well represented in Spain. Setting up an account is simply a matter of completing a few forms. Although some people may be more confident

opening an account with a Spanish branch of a UK bank, they will find
that the Spanish branches of British banks function in just the same way as
the Spanish national banks and are totally separate from their UK parent
companies. Foreign banks also tend to be concentrated around the coastal
resorts, so if you are moving inland then a Spanish bank may be a safer bet.

British Banks in Spain	
Barclarys Bank España	www.barclays.es
Halifax Hispania	www.halifax.es
Lloyds TSB España	www.lloydstsb.es
Royal Bank of Scotland	www.rbs.com
Spanish Banks in the UK	
Solbank	☎937-453956; www.solbank.com
Banco Santander Central Hispano (BSCH)	☎020-7332 7766; www.bsch.es
Banco Bilbao Vizcaya Argentaria	☎020-7623 3060; www.bbva.es

For details of banking once you have arrived in Spain see the banking section in the chapter *Personal Finance*.

Medical Matters

One essential part of your preparations should be a visit to your GP in order to inform him or her of your decision. A final check-up before moving
abroad is also a good idea, and you should certainly ensure that you know
what the Spanish equivalents are of any regular prescriptions that you are taking. It will not be possible to take your medical records away with you, but
once you have found a doctor in Spain these can easily be forwarded on.

You should also visit your dentist and optician as although pensioners in
Spain are entitled to free medical care and prescription medicine, Spanish
social security does not cover dental treatment, dentures or spectacles.

Before leaving, anyone who receives a state pension should obtain form
E121 from the UK Department for Work and Pensions (see below).
This form will give you access to the Spanish healthcare system. If you
are retiring to Spain before having reached pensionable age and are not
intending to work in Spain (therefore not contributing to Spanish social
security), it is still possible to receive free healthcare for a limited time by

applying to the DWP for form E106. Not everyone is eligible for the E106, so it is wise to check with the DWP.

Far too many expats in Spain believe that they are covered for healthcare by the E111, which has now been replaced by the EHIC (European Health Insurance Card). However the EHIC is intended for tourists and covers only emergencies within three months of your departure.

Details of all of the above are available in the DWP leaflet SA29 – *Going Abroad and Social Security Benefits*. Further information on all medical matters can be found in the *Healthcare* chapter.

DWP Contact Details

Department for Work & Pensions: The Pension Service, International Pension Centre, Medical Benefits Section, Tyneview Park, Whitely Road, Newcastle-uponTyne NE98 1BA; ☎0191-218 7547; www.dwp.gov.uk.

Mail Forwarding

Whether you have sold your UK property, are letting it out, or are simply leaving it vacant, then you will need your post to be forwarded on to your new address in Spain. If you are keeping your UK home and therefore address, this is likely to generate more post than if you have sold up your UK assets and left the UK entirely. If you have a trusted neighbour, or your tenants are friends you can ask them to check your post, throw away obvious junk and readdress any important looking mail to you in Spain. Alternatively you can arrange to have your post redirected by The Royal Mail. You can arrange this at any post office. The time limit for redirecting mail is two years and it costs £60 per surname, per year. Special Delivery and signed for mail cannot be forwarded. Alternatively, there are commercial Accommodation Address mail forwarding services, which can be found with a simple Google search. These services allow you to use their address and forward your mail on once a week, for a fee of around £15 per month.

Pensions

You should arrange for your occupational and state pension payments to be paid into your bank account in Spain. To do this you need to contact the pensions service in the UK (www.thepensionservice.gov.uk;

☎0845-6060265) and search/ask for details of Overseas Direct Payment in local currency. For occupational and private pensions contact your provider.

Those who move to Spain before reaching retirement age, but do not intend to work, should arrange to continue paying national insurance contributions in the UK in order to qualify for a British state pension when they reach 65. Before you go, seek advice on this issue from the Inland Revenue National Insurance Contributions Office (☎0845-302 1479; www.hmrc.gov.uk/nic/). For more details see *Pensions and Exportable UK Benefits* in the *Personal Finance* chapter.

Pets

Cats and dogs may be brought in and out of mainland Spain, the Balearic Islands and the Canary Islands under the Pet Travel Scheme. This scheme makes travelling with animals far more straightforward, although it can be a fairly lengthy and expensive process. To obtain an EU pet passport, your pet must be micro-chipped, and given a rabies vaccination at least twenty-one days before departure. The procedure must be carried out by a government authorised vet and the total cost of the process is around £200.

The scheme is managed by the Department for the Environment, Food and Rural Affairs (contact details below) and they will have the latest details of import conditions. Animals other than cats and dogs may be imported but are subject to specific rules. Further information is available from the nearest Spanish consulate or the PETs helpline: ☎0870-241 1710.

Every time the animal returns to the UK it must be treated against tapeworm and ticks 24-48 hours before departure. The vet will issue an official certificate bearing the vet's stamp with the microchip number, date and *time* of treatment, and the product used.

Some but not all ferry companies and airlines will take accompanied pets. There is also a list of carriers on the DEFRA website: www.defra. gov.uk/animalh/quarantine/pets/contacts.htm. Once in the country the animal's documentation will be checked before being taken to the Animal Aircare Centre and then released to the owner. Note that in some cities in Spain dogs have to be registered and insured and a dog licence required or a tax levied. Information on the registration formalities once in Spain will be found at the local town hall (*ayuntamiento*).

Useful Contacts

Pet Travel Scheme:	Department for the Environment, Food and Rural Affairs, Area 201, 1a Page Street, London SW1P 4PQ; ☎0870-241 1710; fax 020-7904 6834; e-mail pets.helpline@defra.gov.uk; www.defra.gov.uk.
Airpets Oceanic:	☎01753-685571; www.airpets.com. Pet exports, pet travel schemes, boarding, transportation by road/air to and from all UK destinations.
Pet Plan:	☎0800-107 0204; www.petplan.co.uk. Offers travel insurance for pets.

Removals

When considering what to take with you to Spain and what to leave behind or sell at a car boot sale, start with a list of essential items and then try and cut this down again. Anything one decides to take must be carefully considered to ensure that it really is practical, and necessary. Anything of substantial weight will be very expensive to ship abroad.

You should also bear in mind that furnishings are often included in Spain if you are buying a resale property, as expats Mac and Meryl Macdonald discovered:

We brought almost nothing with us. Out here it seems to be the rule that when you buy a house, you buy everything with it – they leave it fully furnished, right down to the crockery and linen! Some friends of ours recently bought a house and actually had a car included. It was ideal for us. Within ten minutes of arriving at our new house we were sitting down and eating lunch.

The approximate charge for transporting your belongings from the UK to Spain is £120 to £150 per cubic metre plus a fixed fee for administration and paperwork. Typically you should expect the total cost to come to around £3,000-£4,000 and the whole process will take a couple of weeks.

There are numerous removal firms, many of whom advertise in Spanish property magazines. Look for those who are members of the British Association of Removers (www.removers.org.uk; ☎ 01923-699480) as these are likely to be more reputable companies. BAR has set up International Movers Mutual Insurance so that clients of any of its member companies will be compensated for loss or damage, or in the case of bankruptcy, the removal will be completed by another BAR member.

Before you start phoning around for quotes, there is a useful website which does the bulk of the work for you: www.reallymoving.com. Simply type in the pick-up and drop-off points and a rough estimate of how many cubic feet you'll be moving (their estimator will work this out for you) and the site will email your request to several shipping companies. Over the following few days personalised quotes will trickle into your inbox.

Removals Checklist

- Any EU citizen intending to take up permanent residence in Spain may import their household effects and personal possessions free of customs duty.
- Before moving you should compile an inventory of all the goods to be transported to Spain. This list should then be presented to the Spanish Consulate with a completed customs clearance form where the inventory will be stamped for a small fee. The removals company should handle most of the paperwork for you. Anyone thinking of taking their household effects out to Spain in a private truck or van should first consult their nearest Spanish embassy or consulate for the most up to date regulations and advice.
- Furniture and other large items from your English home might not be suitable for your beachfront villa. Bear in mind that it is easy to buy cheap second-hand furniture in Spain.
- Electrical items are slightly more expensive in Spain and it may be worth taking yours if they are compatible, although spare parts may be a problem in Spain.
- Decide what smaller items you can transport yourself by car to Spain.
- If you are moving slightly unusual things such as vintage cars, or horses, try Brookfields Removals (www.brookfields-removals.co.uk). The company will give you a quote for moving nearly anything.

Odds and Ends Checklist

- Cancel any regular subscriptions to newspapers, magazines, etc., or arrange to have them redirected if possible.
- Dispose of anything you don't want to take with you via ebay, a car boot sale, or charity shops.
- Book disconnection of mains services.
- Decide whether to take your current car or sell it and buy a new one in Spain (see *Adapting to Your New Life*).
- Notify bank, credit card company, car registration, passport office etc. of change of address.
- Cancel gym or other UK club memberships.
- Cancel the milk/newspapers.
- Return library books.
- Cancel contracts with gas, electricity and telephone companies and settle accounts.
- If you are renting out your UK home, take meter readings for gas and electricity and settle bills before tenants move in and make an inventory of items left in the house to be attached to the tenancy agreement.
- Notify dentist, doctor, optician, vet.

Part two

A New Home in Spain

Where to Retire

Your New Home in Spain

Housing Finance

Where to Retire

CHAPTER SUMMARY

- When seeking the location for your retirement it is a good idea to list your priorities and realise that you may have to compromise on some of them.
- The majority of people head for the coast, attracted by the beaches and the holiday lifestyle, but beachfront properties are considerably more expensive, and you will also have to contend with the tourist hordes that invade in high season.
- You will have to decide whether you wish to live amongst your compatriots. Many find the presence of so many expatriates to be a useful way to ease themselves into Spanish culture.
- Spain is developing and changing so quickly that wherever you buy, you should consider how the area might change in the coming years.
- It pays to consider the future. A beautiful remote spot might be ideal in your fifties, but as you get older the long trek to the nearest amenities may become a real burden.
- 30% of British citizens who are resident in Spain have chosen to live in Andalucia, the most populated region of Spain with year-round sunshine and four very popular costas – the Costa de la Luz, Costa del Sol, Costa Tropical and Costa de Almería.
- The Costa Blanca has long been popular with retirees, but prices here are high. A little further north, the Costa del Azahar is less developed and offers lower prices. A new airport on this coast in due in 2007 which will push prices up.
- A large number of foreigners choose to live in Madrid where there are many facilities for expatriates. However, property prices here are the highest in Spain.
- Galicia is not a common place for expats to relocate to due to it's damp climate, but retirees who are a little more adventurous will find a wealth of cheap renovation homes here.

CHOOSING THE RIGHT LOCATION FOR RETIREMENT

There is nothing more important than finding the right place to spend your retirement. Spain is a fabulously diverse country and each area has its own attractions. It is sensible to spend time during different parts of the year in the area where you think you would like to buy. Many expats spend hours researching the areas that interest them in libraries and on the internet. Others buy on gut instinct having fallen in love with the area. For some this can work out very well, but expat David Austen advises against it:

There are so many people who come out here and buy without thinking. I think it is a good idea to have a good look around. We took a year before we bought our villa. Having found an area that we really liked, we rented a place and waited for exactly the right property to become available. This gave us time to really get to know the area and be sure that we had made the right decision. Then, when the right property came up, we were in the right place to swoop in with an offer. One of the houses around the corner from us sold in three days, so it pays to be in situ, and on the ball.

It is vital to decide on your criteria early on. Are you a true urbanite who needs the bustle of at least a decent sized town or are you looking for tranquillity and solitude? Do you crave the healthy salt air and the holiday atmosphere of the coast, or is it the rugged mountains of the interior that appeals to you? Expat Meryl Macdonald advises that you spend some time thinking this through:

You need to sort out your criteria and be aware that you may have to compromise on some of them. We bullet pointed around ten priorities and stuck to them. In the end the only thing we compromised on was being able to walk into town, but it was a trade off – if we had bought a townhouse then we wouldn't have the privacy and tranquillity that we have here.

Below are some of the factors that you should take into consideration.

Coast Vs. Inland

The majority of people head for the Mediterranean coast. Living beside the sea is a dream for many people, inspired by glorious summer holidays lying on Spain's superb beaches. And why not? During the hot summer months the sea breezes make the temperatures more bearable and the appeal of water sports for many is a big draw, sailing out into the Mediterranean, surfing, swimming, beachlife etc. After the cold of northern Europe with its grey choppy seas the desire to live beside an azure sea, calm as a millpond, is easily understandable. The downside of the dream, of course, is the reality. Along the Mediterranean coast (less so along the Atlantic coast) the tourist hordes invade in high season and take over those once quiet beaches, pack the roads and verges with hire cars and motorbikes and coaches and party loudly into the early hours. Also, being on holiday in Spain is a world away from actually living there, as expat Joanne Kitching points out:

We were very naïve. My idea of Spain was very much influenced by package holidays during my student days. Lying by the pool in the sunshine may be heaven for two weeks, but when you actually live here things are very different. It doesn't take long before you become like the Spanish, and stay out of the hot sun as much as possible. You need much more than just the sun to have a fulfilling retirement, but there are many interesting aspects to life here.

Another problem is that properties within spitting distance of a beach and the sea are now fiercely fought over and as a consequence are very expensive. There may also be problems with building regulations if you plan to buy a property, or build one on land within a kilometre of the high water mark. The 'Law of the Coasts' (*ley de costas*) prohibits any new building on the coast.

Much of Spain, inland and away from the costas is still pretty sedate and what is strangely termed 'real Spain' still survives. Plots of land can be had much cheaper here than on the coast and though the infrastructure may be less developed there will be a more established sense of community and, depending on how you integrate yourself into a community, you may find it more rewarding being the foreigner on the hill than merely one of many.

Do You Want to Live Among Your Compatriots?

Because of the sheer volume of foreigners who have bought property in Spain over the years, you will be unlikely to find a property too far away from another owned by someone from Germany, Holland or Britain or Scandinavia unless you have decided to buy in the *meseta*. Even houses in the villages up in the hills and hinterland behind the *costas* are increasingly being bought up by foreigners. These villages remain very Spanish and because the foreigners have moved there for precisely that reason, they try to integrate into the Spanish community as best they can. Don't be under any illusions that you will find a 'traditional' and culturally intact village up in the hills where you will be the only foreigner – those days are long gone.

If you choose to live on the Mediterranean coast, then living amongst a purely Spanish community is almost impossible. In areas such as Torremolinos on the Costa del Sol, and Torrevieja on the Costa Blanca the British live in expat ghettoes. There are *urbanizaciónes* where all the owners of the villas or apartments are foreign and you will rarely see a Spanish face.

Nevertheless, there are many advantages to living in an area where there are a large number of expats. The British in these areas form social clubs and offer all sorts of sports and leisure activities, making it far easier to settle in and make new friends. In such areas it is also fairly easy to find familiar services offered in English, alleviating some of the difficulties and fears that the language barrier can create. For many, the presence of so many fellow countrymen is a real draw to a certain area. For expats Mac and Meryl Macdonald, who moved to Spain to lead a more active, outdoor lifestyle, it was a deciding factor:

> *It was never our intention to completely immerse ourselves in a different culture. We spent quite a lot of time looking at different areas to live in, but the fact that there were a lot of expats in Javea, and that there were very good sporting facilities really made up our minds.*

Many find the presence of Brits a useful way to ease themselves into Spanish culture. This was the experience of expats Andrew and Margaret Slepyan:

We didn't really realise the sort of culture we were buying into, but it has worked out well. If we had gone straight to the interior, we'd have been completely lost; we wouldn't have known the language or understood anything. Now, although we still like it here, we are looking for more of the real culture of Spain, so we are looking for something away from the coast. The costas have been a stepping stone for us.

How Might the Area Change in the Future?

Spain is going through a period of rapid development and modernisation. Wherever you buy, the area will certainly not remain as you found it, and it is wise to prepare yourself for the future. Andrew and Margaret Slepyan describe the rapid Anglicisation of their town, in just a few years:

Four years ago when we arrived and set up our shop here, we were the only British shop in Oliva and you hardly ever heard people speaking English. Now all of the bars and restaurants are British run and it is more unusual to hear people speaking Spanish!

The estate agents in Spain are constantly looking for new areas that they can sell as 'a slice of the real Spain'; areas that have not been over-run by expats, and where prices are still attractive to the international community. David and Joanne Kitching, tell a story that is indicative of the zealous plans of the developers:

A friend of ours went to look at a new off-plan development being built further north up the coast. She was impressed, but was concerned that there was not much of a British community in the area, to which the developer replied – 'Just give us a year or two'.

If you are buying an off-plan property, find out if there are likely to be further buildings planned – a possible Phase 2 or 3 where your bijou set of apartments is going to be reduced to being merely one of a number of such apartments, part of a small town complete with café, club house and social centre.

Other Considerations

The Weather. The only place where you will be guaranteed sunshine and warm sea temperatures throughout the year is in the Canary Islands. Elsewhere in Spain winter temperatures can get distinctly chilly. You will need to pack warm clothes and make sure that the property has adequate insulation and heating.

Ease of Access. These days, buyers hoping to find cheap properties near the budget airports will have their work cut out, although new routes and destinations are constantly opening up in Spain. Nevertheless, proximity to an airport is a significant consideration. Also consider local and regional transport in the area. How easy is it to get to areas of interest, the beaches and the commercial centres?

The Local Municipal Council. You may find that local facilities, and services are very well run and efficient and that any planning and building regulations are dealt with quickly and efficiently. On the other hand things may be badly run and disproportionately expensive to remedy. It all depends on the local *ayuntamiento*. Good places to find out this sort of information are the English-language magazines and newspapers, as well as other expat property owners.

Planning for the Future. The British Consulate advises people to look ahead when considering where to buy their retirement home. Whilst it may be ideal to live in a beautiful but remote spot in your fifties and early sixties, as you get older the long trek to the nearest shops and amenities may become a real burden. You should also consider the provision of medical facilities in the area where you are hoping to buy.

Leisure Facilities. Depending on what your leisure interests are – golf, sailing, skiing, equestrianism, water sports or bridge, how close to the property are the nearest facilities?

Water Shortages. Areas that get little annual rainfall will naturally succumb to periods of drought (especially Andalucía, the Costa Calida, the Costa Blanca and the Costa Brava) when water restrictions come into force. Indeed, in 2005 Spain was subjected to its worst drought in sixty years, with rivers losing nearly a third of their volume. Talk to the locals and other foreigners who have lived in the area for some time to establish how likely a drought may be.

Seasonal Population Fluctuations. Is your property part of a development where neighbouring properties are let out continually to holidaymakers intent on a raucous two-week knees-up throughout the high season? Does the area turn into a ghost town during the winter? Try to visit the area in both high and low season

THE TEN MOST POPULAR REGIONS FOR RETIREMENT

Spain as we know it today has grown out of a number of separate states and kingdoms, making it a complex country with a mix of peoples and cultures. The regions and provinces described below represent the current political make-up of Spain and are listed in order of their popularity with British expatriates (according to official residencia application figures). The average price of a second home in Spain is €207,260.

1. ANDALUCÍA

British residents in Spain who have chosen this region: 30%
Provinces: Almería, Cádiz, Córdoba, Granada, Huelva, Jaén, Málaga and Sevilla.
Main City: Sevilla.
Airports: Almeria, Córdoba, Gibraltar, Granada, Jerez de la Frontera, Málaga, Sevilla.
Regional tourist office website: www.andalucia.org.

Andalucía is the second largest autonomous region of Spain covering 17% of Spain's total area. It is the most populated region with around seven million inhabitants, all enjoying 300 days of sunshine per year. Andalucía takes its name from al Andaluz, which was the stronghold of Muslim Arabs and Berbers who crossed from North Africa in the eighth century. The region's Moorish past can be seen in the great monuments that survive from the period, such as the Mezquita in Córdoba and the Alhambra palace in Granada, regarded as one of the world's greatest buildings.

Some see Andalucia as having the most distinctive character of any of the regions: it is the home of the gypsy guitar and flamenco, has its own very strong accent, and a regional government that enjoys far more autonomy than many. Those who choose to live in Andalucia, away from the enclaves of expats, will discover a new world filled with the customs and traditions of local life.

Foreigners who relocate to Andalucía tend to gravitate to one of the region's four costas: the *Costa de la Luz*, the *Costa del Sol* (one of the most popular tourist destinations on earth), the *Costa Tropical* and the *Costa de Almería*. These areas are discussed below:

The Costa de la Luz

Average House Price: €202,184.

The Costa de la Luz (Coast of light) is becoming increasingly popular as it is less developed than the Costa del Sol, with quieter beaches and cheaper land. This coastline is at the western end of the Andalucían coastline, facing out to the Atlantic. It covers the coastline of Huelva - from the Portuguese border to Doñana National park and the region of Cadiz - from Jerez to Tarifa. The temperatures are slightly milder than on the Costa del Sol and the golden sand beaches are more spread-out, and often backed by sand dunes and pine trees. This part of the coast has not yet seen the high-rise hotel development of other areas. At present property prices on the Costa de la Luz are rising fast as more and more people are discovering the potential of the region.

Titan Properties choose the Huelva coastline of Costa de la Luz for a variety of reasons. Faro Airport, gateway for golf, good times and grandchildren, hosts flights from 20 UK airports. Only 30 minutes away is the beautiful and friendly, 70-km south-facing coast, from Ayamonte to Punta Umbria. This under-developed, but fully serviced coast attracts an exciting mix of cultures, international and Spanish. All resources are nearby, including excellent medical facilities. Buying for up to 40% less than Spain's other costas, retirees can enjoy the growth of their investment as well as 'la vida' on the white beaches, amongst the pine forests, 7 golf-courses, and the fresh food of beachside restaurants.

RETIREMENT HOTSPOT

Nuevo Portil. Built amongst natural pine forests and running alongside golden sand beaches, Nuevo Portil is an attractive, tranquil development. The 18-hole golf course is surrounded by low density luxury villas and some townhouse developments. Nuevo Portil golf resort blends into the small town of El Portil, which has bars, shops and restaurants. Across from the beach there is a natural sand barrier offering a perfect natural marina for yachts. The area is very accessible for international tourists: less than one hour from Faro airport and Seville airport. There are also plans for an international airport to be built in Gibraleon, close to Huelva.

Regions & Provinces of Spain

The Basque Country
Biscay
Guipuzcoa
Alava
Navarre
Rioja
Huesca
Lérida
Gerona
Soria
Aragon
Catalonia
Zaragoza
Barcelona
Tarragona
Guadalajara
Teruel
Cuenca
Castellón
Balearic Islands
Menorca
Mallorca
Mancha
Valencia
Ibiza
Albacete
Formentera
Alicante
Murcia
Almeria

Mediterranean Sea

La Palma
Lanzarote
Gomera
Tenerife
Hierro
Fuerte-Ventura
Gran Canaria
The Canary Islands

Typical Properties for Sale on the Costa de la Luz			
Location	Type	Description	Price
Chiclana de la Frontera	Town house	3-bedroom house with small terrace, close to town centre.	€130,250
Sancti Petri	Apartment (within an urbanización)	2-bedroom apartment with private garden and garage. 500m from the beach and 10km from the town.	€291,000
Costa Esuri golf resort	Apartment	2-bedroom apartment overlooking golf course.	€160,646
Nuevo Portil golf resort	Townhouse	3-bedroom townhouse in heart of golf course and 500m from the beach.	€268,000

The Costa del Sol

Average House Price: €232,260.

UK residents account for 200,000 of the permanent population of the Costa del Sol. Most of the development so far has taken place west of Málaga, with perpendicular concrete running virtually all the way to Marbella. The western reaches of the Costa del Sol – between Málaga and Cádiz – has one of the most developed coastlines in Europe. The notorious tourist centres of Fuengirola, Torremolinos and Calahonda are along this stretch, as well as the more upmarket towns such as Marbella, Estepona and Puerto Banús. Property for sale along this stretch is either new or fairly new re-sale buildings. The highest prices will be asked for property lying between the N340 and the sea and in the environs of Marbella. Inland there are still some bargains to be had, but the more beautiful the setting (e.g. towns such as Ronda and Mijas), the higher the price of property.

At the most westerly point of the Costa del Sol lies Gibraltar, still British and a banking and money moving centre. Luxury housing developments are beginning to sprout in the vicinity, notably at Sotogrande and La Duquesa, and many people are choosing to live not too far from English-speaking Gibraltar. Now that the final stretch of motorway linking Estepona to Sotogrande has been completed, it is possible to travel to the western part of the Costa del Sol from Málaga airport within an hour.

East of Málaga, development has been a little less rampant but concrete does proliferate, especially around the resort of Nerja. The eastern Costa del Sol does not have the same long swathes of beaches as the west, but the area has managed to hold onto its roots and prices here are generally cheaper.

For years now the Costa del Sol property market has been booming, and many people have been able to double their investment in as little as two years. However, in 2005 prices began to stabilise, and in some areas prices of new second homes dropped for the first time in years when supply finally outstripped demand. Although for years people have been expecting the "bubble to burst" on the Costa del Sol, it seems more likely that the next few years will see a slow levelling off of house prices, rather than a dramatic crash.

RETIREMENT HOTSPOT

Mijas. Located on a mountainside 8km inland of Fuengirola, Mijas is a typical Andalucían white village with Moorish origins. The walled town is picturesque with winding lanes and little squares filled with restaurants and shops and a miniature bullring. Mijas is the place of choice for many permanent, expat residents. The many hilltops surrounding the town and along the descent to the coast are natural attractions for a dream villa with magnificent views. While enjoying the tranquillity of the mountain setting, the coast is only minutes away and below Mijas proper is Mijas Costa, a series of residential developments. Property here is cheaper than in the village itself, but does not have the same charm.

Typical Properties for Sale on the Costa del Sol			
Location	Type	Description	Price
Mijas	Apartment	2 bedrooms, views of the coast and mountains from terrace, sauna.	€341,250
Estepona	Apartment	2-bedroom ground-floor apartment with communal garden and pool.	€210,000
Torremolinos	Apartment	Fully-furnished studio apartment in the town centre.	€72,000
Lake Iznajar (inland)	Farmhouse	8-bedroom farmhouse overlooking the lake, with 1.5 acres, pool, tennis court.	€350,000

The Costa Tropical

The Costa Tropical takes its name from the sub-tropical climate, which allows the cultivation of exotic fruits and crops such as avocados, mangoes and bananas. Until a few years ago it was lumped in with the Costa del Sol but it has now been re-branded in an attempt to highlight the region's distinct character.

Whilst there are similarities with the Costa del Sol, Tropical has managed to avoid mass tourism and some of the uglier high-rises. From Salobreña to Motril the coastline remains entirely undeveloped, although there are plans to extend Motril's golf course and there are even proposals to build a yacht marina.

The warm micro-climate found on this coast is created by the shelter of the Lujar and Chaparral mountains near the coast, and the Sierra Nevada behind, with some of the highest peaks in Europe. The warm winds coming across from North Africa give this sheltered *costa* mild temperatures all year round. As a result the coast is filled with dense orchards, which are guarded by Moorish watchtowers and fortresses nestling on the cliffs.

The coast is a mere forty-five minutes from Granada and it takes just over an hour to get to the Sierra Nevada. This leads to the fairly bizarre situation between October and April, when you can ski in the Sierra Nevada in the morning and sunbathe on the coast in the afternoon. The ski fields are approximately an hour away by car. Diving is also a very popular pastime on the Costa Tropical.

RETIREMENT HOTSPOT

Salobreña. Located 2km inland from the coast, Salobreña is set high on a crag surrounded by a tropical plain. The town has been far less developed than many other coastal towns and the old centre is a maze of narrow streets leading up to a Moorish castle from which there are breath-taking views of the mountains and the plain. Salobreña town hall is very conscious of preserving the town's traditional image and in recent years has invested in freshly cobbling the streets. Development in the area is therefore restricted. Beneath Salobreña is a modern development of low-rise attractive apartments, bars and restaurants, and the commercial centre where you will find shops, supermarkets, banks and the town hall. The seafront is lined with *chiringuitos*, simple beach bars. The amount of construction currently underway along the front means that there are plenty of off-plan opportunities for the homebuyer.

Inland from the Costa Tropical – Alpujarras. Only fifty kilometres in from the coast, the Alpujarras region is a beautiful and unspoilt area of mountain villages and deep valleys tucked away in the foothills of the Sierra Nevada. The area boasts spectacular scenery of laden orchards, deep gorges, lush green valleys and pine forests. Hidden amongst this dramatic landscape is a string of seventy or so villages, some of the most picturesque to be found anywhere is Spain. Whitewashed houses built haphazardly on top of one another tumble down steep slopes, each balcony is strewn with geraniums, carnations and wild roses, while red peppers and corn are hung up to dry against the thick stone walls. After centuries of isolation, newly constructed roads are opening the region up and many ramshackle houses are being snapped up by foreigners.

Typical Properties for Sale on the Costa Tropical			
Location	Type	Description	Price
Almuñecar	Townhouse	3-bedroom house, central location, 200m from beach.	€140,000
La Herradura	Apartment	Frontline beach apartment. 2 bedrooms, 2 bathrooms, big terrace, sea views.	€283,000
Salobreña	Villa	3-bedroom, brand new villa with swimming pool and sea views.	€525,000
Alpujarras	Cortijo (farmhouse)	2-bedroom traditional farmhouse.	€72,000

The Costa de Almería

Average House Price: €154,335.
Almería is now one of the wealthiest regions of Spain, largely because of its thriving agricultural industry. Would-be second homeowners are attracted to the hottest corner of Europe because of its unspoilt and dramatic coastline, and 190km of clean, sandy beaches. The Costa de Almería is not yet as overcrowded as most other Spanish tourist resorts. Made up of bays, inlets and cliffs, it is an ideal place for those who want to get away from it all and live in a more traditional Spanish environment. The climate in Almería is subtropical, with an average winter temperature of 16° Celsius. It has the most sunshine hours of the whole of Spain, 3,000 per year. The area is great for water sports and there are a number of golf courses, such as the 18-hole golf course Marina Golf at Almería's main resort, Mojácar Playa. The international airport is 8km from Almería city (which also has a train station), and other airports at San Javier in Murcia and Alicante serve the area.

RETIREMENT HOTSPOT

Almerimar. Almerimar was purpose built to provide facilities for holidaymakers and those who wish to retire from the irritations of modern life. The beach is wide and sandy, with crystal clear waters, and the marina, which was built around the original harbour, houses boats from all over Europe. Golfing fans may be attracted by the resort's 18-hole course around which there are numerous villas and apartments for sale. The only problem with buying in Almerimar is that there are hardly any resale properties available. However, there is a selection of high quality, attractive new-build apartments under construction near to the marina.

Typical Properties for Sale on the Costa de Almería

Location	Type	Description	Price
Almerimar	Apartment	2 bedrooms, overlooking golf course, views of the beach and Sierra Nevada.	€130,000
Mojacar	Apartment	2-bedroom luxury apartment close to the beach with sea views.	€337,323
Roquetas de Mar	Townhouse	4 bedrooms, 2 bathrooms, 200m from beach, central location.	€183,600
Tabernas (inland) – Oasis de Tabernas development	Villa (off-plan)	3 bedrooms, 2 bathrooms, private swimming pool.	€165,000

2. VALENCIA

British residents in Spain who have chosen this region: 28%
Provinces: Valencia, Alicante, Castellón.
Main Towns and Cities: Torrevieja, Alicante, Benidorm, Jávea, Puerto de Gandía, Valencia, Sagunto, Castellón de la Plana, Vinaroz.
Airports: Alicante, Valencia. New airport due at Castellón de la Plana in 2007.
Average House Price: €158,778.

The Valencia region has strong historical associations with the Catalonian/Aragonese partnership which conquered it in the twelfth century, and shares a linguistic heritage with Catalonia, although arguments still rage as to whether Valencian is in fact a language in its own right or a dialect of Catalan.

In the province of Alicante lies the Costa Blanca ('White Coast'), which has a thriving community of expatriates. The beaches and resorts of the

Costa Blanca: Denia, Jávea, Calpe, Altea, Benidorm and Villajoyosa to name but a few; are incredibly popular with both tourists and property buyers. Access to the Costa Blanca is easy from Alicante airport.

The White Coast gets its name from Greek traders who founded *Akra Leuka* or the blank foothill there around 2,500 years ago, but it was only really in the 1960s, when the picturesque village of Benidorm began attracting package tourists that the area started to take shape as the holiday haven it has become today. The Costa Blanca may have been over-developed in places but this does not detract from its natural beauty and serenity. Indeed, the World Health Organisation cites this stretch of coastline as one of the healthiest places on earth due to its climate, recreational facilities and relaxed way of life.

There is quite a large north/south divide on the Costa Blanca. Property prices are far cheaper in the south and as a rule, the north attracts a more refined crowd searching for a villa with private swimming pool, whereas in the south property-buyers are usually young families or couples looking for an apartment.

In the provinces of Valencia and Castellón is the Costa del Azahar, which runs from just north of Denia to the town of Vinaroz. It offers some breath-taking scenery, mild winters and real value for money when it comes to buying property. In the centre of this coast lies Valencia, Spain's third city which provides an enticing blend of the traditional and the contemporary avant-garde.

Costa Blanca South

The southern region of the Costa Blanca, running from the border with Murcia up to Alicante, is generally cheaper to buy property in than the northern reaches and offers far better value for money. There are some excellent, blue-flag winning beaches here and some of the resorts are developing excellent sporting facilities, hotels and nightclubs. Although the up and coming regions are considered to be Almeria and Murcia, this area offers some strong competition and is an ideal choice for those with families.

Heading inland from the southern Costa Blanca there are many comparatively unexplored areas where fincas can be bought for as little as €70,000.

RETIREMENT HOTSPOT

Torrevieja. Torrevieja is over-developed and is one of the fastest growing resorts on the Costa Blanca (the town has swelled by 100% since 1998), but that fact doesn't mean that one has to write off the whole area. The superb climate, great beaches, first class sport, recreation and health facilities and the low cost of living, as well as being just 35km south of the airports at San Javier and Alicante, go some way to explaining why so many Britons have chosen to retire here. Torrevieja also offers stunning cliff walks, many natural beauty spots, a well-served marina and the two attractive lagoons of Las Salinas. Prices around Torrevieja are among the cheapest on the Costa Blanca. Heading south along the Orihuela Costa, there are excellent golf courses, a dozen varied beaches, two good marinas and plenty of restaurants and bars.

Alicante and the Costa Blanca North

Alicante was called *Lucentum* – City of Light – by the Romans. The city has good medical care facilities and an infrastructure that supports the large number of retirees who have decided to move into the area.

As the main city of the Costa Blanca, Alicante has much to offer with the architecture, arts, crafts and cuisine a wonderful fusion of styles, together with miles of coastline. The San Juan de Alicante beach is to the east of the city and is over 7km long. Gran Alacant, at the southern-most reach of Alicante's influence, is located just south of the regional capital and close to the airport. It is also convenient for Benidorm, Terra Mítica and the North Costa Blanca, making it a very popular resort town.

South of Alicante property is relatively cheap, and there is plenty of it, though over the last three years prices have increased by 20% a year. North of Alicante, the coastline can be quite spectacular and, except for the blot of Benidorm, the northern reaches of the Costa Blanca have had restricted development, which has led to a rather exclusive and expensive area of property acquisition. The 'golden triangle' of Denia, Javea and Calpe are sought after and property prices are high compared to those south of Alicante.

RETIREMENT HOTSPOT

Jávea (Xábia). Jávea is an attractive town, and the area is a favoured venue for naturalists, scuba divers and water sports enthusiasts. The town consists of three parts with the pretty and laid-back old town lying inland, and the port and marina 3km away. Nearby is the main beach resort of El Arenal, the beginning of 25km of coastline. Villas here start at around €300,000, so it is not a cheap place to buy. However, the area has for many years been popular with foreign property buyers and 20% of the town's population are British expatriates, making their presence felt with an enthusiastic cricket, bowls and bridge scene. It is easy to see why people are drawn here. Jávea is relatively quiet for most of the year and only the resort of El Arenal endures the excesses of the tourist season in July and August.

Typical Properties for Sale on the Costa Blanca			
Location	Type	Description	Price
Torrevieja	Apartment	3 bedrooms, first floor, near to town centre, small balcony, semi-furnished.	€132,450
Jávea	Villa	3 bedrooms, 3 bathrooms, close to city centre, swimming pool.	€450,000
Moraira	Bungalow	2 bedrooms, panoramic views, next to beach, communal pool.	€220,000
Benidorm	Apartment	1 bedroom, sea view and large terrace. Located in development with pool, tennis and gym.	€145,145

Valencia and The Costa del Azahar

Valencia, Spain's third largest city, is a truly exciting and vibrant place, accurately labelled 'the City of Contrasts'. Founded by Roman legionaries in 138 BC, Valencia has a traditional atmosphere with an impressive array of architecture going back to the Middle Ages. However, in recent years Valencia has seen a huge amount of investment and modern development and the brand new area, the City of Arts and Sciences has been praised for having brought ultramodern urbanism right into the heart of its traditional town. The modern-day city of Valencia has sprawling suburbs of high-rise blocks and its fair share of beggars; however, the city is forever linked with the romantic figure of El Cid. Cheap housing is available around the outskirts of the city, but for those who wish to live fairly centrally, prices are still at least thirty per cent lower than in Barcelona or Madrid.

The coastline along the provinces of Valencia and Castellón is lined with magnificent orange plantations amidst lush green vegetation giving it the name – the Costa del Azahar or the Orange Blossom Coast. The strong smell of pines drifting down from the mountains mixed with the intoxicating smells of orange trees in blossom and the almond groves really brings this 112km stretch of coast to life. Surrounded by the extensive, spectacular La Safar mountain ranges and excellent white sandy beaches, the Costa Del Azahar offers views of stunning and contrasting landscapes.

Dotted along the shoreline are small summer resorts, perhaps the best known of which is the ancient fortified town of Peñiscola. The coast here boasts miles of sandy beaches and very calm waters, particularly safe for bathing and for practising all kinds of water-sports.

RETIREMENT HOTSPOT

Gandía. Gandia itself is slightly inland, but most people look for property in the Gandia Playa coastal resort, with over four miles of palm-lined beaches. It is a clean, pretty and relaxed stretch of coastline with mountains to the west and 18km of magnificent white sandy beaches to the east. Property prices are lower here than further south and the cost of living is certainly cheaper. In the last five years the expat community has increased massively. There are now many English-speaking clubs and organisations.

Properties along this lesser-known coastline are bought mainly by Spaniards, but appeal to foreigners as prices remain reasonably low and access is relatively quick and direct from Valencia airport, which is now served by several of the budget carriers. The new airport at Castellón de la Plana is due to open in 2007 and will make the area far more accessible to foreign homebuyers, almost certainly creating a huge surge of demand.

Typical Properties for Sale on the Costa del Azahar			
Location	**Type**	**Description**	**Price**
Gandia	Apartment	Small 3rd-floor apartment situated in the city centre, 3 bedrooms.	€57,459
Peñiscola	Villa	3 bedrooms, close to the beachfront, sea views.	€202,080
Oliva	Town house	2 bedrooms. Single storey town house with patio and terrace. Situated in town centre.	€105,268
Benicarló	Villa	4 bedrooms, 2 bathrooms. Private pool and gardens. Quiet area 3km from beach.	€264,300

Those planning on buying property in the Valencia region should be aware of the infamous LRAU, the land-grab laws that have seen many expats lose their homes. For further information see *Your New Home in Spain.*

3. THE CANARY ISLANDS (LAS ISLAS CANARIAS)

British residents in Spain who have chosen this region: 13%

Principal islands and resorts: Gran Canaria: Las Palmas; Lanzarote: Arrecife; La Palma: Santa Cruz; Tenerife: Santa Cruz.

Airports: Gran Canaria, La Palma, Tenerife South, Tenerife North, Fuerteventura, Lanzarote.

Regional Tourist Office Website: www.canarias-saturno.com.

Average House Price: €252,210.

The Canary Islands became Spanish territory as long ago as the fifteenth century. For retirees the draw of the Canaries is obvious: the 'eternal spring' of the islands' subtropical climate. The islands are warm throughout the winter and, with the exception of Lanzarote, do not become unbearably hot, even in the height of summer. The best known of the Canary Islands are also the largest: Gran Canaria, Lanzarote and Tenerife and it is on these islands that the largest enclaves of foreign residents are situated, offering retirees a full range of English-speaking services. Ferries and jetfoils link each of the islands and commmunications with the rest of Europe are good, although many find the three and a half hour flight from the UK off-putting.

There are seven islands altogether, located about 70 miles off the Moroccan Western Sahara coast. The smaller islands are Fuerteventura, Hierro, Gomera and La Palma. With the exception of Lanzarote, which is comparatively flat, all these islands are characterised by high central mountains, and the consequent change of climate and spectacular scenery, a legacy of their volcanic origins. The central island, Gran Canaria, is described as a 'miniature continent', with a range of climates from dry and desert-like around the periphery; lush and sub-tropical; to a more temperate climate as you climb the central mountains. The mountains are volcanic, like the islands themselves, which emerged from the Atlantic some 40 million years ago. The atmosphere of Gran Canaria today is surprisingly cosmopolitan and the island is certainly not a backwater. Ikea and Benetton have stores there as does El Corte Inglés, the ubiquitous Spanish department store. The capital, Las Palmas, has all the facilities of any large Spanish city and its own beach – a centre for sunbathing and socialising – while the coastline further to the southwest has Puerto de Mogan, which retains its old-fashioned charm and is a favoured stopping-off point for yachts. The facilities make Gran Canaria an excellent place to live, especially away from some of the overcrowded resorts.

The Canaries have greater autonomy from central government than other regions of Spain and the two provinces they form are regulated from Las Palmas-Gran Canaria and Santa Cruz-Tenerife. The three main islands have long been popular with tourists from all over the world and in recent years they have also become increasingly popular with timeshare and villa owners, many of whom have holidayed in the islands before settling there. The most popular places for foreign residents are also the tourist centres: in the Orotava Valley of Tenerife, and the south of Gran Canaria where there are several tourist developments including the Playa del Inglés and San Agustin. Apart from the three main islands there are also smaller foreign communities in Fuerteventura and La Palma. Hierro and Gomera are less visited and further from the convenience of facilities and services that many expats expect.

> The local tax in the Canary Islands on new homes is 5% compared to the 7.5% on the mainland. Tax on building plots remains 5% compared to the 16% on the mainland which is an incentive for those who are prepared to tackle the bureaucracy involved in self-build.

Property prices are rising in the Canary Islands by up to 20% a year. The British tend to plump for property on Tenerife (and many retirees relocate to the main towns like Playa San Juan or the resorts along the Costa Adeje), Lanzarote and Fuerteventura. Property on the northern coast of Tenerife is still cheaper than that in the south as it rains more. Prices in Lanzarote and Fuerteventura are slightly cheaper (by 10%-15%) than on Tenerife. Because of an embargo on new developments on all the Canary Islands, prices are likely to rise considerably as demand outstrips supply. Germans seem to abound in Gran Canaria, and to a lesser extent are buying up properties in the smaller off the track islands of Gomera, La Palma and Hierro.

RETIREMENT HOTSPOT

Puerto de la Cruz. The northern coast of Tenerife is quieter and more secluded than the resorts of the south and has therefore proved popular with retired Brits. Puerto de la Cruz is the main resort here, and is also a thriving, cosmopolitan city, with plenty of English-speaking amenities and services, including excellent sporting facilities and an annual season of classical music concerts. Nearby, there is superb walking in the Oratava Valley national park.

Typical Properties for Sale in the Canary Islands			
Location	**Type**	**Description**	**Price**
Arrecife (Lanzarote)	Villa	Large detached 3-bedroom property with terrace and swimming pool.	€425,000
Playa de las Americas (Tenerife)	Villa	Furnished 1-bedroom villa with easy access to beach and amenities. Complex has 2 communal pools. Spectacular views.	€149,999
Las Palmas (Gran Canaria)	Detached house	Traditional 3-bedroom house. Completely renovated with fantastic views over the valley, patio and roof terrace.	€316,000
Fuerteventura	Apartment	Ground floor property with panoramic views, situated on a golf course.	€205,919

4. THE BALEARIC ISLANDS (LAS ISLAS BALEARES)

British residents in Spain who have chosen this region: 9%
Main Towns and Cities: Palma (Mallorca); Mahon (Minorca); Ibiza Town; Sant Francesc Xavier (Formentera).
Airports: Palma, Mahon (Maó in Catalan), Ibiza Town.
Average House Price: €219,603.

The Balearic Islands lying off the Valencian and Catalonian coasts have been under Spanish sovereignty since the Romans incorporated them into their province of Hispania. Together the four main islands of Mallorca, Menorca, Ibiza and Formentera make up less than 1% of the area of Spain, with a total population of around 750,000.

Because of government restrictions on development and limited land availability, prices on the islands are higher than on the mainland and it is difficult to find a well located property for less than €200,000. The islands are therefore the number one choice for buyers looking for luxurious properties, glamorous surroundings and the best weather. The largest island of the group is Mallorca, which attracts an estimated three million tourists a year. The other islands are mainly summer resorts and are fairly quiet out of season. The liveliest and most up-market is certainly Ibiza. Menorca is more sedate and family-orientated.

Access to the Balearic islands from the UK is easy as there are numerous charter flights all year round. There are ferry connections to Ibiza from Denia and Barcelona and from Valencia to Ibiza and Palma. It is also possible to reach Mahon in Menorca by ferry from Barcelona.

Mallorca

Mallorca has become an extremely desirable place to live. Although there are areas of the island that were ravaged by developers in the sixties and seventies, most of the island retains its staggeringly diverse natural beauty. The island's capital Palma has also been much maligned in the past, and those who visit, more often than not, have their preconceptions shattered by a lively, vibrant city steeped in history and culture.

RETIREMENT HOTSPOT

Puerto Pollensa (Port de Pollença). The Badia de Pollença is a sweeping, horseshoe shaped bay, with sheltered waters that are ideal for swimming. The focus of the bay is Port de Pollença. Once a small fishing village, the town has retained its intrinsic character and charm and offers a relaxed and fairly traditional way of life, there are none of the noisy nightclubs and high-rise buildings of other resorts. Pollença is a place for relaxation. Set in an area of natural beauty, Pollença offers long, sandy, blue flag beaches and an attractive backdrop of the Boquer mountain range. Many bars and cafes are centred around the marina which offers superb views across the wide bay.

It is estimated that there are 15,000 British residents on the largest of the four islands. The majority of foreign buyers are attracted to the south-west corner of Mallorca, which has better weather, a popular coastline and exclusive residential areas. However, more and more buyers are considering inland villages, due to the lower prices and the lack of tourist activity. Those who live in the main tourist areas, particularly the east coast of the island, point out that the end of season exodus and the subsequent closing of businesses can be quite depressing. Property prices in Mallorca are currently rising by around 25% a year and as long as development restrictions on the island remain, demand will continue to increase.

Menorca

Menorca is the Balearics' second largest island, but unlike parts of Mallorca, it has remained relatively untouched by tourism. Menorca's charms lie in its relaxed atmosphere, picturesque towns, stunning scenery and deserted beaches with crystal clear waters. There are more than a hundred idyllic beaches on Menorca and although the government here has been trying to improve access to the more remote ones, there are still many beaches that can only be reached by foot. There is nothing more satisfying than a scenic hike to your own private beach.

Expatriates cite such aspects of island life as the minimal crime index, peace and quiet, and the friendly familiarity of the locals as the main reasons for choosing Menorca as the location for their retirement. Around 70-75% of property buyers in Menorca are British. According to Drew Galloway of Vil-la Inmobiliari, *'Whereas previously most people were looking for a holiday home, these days people are seeing the long-term advantages of living on the island and are looking to either retire there permanently or split their time equally between a home in Menorca and a home elsewhere'.*

Ibiza

Ibiza offers something to please everyone, from the culture, fashion and superb cuisine in Ibiza town and the stunning coves and beaches on Ibiza's coastline to the wild twenty-four hour clubbing in San Antonio and hippy chic in Santa Eulalia. Those worried about Ibiza's culture of excess will find that the clubbers and revellers are concentrated in Ibiza Town, San Antonio and Santa Eulalia. Away from the resort areas is a stunningly beautiful island with dense pine forests, towering cliffs and some of the best beaches in the Balearics. Property on Ibiza is expensive and the island is home to numerous millionaires. The restrictions on development in the Balearics have caused prices in Ibiza to soar even more than on the other islands.

Typical Properties for Sale on the Balearic Islands			
Location	Type	Description	Price
Palma (Mallorca)	Apartment	3 bedrooms. Situated close to the beach and amenities. Terrace.	€338,000
Puerto Pollensa (Mallorca)	Magnificent country house	4 bedrooms – each with private terrace, 4 bathrooms. 14,000 sq.m. of land. Private swimming pool and garden. 5 minutes from golf course.	€1.5 million
Cala Llonga (Menorca)	Villa	5-bedroom harbour side villa with incredible views, terrace, swimming pool and parking.	€504,799

5. CATALONIA (CATALUÑA)

British residents in Spain who have chosen this region: 7%

Main cities and provinces: Barcelona, Girona, Lleida (Lérida), Tarragona.

Airports: Barcelona, Gerona, Reus.

Catalonia, is one of the regions of Spain which has its own distinct historical, and some would say national, identity, with its own Catalan culture and language. Although covering less than 7% of the total area of Spain, Catalonia is home to over six million inhabitants; about 16% of the total population of Spain. This has long been one of the most exciting and cosmopolitan parts of Spain, and Barcelona is a fascinating centre of politics, fashion, commerce and culture. Despite being heavily repressed under the Franco regime, Catalan nationalism is still prevalent and although Spanish is universally spoken, Catalan is favoured in schools and universities.

The northern costas, the Costa Brava and the Costa Dorada were the first to be invaded in the 1950s by tourism and property development. There is a large Spanish presence among the property owners in this region so it has remained pretty culturally intact, unlike the Costa del Sol. Because of Catalonia's proximity to the French border, overland travel between the UK and Spain is pretty fast. Low cost flights from UK airports have made Spain's northern costas even more accessible.

The Costa Brava

Average House Price: €222,999.

For many the Costa Brava ('the rugged coast') is the only place in which they would consider buying property. The beauty of this coastline, with its cliffs and coves led to the beginnings of mass tourism in Spain, which in turn has led to the over-development of the area. Between Blanes and Sant Feliu de Guixols some of the worst aspects of mass tourism can be seen, but the further north toward the French border you travel the less sprawling the development. Property is still being developed along the coast but there is increasing demand due to the recent decision of Catalonia's new government to clamp down on coastal building. Property remains comparatively expensive in the Costa Brava, partly due to the Spanish and French love affair with the region, and this ban will undoubtedly push prices even higher.

At the northern end of the Costa Brava are the small and unspoilt resorts of Calelle de Palafrugel, Figueres and Cadaques. This area is still relatively unknown to many British holidaymakers and there are almost no noisy nightclubs and lager louts, only beautiful scenery and peaceful, sandy bays and coves. For those interested in water sports, this area has excellent wind surfing at the resorts of Roses, Estartit and Platja d'Aro and snorkelling at Aigua Blava. Proximity to the Pyrenees offers possibilities for hiking in the summer and skiing in the winter.

RETIREMENT HOTSPOT

Blanes. About an hour's drive north of Barcelona and situated at the southern end of the Costa Brava, Blanes is a colourful resort town. The sandy beach is one of the longest on this stretch of coast and the international airports at Girona and Barcelona are half an hour and just over an hour away respectively. Local road and rail links are excellent. There is a marina, a port, an aquarium and two botanical gardens. Rather unusually this resort manages to combine modern facilities with the traditional feel of a Mediterranean fishing town. For golf aficionados there is the Club de Golf l'Angel and the area boasts two water parks. Andorra, which offers excellent skiing, is only two hours away by car. Property here is fairly cheap, as is the cost of living. Two bedroom apartments sell for as little as €100,000.

Barcelona

Barcelona city, much to the chagrin of the capital Madrid, is held by many to be the most lively and interesting city in Spain. Not only is it a huge industrial centre and port (with a population of three million), and the spiritual home of individuals of such startling originality as the architect Gaudí and Pablo Picasso, it is also the most liberal (or decadent, depending on your viewpoint) city in Spain and currently one of the most fashionable in Europe.

Barcelona airport, Prat, is 14km from the city centre and although the airports of Gerona and Reus are further away, the low cost fares available to these airports may make the extra journey worthwhile.

Property in the city itself is fairly expensive. In the centre it is very rare to find anything other than apartments. In top notch central areas expect to pay around €5,890 per square metre of apartment. Barcelona's townhouses and villas are mainly located in the north (Pedralbes, Tres Torres and Sarria) and west (Les Corts) of the city.

Typical Properties for Sale on the Costa Brava and in Barcelona			
Location	Type	Description	Price
St. Feliu de Guixols	New apartment development	4 bedrooms, 5-minute walk to beach, communal pool.	€211,872
Lloret de Mar	Apartment	3 bedrooms, balcony. Quiet area with few neighbours.	€110,182
Blanes	Spanish style villa	3 bedrooms, 2 terraces. Superb views of the Pyrenees. Beach and 2 international golf courses nearby. Large private pool.	€360,000
Pedralbes (north Barcelona)	Townhouse	3 bedrooms, spacious living area, quiet location.	€375,000
Bario Gótico (central Barcelona)	Apartment	1 bedroom, beautiful area, small balcony.	€433,000

The Costa Dorada

Average House Price: €278,177.

The Costa Dorada (the Golden Coast), running south of Barcelona to the Delta de l'Ebre, is less wild than the Costa Brava and the closer you are to Barcelona the higher the cost of property. There are fewer coastal centres of population along this coast, with most development around Vilanova in la Geltrú and Torredembarra, and the terrain becomes less attractive and flat as you head south toward Tarragona. Sitges, a fashionable resort since the late 19th century, is the star of this stretch of coast but because of its status property here is more expensive than elsewhere and apartments in town can be very hard to find.

The Costa Dorada is less of a draw to holidaymakers than the Costa Brava or Costa del Sol and for this reason property is somewhat cheaper than on those coastlines. Against this is the fact that many of the resorts along the Costa Dorada become ghost towns during the winter, and both the busy main coastal road (the N-340), and the Barcelona-Valencia railway line run parallel to the beaches.

Calafell, Cubelles, Altafulla, Cambrils and Tarragona are all places worth looking for property due to their proximity to the beaches. There are several marinas along this coast and four golf courses.

Although the Costa Dorada does not have the density of foreign residents of other places in Spain, the number of foreign visitors to the area means that there is access to English-language newspapers and magazines as well as the supermarkets stocking certain foods from 'back home' and pubs and restaurants catering for those after non-Spanish cuisine.

Typical Properties for Sale on the Costa Dorada			
Location	Type	Description	Price
Tarragona	Studio apartment	2 bedrooms, near to Tarragona port. Spacious living area.	€121,401
Salou	Villa	3 bedrooms. Beachfront with panoramic sea views. Large terrace.	€354,496
Miami Platja	Studio apartment	Beachfront property. Large terrace with sea views.	€82,939

6. MADRID

British residents in Spain who have chosen this region: 6%
Airports: Madrid-Barajas, Madrid-Cuatro Vientos, Madrid-Torrejón.
Regional Tourist Office Website: www.madrid.org/turismo.
Average House Price: €401,806.

It is not by chance that the capital looks like a bull's eye on the map of Spain: located on a high plateau with impossible extremes of climate, the town had little else going for it other than its strategically central and easily defended position, until, that is, the capital was moved here in the seventeenth century. All distances in Spain are measured from Puerta del Sol in the city centre. It is the seat of the Spanish parliament and famed for the

Prado museum and its dizzy nightlife, which lasts from dusk till dawn.

Madrid and the surrounding area together form the autonomous community of Madrid, which is the most densely populated region of Spain, with about 600 inhabitants per square kilometre. Madrid city, as opposed to the region, has a population of just over three million inhabitants – referred to as *Madrileños*. Unfortunately, in common with other giant metropolises, Madrid has its fair share of eyesore high-rise suburbs. However, the capital has many advantages for those not wedded to the sun, sea and sand lifestyle offered by the Mediterranean coast: limited heavy industry and strict pollution controls, and a programme of tree-planting which has transformed the cityscape, have quite literally given Madrid a better atmosphere. Some of Spain's most stunning sights are within easy visiting distance of the capital, notably the cities of Segovia, Avila and Toledo.

Madrid is the hub of all lines of communication in Spain and is served by Barajas Airport, which lies 16km east of the city and can be reached by metro from the city centre. A large number of foreigners live in Madrid (around 100,000) and because of this there are the facilities available to cater for their needs. There are social clubs, Anglican churches, English-speaking doctors and dentists and international schools. There are also two English-Language free sheets (*The Broadsheet* and *Guidepost*), published monthly.

The price of property here is the highest in Spain and mainly consists of apartments and flats. A two-bedroom apartment can fetch anything from €200,000-€500,000. While Madrid is one of the cheapest capital cities in Europe, it is also one of the most expensive places to live in Spain.

Typical Properties for Sale in Madrid			
Location	Type	Description	Price
Madrid	Apartment	Modern 1-bedroom luxury apartment with 24-hour security and metro within 100m. Communal garden and pool.	€485,000
Madrid	Apartment	3-bedroom flat overlooking the street in Austrias district.	€349,140
Madrid	Apartment	Recently refurbished 2-bedroom property near Parque del Retiro. Large balcony overlooking the street.	€570,961

7. MURCIA AND THE COSTA CALIDA

British residents in Spain who have chosen this region: 4%

Main City: Murcia.

Airports: San Javier Airport (47km from Murcia). There are also plans for a new regional airport near to Corvera, which is due to open in 2007.

Regional Tourist Office Website: www.murciaturistica.es.

Average House Price: €149,715.

Murcia, the driest part of Spain, consists of a single province of that name; and neither historically nor nowadays does it have as strong a regional identity as its Valencian neighbour. However, the region has a lot to offer. For nature lovers there is the stunning Sierra Espuña National Park and the Sierra de Carrascoy mountain range. For beach-lovers, the Costa Cálida, which runs from Aguilas to La Manga, boasts white sandy beaches and crystal clear water. For those interested in sport, the region offers excellent facilities. At the upmarket La Manga Club there are international golf courses and tennis centres and the Mar Menor, Europe's largest salt-water lagoon offers sailing, windsurfing, diving and jetskiing. Inland the landscape is dominated by vineyards, rivers, mountains and apricot trees.

Murcia is currently the fastest-growing area in Spain for new *urbanizaciónes*, custom-built villa communities, mainly for the expat market. New marinas, golf courses and hotel developments are all in the process of being built, but it is hoped that the developers here will have learned from the 'too much too soon' construction of some of the other costas and will manage to retain some of the coast's present charm. In the past development in the Costa Cálida was restricted by poor infrastructure. However, improved roads and the evolution of San Javier from an ex-military airport with one flight per week, to an international airport delivering 600,000 visitors a year to the region have improved accessibility. As a result house prices here are on the up, and demand is set to continue, especially when the new custom-built international airport opens in 2007, with the capacity for 22 planes per hour.

Typical Properties for Sale on the Costa Cálida			
Location	Type	Description	Price
Mar Menor	Villa	Modern 3-bedroom villa situated on a golf course.	€407,800
Murcia	Town house	Centrally located, 2-bedroom town house.	€226,000
Club La Manga	Luxury villa	2 bedrooms, private pool and grounds, full access to facilities at Club La Manga.	€850,000
Lorca	Farmhouse	4 bedrooms, 2 bathrooms, located on outskirts of Lorca with 200 olive trees in grounds.	€359,404

8. PAÍS VASCO (THE BASQUE COUNTRY)

British residents in Spain who have chosen this region: 0.9%

Provinces: Alava, Guipuzcoa, Vizcaya (Biscay).

Main city: Bilbao.

Airports: San Sebastián.

Regional Tourist Office Website: www.basquecountrytourism.net.

The Basque Country (*Euskadi*) has a huge amount going for it: gourmet restaurants, undiscovered vineyards, beautiful countryside, vibrant beaches and spectacular architecture, to name but a few. It also has the most determined separatist movement; and a terrorist organisation, Euskadi ta Azkatasuna (ETA) which came into being as a direct result of the repression of the Basques, their culture and language (*euskera*), and their national aspirations, by the Franco regime. In 2006 however, ETA have for the first time announced a 'permanent' ceasefire and this is likely to make the area far more popular as both a place to visit and a place to live. The Basques themselves see the ceasefire as heralding a new era of calm and are expecting a huge rise in the number of visitors.

Food lovers will be particularly attracted to the region, which has more Michelin stars per head than anywhere else in the world: 22 in all. Basque food is renowned for being the best in Spain and you do not need to visit famous restaurants to get an idea of the diversity of cuisine available. There are downsides to this region though; one being the weather. Because of the cooler Atlantic sea temperatures and the amount of annual rainfall, the British are likely to feel very much at home. Similarly the language is a drawback. The Basque language bears no resemblance to other European languages, and will be extremely difficult to learn.

Nevertheless the region has never been so accessible: easyJet flies to Bilbao and Ryanair flies to Vitoria, the city with one of the highest standards of living in the country. It is also possible to sail from Portsmouth to Bilbao with P&O.

Typical Properties for Sale in the Basque Country			
Location	Type	Description	Price
Bilbao	Town house	3-bedroom property, centrally located over 2 floors, large living room.	€347,000
Hondariribia	Town house	Luxury town house on 4 floors, with loft conversion. Parking and garden. Completely renovated.	€570,960
Zumaia	Detached house	4 bedrooms, large living area, stunning views.	€540,911

9. GALICIA

British residents in Spain who have chosen this region: 0.6%

Provinces and main towns: A Coruña, Lugo, Orense, Pontevedra.

Airports: Labacolla (13km east of Santiago de Compostella).

Regional Tourist Office Website: www.turgalicia.es.

It is hardly surprising that Galicia rates as one of the least developed and poorer regions of Spain. Its inland provinces of Lugo and Orense have a reputation as being among the most backward in the country. Galicia sits in the northwest corner of the peninsula, isolated geographically and with poor communications with the other regions. Nevertheless, for the more adventurous, Galicia has a great deal to offer.

The region has a Celtic past of which traces survive, including the bagpipes (*gaita*), and the Galician language, *galégo* (which also gave rise to Portuguese) – a separate language from Spanish, spoken by about 80% of the inhabitants, in a variety of dialects. This region is often compared to Ireland because of a shared Celtic heritage, similar climate and a west coast shaped by the Atlantic into deep inlets.

In contrast to the countryside, the coastal cities of La Coruña, Pontevedra, Vigo and Santiago de Compostela are relatively prosperous and tend to be Castilian-speaking. Galicia has charm with its mixture of the traditional and the modern. Increasingly new highways make it easy to discover the beautiful Atlantic coast, which has some of the best beaches in Spain. Madrid is three hours away from La Coruña by road.

Galicia's average property price is just €925 per square metre, the third lowest of all the autonomous regions and just 61% of the national average. Galicia offers a wealth of cheap renovation homes, ideal for investment. Property prices in Galicia have risen for the last ten consecutive years yet this is one of the last chances to pick up a house in Spain for less than €75,000. In spite of Galicia's charm and the low price of property, there are few foreigners living in this region.

Typical Properties for Sale in Galicia			
Location	Type	Description	Price
Santiago de Compostella	Town house	Attractive 3-bedroom house close to city centre and amenities.	€168,595
Pontevedra	Apartment	2 bedrooms, central location and close to beach and a natural thermal spa.	€46,999
Pontecaldelas	Rural property	Fully restored 3-bedroom house with 5,000m² of private land.	€190,500
Vigo	Town house	Small 2-bedroom town house, central location.	€75,000

10. CASTILLA-LEÓN (OLD CASTILE)

British residents in Spain who have chosen this region: 0.4%
Provinces: Avila, Burgos, León, Palencia, Salamanca, Segovia, Soria, Valladolid, Zamora.
Main City: Valladolid.
Airports: León.
Regional Tourist Office Website: www.jcyl.es/turismo.
Average House Price: €202,934.

The nine provinces of the region of Castilla-León make it the largest region of Spain, covering almost a fifth of the surface area; but it has less than half the population of the next largest region, Andalucia. Castilla-Léon is frequently referred to as Old Castile while the region of Castilla-La Mancha to the south is New Castile. Aragón-Castile became known as Spain in the wider world.

The great river Douro flows right across the *meseta* of Castilla-León and on through Portugal to Oporto at its mouth. The meseta is characterised by its huge prairies, given over largely to cereals, and by its lack of inhabitants.

Some of the most beautiful cities in Spain are to be found here: Salamanca, León, and the walled city of Avila. The most scenic province is probably Soria which is full of the fine castles (*castillos*) giving rise to the region's name. Burgos, the city as opposed to the province, was the former capital of Old Castile, though its significance nowadays derives from its position as a main garrison of the military.

The people of Castilla-León are known as fairly conservative and formal, although people from the vibrant cosmopolitan city of Salamanca are the exception to this rule.

Typical Properties for Sale in Castilla-León			
Location	**Type**	**Description**	**Price**
Toro	Traditional house	3-bedroom property with large garden, swimming pool, tennis court. Close to amenities.	€180,304
Segovia	Town house	4-bedroom property in suburbs of Segovia, good links to Madrid.	€245,495
Salamanca	Apartment	2-bedroom apartment in centre of town.	€108,500
Santiz	Finca	Large 7-bedroom property in a rural setting, near to Salamanca. Large gardens, patio, swimming pool.	€300,799

UNDISCOVERED SPAIN

The following regions have yet to be discovered by any but the most adventurous of British expatriates. Only 1.5% of British residents of Spain live in the combined regions below. This is not to say that they are necessarily wild and inhospitable, merely that they have yet to capture the British public's imagination. However, trends change rapidly and each region has its own distinct charm.

Aragón

Regional Tourist Office: www.turismoaragon.com.
The Aragonese provinces (Huesca, Teruel, Zaragoza) comprise 9.5% of Spain but like Extremadura are heavily under populated with a total of only around 1.2 million inhabitants. Pyrenean Aragón is fast becoming popular with hikers, particularly in the Ordesa National Park. There are also several ski resorts of which the most chic is Benasque.

Geographically the province of Teruel reaches out to the south rather than the Pyrenees and is one of the most unexplored areas with few inhabitants and poor roads. Property for sale in Aragón is scarce. Nevertheless, the lively city of Zaragoza does offer some interesting prospects for house-buyers. Zaragoza has been largely untouched by tourism despite frequent Ryanair flights there, and therefore has a far more Spanish feel than many other northern cities. Prices in Zaragoza are higher than in much of northern Spain, but the city is attractive, exciting and also a commercial centre. The average house price in the region is €165,244.

Cantabria and Asturias

Regional Tourist Offices: www.turismo.cantabria.org; www.infoasturias.com. Both the coastline and the interior of the spectacularly mountainous regions of Cantabria and neighbouring Asturias are capable of stunning the visitor. This is also the last place in Spain where you will find unspoiled coastline. Bear in mind however that it is not known as la Costa Verde (the green coast) for nothing and the rainfall and cool temperatures here may put off some prospective retirees.

The Picos de Europa, a large mountain range, form a natural barrier between Asturias and Cantabria to the east. The small region of Cantabria is centred on the port of Santander, an elegant resort popular with Spaniards from the capital. There are many smaller resorts east of Santander including Laredo which is to the French what Benidorm is to the British.

Homes here are a lot cheaper than those found on the Mediterranean coastline. The average house price is €156,777 in Cantabria and €150,270 in Asturias. There are many properties for restoration available to those with the ambition and money to take on such a project. The main places to look are Santander, Gijón, Cudillero, Laredo, Comillas, Castro Urdiales, Llanes, Noja and San Vicente de la Barquera.

Extremadura & Castilla-La Mancha (New Castile)

Regional Tourist Office: www.turismoextremadura.com; www.castillalamancha.es
Extremadura and Castilla-La Mancha are two of the regions of the *meseta* (the central tableland) which together comprise about a quarter of Spain's surface area but contain just over a sixth of its population. Extremadura is

Villa terrace, Majorca

Barcelona fruitstall

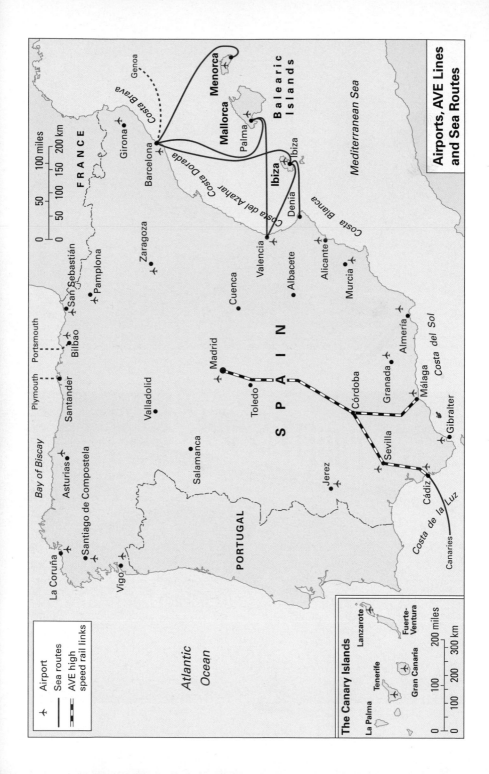

Airports, AVE Lines and Sea Routes

Airport
Sea routes
AVE high speed rail links

Atlantic Ocean

Bay of Biscay

FRANCE

La Coruña
Santiago de Compostela
Vigo
Asturias
Santander
Bilbao
San Sebastián
Pamplona
Zaragoza
Valladolid
Salamanca
Madrid
Toledo
Cuenca
Valencia
Albacete
Alicante
Murcia
Almería
Granada
Córdoba
Sevilla
Jerez
Cádiz
Gibralter
Málaga

PORTUGAL

S P A I N

Costa del Sol
Costa de la Luz
Canaries

Girona
Barcelona
Costa Brava
Costa Dorada
Costa del Azahar
Costa Blanca
Denia
Ibiza
Palma
Mallorca
Menorca
Balearic Islands
Ibiza

Mediterranean Sea

Genoa

Portsmouth
Plymouth

100 miles
100 km
0 50 100 150 200 km
0 50 100 miles

The Canary Islands

La Palma
Tenerife
Gran Canaria
Lanzarote
Fuerte-Ventura

0 100 200 miles
0 100 200 300 km

dominated by ranges of mountains and reservoirs. Cáceres, the main town, was originally built with spoils from the activities of the local nobles in the New World. There is a famous six-arched Roman bridge at Alcántara near the Portuguese border and further extensive Roman remains at Mérida. The climate here swings between the extremes of boiling summers to freezing winters, and perhaps as a result, this is the part of Spain that has least been affected by mass tourism.

Castilla-La Mancha contains what is probably one of the most beautiful towns in Spain, Cuenca, perched precariously on the side of a cliff. It also has one of the most famous: the medieval capital of Spain, Toledo, which sits on a craggy rock in a loop of the Tajo River.

Few foreigners live in the region, at least partly because it contains no international airports. Nevertheless Extremadura has some of the cheapest properties in Spain and it is possible to buy habitable properties here for as little as €50-60,000.

Navarra (Navarre) and La Rioja

Regional Tourist Offices: www.cfnavarra.es/turismonavarra; www.larioja.org/turismo
Navarre is one of the smaller regions comprising 2.06% of Spain's area and home to 1.35% of the population. A stretch of the Pyrenees fills the northeastern part of the province and includes the historic pass of Roncesvalles on the route taken by medieval pilgrims to Santiago. The south of Navarre is on the north-eastern edge of the meseta and is a region of vineyards and other agriculture. The main city of the region is Pamplona, whose bull-running festival, the Fiesta of San Fermín, takes place in July and attracts capacity crowds from all over Spain and beyond. The average house price in the region is just €165,244.

Rioja to most Britons means wine. La Rioja is the smallest of the Spanish regions occupying just 1% of its surface area and home to a mere 0.67% of the population, or just over 50,000 souls. This single-province region takes its name from the Rió Oja, a minor tributary of the great Ebro river which provides the water for the famous vineyards of the region. The main city of Logroño, replete with fine architecture, is on the pilgrim way to Santiago. The average house price here is €202,934.

Your New Home in Spain

CHAPTER SUMMARY

O Recent years have seen a downturn in the Spanish property market. Experts estimate that property prices will continue to rise, but at a slower, more sustainable rate.

  O Properties are taking longer to sell and buyers are in a very strong negotiating position.

O **Estate Agents.** There are hundreds of British estate agents with local knowledge and Spanish agents with experience of dealing with foreigners. Whatever their origins, make sure they are properly licensed.

  O Commission rates vary. The Commission recommended by the official organisation API is 3%.

O Finding a rustic home is a dream for many, but the reality will involve a lot of hard work and renovation costs are high.

O Two years ago only around 5% of overseas enquiries were for city apartments, but this has increased to around 20%.

O Some of the over 55 age-group are choosing to buy into purpose built retirement villages, which offer wonderful facilities and 24-hour security.

O Those buying in the Valencia region should be particularly aware of the land-grab law issues in the area.

O The total costs involved in the purchasing process come to around 10% of the property price (7-9% in the Canaries).

O The signing of the property's title deeds (*escritura*) must be witnessed by a notary (*notario*). Following signing and payment, the notary will pass the purchaser a copy of the deeds and the keys to the property.

O Renting is an alternative, but the Spanish market for long-term rentails is not as well developed as we are used to in the UK.

OVERVIEW OF THE SPANISH PROPERTY MARKET

By 2008 it is estimated that the number of foreign buyers in Spain will have exceeded Spanish owners in popular tourist areas. For many years Spain has been the property buyer's paradise. Traditionally cheap property, the availability of timeshares and a welcoming atmosphere for expats, have all contributed to its attraction for second-home buyers and potential residents.

For the last ten years, Spain has been experiencing what some have termed a 'property bubble', with property prices rising dramatically in most areas of Spain. Over the last seven years the average property price increase in Spain has been 144%, according to one report, and the biggest increases were in the Balearics (215%), Murcia (209%), Madrid (168%) and Andalucia (162%). Even in the area with the lowest property price increase, Galicia, prices still rose by a substantial 83%.

However, the situation now seems far less clear-cut. The problem with property bubbles is that there is always the possibility that they will burst, causing prices to plummet. The Bank of Spain, in its annual report in 2005, suggested that prices had risen to wholly unrealistic levels: between 24% and 35% above the actual value. In the bank's opinion, if measures are not introduced to guide the property market to a soft landing, then this unrealistic pricing presents a severe threat to the health of the Spanish economy. Indeed prices in 2006 could drop by 10% or more according to *Tribune Properties*.

One of the main problems, according to Spain's Council of Architects (*Consejo Superior de Colegios de Arquitectos*), is that new properties are being built at a rate which by far outstrips demand, a situation which is clearly not sustainable in the long term. This excess comes at a time when foreign investment in Spain has taken a down turn. The British represent a driving force in the Spanish property market, but the slowing of the UK property market in 2005/6 has taken its toll and created a climate of declining buyer confidence. Whereas previously middle-market developments were snapped up by British buyers who remortgaged at home to finance their purchases, people are being more cautious now, especially when it comes to putting their money into speculative off-plan schemes. Many quick-buck profiteers have turned their attention away from Spain to emerging property markets such as Bulgaria and Romania. As a result properties in certain areas are taking far longer to sell.

The evidence therefore appears to point to a downturn in the Spanish property market. Nevertheless, the authorities disagree about what form this will take. Some organisations outside of Spain such as the European Central Bank, the IMF and the OECD have implied that a sharp fall in prices is a distinct possibility. Nevertheless, many of the banks, estate agents and official organisations suggest that property prices will continue to rise but at a slower, more sustainable rate. BBVA, one of Spain's largest banks, estimates that property increases will slow down to 5% during 2006 (from 17% in 2004).

In essence what these new trends suggest is that Spain doesn't offer the rich pickings for the amateur investor that it once did. However most retirees are not looking for a quick buck and Spanish property still offers a sound investment in the longer term, especially for those buying as an owner-occupier who will be able to make use of the property whilst the market levels itself out over the coming years. Be aware that estate agents keen to make sales to the foreign investor may be prepared to be unrealistically encouraging about the market and about the ease of letting a certain property. Keep in mind that buyers are likely to be in their strongest negotiating position since the mid 1980s, as owners, who have been unable to sell their property, are likely to drop their asking prices in order to secure a sale.

It is also advisable, given the slowing British property market, that you do not buy anything in Spain until at least having reached the contract stage in the UK. Many retirees are renting in Spain as a stopgap until they have managed to sell their UK property.

FINDING A PROPERTY

When you begin looking into the possibilities of buying a property in Spain you will very quickly become aware of the vast number of companies out there who are looking to persuade you to do business with them. Take out a subscription to one of the property or lifestyle magazines (see the *Media* section of *Adapting to Your New Life*) and you will find their pages rammed with advertisements placed by property developers, estate agents, removals firms, lawyers, insurers and accountants. The property pages of the weekend national newspapers frequently have articles on buying property abroad and these pieces will include sample prices of properties and details of the companies featured.

Estate agents and property developers are increasingly using the web as a marketing tool as a relatively cheap way to get their name known internationally. There are now internet portals, which deal exclusively with properties for sale from thousands of leading agents and developers. A few sites worth looking at, especially for those looking to buy at the top end of the property market, are Knight Frank (www.knightfrank.com), Hamptons (www.hamptons.co.uk), www.primelocation.com (which includes property from 250 estate agents), www.propertyfinder.com (property from 900 agencies), www.altea.com and www.newskys.co.uk.

There are also a number of property exhibitions held in venues across the UK and Ireland. These are a good opportunity to get hold of information, brochures, and an idea of the kinds of properties and prices available.

Organisers of Property Exhibitions	
Fresh Start Media Ltd:	☎01273-201 384; www.freshstartmagazine.co.uk.
Homes Overseas:	☎020-7002 8300; www.blendoncommunications.com.
Homebuyer Events Ltd.:	☎020-8877 3636; www.homebuyer.co.uk.
Interealty:	☎952 900 550; www.interealtynet.com.
International Property Show:	☎01252-720652; www.internationalpropertyshow.com.
Spain on Show:	freephone 0500-780878; www.spainonshow.com.
Town & Country:	☎0845-230 6000; www.spanishproperty.uk.com.
World Class Homes:	☎01582-832 001; www.worldclasshomes.co.uk.

Estate Agents

The British have been buying up properties in Spain ever since the 1960s and the market has been growing steadily. As a result there is no shortage of UK based estate agents with a portfolio of properties in Spain, British estate agents based in Spain, and Spanish estate agents with vast experience of dealing with British clients. These agents will be more than willing to offer advice on the costs involved and to help handle the property buying transaction for you.

Jerry Whitehouse of Mallorca Casa advises that buying a property in Spain is a relatively straightforward process provided that the Estate Agent is diligent. He strongly recommends that all those intending to purchase a property thoroughly investigate the Estate Agency that they propose to use. Time and time again he has heard stories of so-called

'Estate Agents' failing to deliver the follow-up services and help that they had promised and charging additional fees.

Depending on the time scale you have allowed yourself to find and buy a property in Spain, before dealing with estate agents you should decide first on the area where you want to buy. By all means look in estate agents' shop windows and check out price ranges and property on offer in different parts of the country, but don't tie yourself immediately to one or several estate agencies before you are sure about where you are hoping to buy. It will also be far more productive for those looking for an individual property, rather than a new-build, to research properties (and estate agents) on the ground in Spain. Once there, you will be able to get a feel for the reliability and efficiency or otherwise of a particular agent as well as being able to see the most recent properties that have come onto the market.

UK Estate Agents may act as agents or middlemen for Spanish estate agents who do not have the contacts, the marketing know-how or the fluency in English that a British estate agent has. Because they may well have an office in the UK, contacting such agents is a good starting place for sounding out the prices and property available, above all if they deal with the region/s where you are interested in buying. Agents have experience of dealing with Spanish property law, regulations and red tape and can therefore be very helpful for anyone who is wary of dealing with Spanish estate agents direct.

Prospective buyers of property should make sure that they are aware of and very clear about everything that is taking place 'on their behalf' during negotiations and to be in control of proceedings. Before entering into a contract through one of these agents, check to see what charges for services are going to be levied and ask for a breakdown of costs and commission. It may work out to be far more expensive going through an agent back home than dealing with a Spanish-based estate agent direct.

Inspection Trips

If you know the type of property you want to buy and where you want to buy it some property firms can arrange inspection flights to Spain. A typical deal involves the estate agency booking the flight to Spain, collecting you from and returning you to the airport and providing free accommodation for the duration of your trip. A consultant will take you round various properties on a one-to-one basis, showing you the area and the facilities on offer. Normally you will only have to pay for your flights and these will be refundable if you eventually decide to buy a property with the agents.

Although there will be no obligation to buy on these inspection trips you should expect a fair amount of high-pressure selling. Inspection trips take the business relationship between a prospective buyer and an agent into a more complex area. Going on an inspection trip means that the agent is investing time and money in you as a client and they will want a return on their investment. Do not allow yourself to be rushed into a decision you may regret.

Spanish Estate Agents (Inmobiliaria), much like British agents, are not required by law to be qualified members of a professional body of estate agents. It is therefore imperative that you ensure you are dealing with an agency belonging to either the *Agente de Propiedad Inmobiliaria* (API) or the *Gestor Intermediario de Promociones y Edificaciones* (GIPE). These agencies display their certificate of registration and identification number on the premises. Any API registered estate agency employs an API accredited lawyer and has paid a bond. They are then bound to act in accordance with regulations of the API and can be sued if they do not.

As in the UK, estate agents in Spain often concentrate on the area around which their office is based. They deal with local properties and have a good knowledge of the possible problems associated with planning regulations, utility provision etc. in their locality. Estate agents dealing with properties on the *costas* are very likely to speak English, and may even *be* British. *Inmobiliarias* out in the wilds may not be used to dealing with English-speakers, though agents will want to bend over backwards in order to make a sale. Spanish estate agents in general provide far less detailed descriptions of property than those which we are used to at home. Photographs of properties and details will be of varying quality, though in general the more expensive the property the better the marketing will be.

When dealing with Spanish estate agents, because of the sometimes 'cash in hand' nature of things in Spain, you may be asked to sign a *nota de encargo* before being shown a property or properties. This document protects the agent's interests, and ensures that he will be paid the commission should you go ahead and buy one of the properties on his books. This is because a property may be placed with several agents all of whom are wanting their commission from the sale.

Once a deal has gone through, any issues that arise over the property will have nothing to do with the agents. It is therefore imperative to get a lawyer (an independent lawyer, rather than one recommended by the estate agency or the vendor) to check all contracts thoroughly before buying a property.

Commission. The commission rate charged by estate agencies can vary. A higher commission is payable on cheap properties than on more expensive ones, and the rate will also vary from region to region – higher rates being charged in more popular resort areas. The commission recommended by the API is, in most regions, 3%.

Useful Contacts

National Association of Estate Agents: ☎01926-496 800; www.naea.co.uk.
Royal Institute of Chartered Surveyors: ☎020-7222 7000; www.rics.org.
European Confederation of Real Estate Agents: www.webcei.com.
The Federation of Overseas Property Developers, Agents & Consultants:
☎0870-3501223; www.fopdac.com.

Estate Agents
Livingstone Estates Costa Blanca: ☎966-881191; e-mail infocb@livingstone-estates.com; www.livingstone-estates.com.
Livingstone Estates Costa del Sol: ☎952-900402; e-mail info@livingstone-estates.com; www.livingstone-estates.com.
Mallorca Casa: Es Capdella, Calvia, 07196 Mallorca; freephone ☎0800-404 6389; phone/fax 971-138562; e-mail contactus@mallorcacasa.com; www.mallorcacasa.com.
Oranges and Lemons: Alcalde Francisco Llorca 15, 1°C, Oliva 46780, Valencia; ☎676-976278; fax 962-855096; e-mail orangesandlemons@wanadoo.es; www.orangesandlemons.com.
Titan Properties: Calle Rio Odiel, Local 5, El Rompido, Cartaya 21459; ☎959-399 968; fax 959-399638; e-mail info@titan-properties.com; www.titan-properties.com.

WHAT TYPE OF PROPERTY?

From tumbledown rural fincas to luxury new villas with sea views, there is an enormous range of idyllic property in Spain and the British are leading the way in buying it up. Buying your Spanish property is an investment in your future life and it should fulfil or exceed your expectations. It is easy to get swept up in the excitement of finding a new home and buy an entirely impractical property, be it in the wrong location or vastly over-budget. It is very important to take into consideration the running and upkeep costs of the property in question. Proximity to facilities is also an important consideration for anyone reliant on public transport. Some of the main types of property for sale in Spain are considered below.

Old Versus New

For a long time the Spanish had no interest in old properties and were looking to move into modern housing and leave their past behind – leaving foreigners the room to snap up and renovate their cast-offs. Today the tastes and the wealth of Spaniards are changing. Many Spaniards now also own second homes and look for places with character to escape to at weekends or on their annual summer holiday.

Fincas

Finca is a generic term used in Spain to describe a large estate or plot of land situated away from centres of population. Included on this land may be a farmhouse, orchards, olive groves, outbuildings, or a modern or derelict detached house. In Catalonia there are large grand farmhouses called *masiás*, in Andalucía such farmhouses are called *cortijos*. Due to their relative isolation *fincas* are highly sought after, especially those situated along or near the coast. Most have been found and renovated. If you can find one, a rebuild, apart from costing a great deal of money (and always more than you will have budgeted for) will need the go-ahead from the local council, the granting of planning permission and much paperwork and bureaucracy, which, if you are not fluent in Spanish, will mean a bit of a headache. It is better to look inland for such properties these days though the extremes of climate and topography may put off all but the most adventurous.

Finding an authentic or rustic home is a dream for many, but the reality will involve a lot of hard work. Renovation costs for such properties can be exorbitant and many old houses don't have (and never have had) adequate sanitation, power provision, access to telephone lines and water etc., which is often why the former owners abandoned them. Adequate insulation is also a problem with old houses, as expats Mac and Meryl Macdonald have found: *'In the winter we find that the central heating escapes, and in the summer there is nothing to keep the heat out!'*.

Town Houses

Town houses can be a good buy and an excellent way to get absorbed into Spanish life instead of peering at it through binoculars from a detached villa in the hills. Houses in villages and towns tend to have shady, rather dark rooms with small patio areas at the back of the property. Properties in the centre of villages are generally joined together in rows along the streets and lanes and may come with roof terraces. It is advisable to get a surveyor to check these houses as they are often of quite an age and may need rewiring, or to have the old water pipes replaced, or have some structural work done to the supporting walls or the roof. These houses in the villages and towns can have a great deal of character, far more than the modern developments and bring the added bonus of placing you right in the heart of Spanish life.

Without some experience of renovating property, what may have seemed like a bargain can end up just being a burden, both financially and mentally. A relatively small initial financial outlay to buy a tumbledown property will be augmented by the need to hire builders and architects and sort out planning permissions. Time, patience, perseverance and, above all, money will be needed to create or recreate the house and grounds of your dreams and without a generous supply of all these the project may falter and the dream die.

Advice for rural buyers – Lindy Walsh

Don't take anything for granted. I know awful cases of people buying land with water running through it, but not being allowed to use one drop; of buying land with trees and finding out too late that they hadn't bought the trees (or their harvest); of buying a 'house' (it looked like a house) and finding that it was registered as a chicken shed and not able to be registered as habitable because it didn't conform to the newest building standards. Check and check again and don't part with any money until you have a copy of a registered escritura that has been looked over by a local (but perhaps not too local as he may be the vendor's brother) gestor or abogado. Better a local gestor who doesn't speak English, and pay the extra to a translator, than an English speaker who doesn't know the area.

By contrast, new properties offer modern luxury designs, effective plumbing and wiring, efficient heating and insulation and all mod cons. You can even design the property yourself, and the building work will be guaranteed by the builders for ten years. Modern developments also offer shared sporting facilities and services. If all of this comfort and luxury is no substitute for tumbledown charm, then you should at least bear in mind the following precautions.

Precautions to Take with Old Properties

- Get a structural survey done before signing any contracts. It may be that there is actually no scope for renovation and demolition is the only option available. If this is the case then you will need to know whether changes to the property are allowed by the planning authorities.
- Find out from the town hall what the planning regulations in the area are. Will you be allowed to demolish and rebuild, to extend beyond the existing structure, or only to renovate the house to the original design? In a town you are likely to be more severely restricted in what you can do with a property than in the countryside. You will also need to obtain a *Permiso de Obra* from the town hall that will allow you to rebuild.
- Title deeds (*escritura*) can be an enormous problem in the countryside. In the worst-case scenario, title deeds for a rural property do not even exist. In this case, it is not worth continuing with the purchase, as it is simply too risky. If you do proceed, be aware of the 205 Procedure. You need to get a 'negative certification' from the Land Registry stating that they hold no title deeds for the property and that, given the evidence of ownership by the vendor, the title of ownership now passes to you. This 'negative certification' is then published so that anyone who may have a claim to the house can come forward to state his or her case. After about a year, if no-one comes forward, you will be officially registered as the owner of the property.
- In rural Spain there are many legitimate claims to property that have never been formally notarised in title deeds. If this is the case, and your lawyer will find out and let you know, a court decision will need to be taken to establish who the rightful owner of the house is. This action, called *expediente de dominio* could take up to two years to complete.
- It is more common that the title deeds simply don't correspond to the amount of land being offered for sale. It is nearly always possible to resolve these difficulties, but you must make sure that they are satisfactory before buying. Once you have bought, the problem becomes yours.

○ Boundary disputes can turn particularly nasty, and sour relations between neighbours. If there is an orchard, or an olive grove, on the property find out it you have the right of harvest. Do you have water rights over any river or well that may be on the land? Is there a right of way over the land that you aren't aware of?

○ Are there any debts on the property? Your lawyer should check this. Remember that under Spain's *Law of Subrogation* any unpaid monies due – such as defaulting on mortgage repayments, locals taxes etc. – are on the property and therefore will be inherited by a new owner leaving the debtor vendor scot-free.

Buying Off-Plan (sobre plano)

At property exhibitions and through estate agents and property developers, prospective buyers will come across opportunities to buy villas and apartments off-plan. Clients will be shown the design and plans of a property with specifications, municipal permissions, a model of the development to be built, and perhaps the interior of a show house. Those clients interested in buying one of the homes on offer will be flown out to view the location of the proposed property and, if happy, will be asked to sign a contract. The contract will contain a clear description of the property, the schedule for completion and the dates when down payments on the property will be due.

> Many investors have successfully bought off-plan and then sold on for a tax-free profit before completion of the project. However, this strategy appears to have had its day in Spain. The oversupply of new-build property has made it considerably more difficult to sell on. Nevertheless, those who want a holiday home and are not simply looking to make some quick cash, can still find some off-plan bargains.

With apartment and *urbanización* developments it is very likely that the builder or agent will already have a standard contract. Nevertheless buyers should always have adequate legal checks carried out before signing a contract. Your lawyer will need to review both the reservation contract and the private sale contract, and confirm that the contracts are legitimate, that planning permission has been granted, and that your stage payments are fully insured. Do not allow yourself to be rushed into signing contracts before consulting a lawyer – the market is moving in favour of buyers, so you have plenty of time to make the necessary checks.

The buyer pays for the house or flat in instalments and will pay an initial – often hefty – deposit, and the final payment once the home is completed. Instalments may be 10% on signing of the contract with two subsequent instalments followed by the final payment on completion. If a property has been partially completed on the signing of the contract, a higher initial payment may be required. All stage payments include VAT at 7%.

Avoiding Pitfalls

Delays can occur in the building process, and clients may not be given information on any further development planned on the *urbanización* or the surrounding land. It is therefore essential that as much information as possible is obtained about the development company's track record, and that an independent lawyer checks the contract before it is signed. Landscaping of the property, access, utility provision, and additional maintenance charges are all matters that may need to be clarified in the contract. If they are not, it may come as a shock after paying the final instalment to find that such things have been left in abeyance. It is vital to get a termination agreement backed up by insurance guaranteeing that every aspect of the property will be professionally finished before you move in.

It is advisable to stipulate that any payments made before the completion of the property be paid into an escrow account – the developer cannot touch money paid into such accounts until the property is completed. An extra charge will be made but the bank will then guarantee your money should the developer go bust or, God forbid, be a rogue. It is, in any case, a legal requirement for property developers to have a bank guarantee to ensure that, should they become bankrupt before the completion of a project, the buyer who has paid instalments will not lose his or her investment.

When buying off-plan you may have to wait for anything from a year to 18 months for a property to be completed. The buyer then takes possession by signing the public deeds of sale before a notary and a further 1% of the property price is charged in stamp duty. Before signing the final deeds, have your lawyer confirm that the developer is not passing on any unexpected debts or charges, and that all the necessary certificates and permits have been granted. Upon taking possession of the property, any initial problems need to be identified as quickly as possible and the developer should put them right immediately.

Villas

There are plenty of villas along the Spanish coastline that are purpose-built for holiday use. A detached villa will sell for more than an equivalent-sized ordinary house in town but will give more privacy as villas tend to be set in their own grounds. Buying a villa is usually a straightforward business as long as the Land Registry has details of any alterations or additions that have been made to the property since the last *escritura* was signed. If such changes have not been registered then delays are likely to occur while negotiations take place between your lawyers and the Town Hall. If extensive alterations have been made to the villa and not registered (say a large conservatory added, or an outhouse converted into a dwelling) then there may be fines to pay and, in the worst-case scenario, even a demand by the authorities for the property to be returned to the state as declared in the *escritura*.

Villas, though they offer a great deal of privacy, lack the security of a flat or a detached house on an *urbanización*. Many of the things to take into consideration when looking to buy a villa are similar to those when looking at old houses (see above). Check out the location of any prospective purchase carefully. Is the villa situated in an area where seasonal tempests or sand storms may cover the house, your car, swimming pool and tennis court in layers of dust? Most villas are relatively modern and you are unlikely to have much problem with access to water, electricity and telephone connections and drainage.

Apartments (Pisos)

Spaniards, especially urbanites, are traditionally apartment-dwellers, and flats in Spain are often large, airy and spacious. In the cities almost all of the available property will be apartments; detached villas and townhouses are rare in the inner city areas. According to a recent report in *The Times,* increasing numbers of Britons are buying property in cities, where they can mix with local people and lose themselves in another way of life – pleasures not always accessible on the more anglicised stretches of coast. Two years ago only around 5% of overseas enquiries were for city apartments, but this has increased to 20%. This change has, at least partly, been wrought by changing holiday patterns and the increasing popularity of city breaks. City apartments are therefore far easier to let to tourists.

A great many holiday flats have been built since the arrival of the tourist hordes in the 1960s, especially around the coastal areas frequented by summer visitors. These flats, though often coming onto the market at a reasonable price, tend to be smaller and less soundproof than other apartments because they were built for short-let holidays and not designed to be lived in on a full-time basis. Older apartments may well be in need of some repair, either cosmetic or structural.

Apartments offer a cheap way to move on to the property owning ladder in Spain and often come with a balcony as standard, and in addition some top floor flats have access to roof gardens. It is important to try and gauge the thickness of the walls and degree of protection from the sound of your potential neighbours. Flats in the middle of town may be great in terms of location but very noisy during the evenings and long into the night as the populace enjoys its *paseo*. In the areas of greatest tourist density, flats along the seafront with great views of the sea may be marred by the noise of those next door taking their hedonistic two-week break in the sun. Choice of location will depend on your predilection. One man's heaven is another man's hell. Flats are generally easy to sell on, and are cheap to maintain.

Urbanizaciónes

If you visit any property exhibition you will come across a number of different *urbanizaciónes*, with a wide variety of properties on offer – from studio and duplex apartments to semi-detached houses and detached villas on huge landscaped estates.

Urbanizaciónes are akin to housing estates – rows of housing (often of an attractive design) running along the crest of a hill or along a beach, or on the outskirts of town. Some are beautifully designed and well run while others may appear bland to the discerning buyer. Because beach frontage property is now at a premium in Spain it may well be worth investing in an urbanización further inland. If you decide to buy into an urbanización away from the beaches or without a sea view you are going to get a lot more for your money in terms of the size of the property and the amount of surrounding land.

Some urbanizaciónes are part of towns and villages while others may have been developed around a marina or golf course (which may mean that they are away from communication centres and correspondingly may become rather desolate places out of season – beware). You may find developments that appear to be entirely populated by one nationality, or are very insular, or where everyone clusters around the communal swimming pool and makes for the local bar every evening – giving a feeling of homely community where you will meet and become life-long friends with people like yourself. Owners of properties on urbanizaciónes may be mainly retirees, or the majority may only visit for a few weeks a year leaving the place a bit of a ghost town for much of the rest of the time.

> The advantages of *urbanizaciónes* are that they can make for a ready made social circle, security will be less of a problem if there are friendly neighbours always milling around, and through them cheaper properties can be found in otherwise expensive areas. It is also likely to be easier to sell on such properties. The disadvantages of *urbanizaciónes* are the possibility of higher community charges for maintenance of the estate (you will be part of a *comunidad de propietarios* – see below), a lack of privacy and space, and the worry of difficult or noisy or boring neighbours.

Urbanizaciónes have sprung up all over Spain since the beginning of the tourist invasion of the 1960s. These developments grew up to cater not only for foreigners looking to buy holiday homes but also for Spaniards, many of whom own second homes where they go at weekends and during holidays to escape the confines of an apartment in the city. Urbanizaciónes vary considerably in the size of the development, the grandiosity of the flats or villas built on it, the infrastructure (lighting, roads, gardens, pools etc.) and the way the *comunidad de propietarios* is run.

LA COMUNIDAD DE PROPIETARIOS (THE COMMUNITY OF OWNERS)

Buying an apartment in a block or a villa in an urbanización will involve you joining a *comunidad de propietarios* whereby you will be involved in the running of the apartment block. This involves attending meetings to discuss the communal aspects of the block – such matters as provision of rubbish collection, the lighting of communal areas (the stairwell, entrance hall, etc.) the maintenance of the lift, entrance hall, gardens, swimming pool, etc. If you are living on an urbanización the comunidad will also be responsible for street lighting, roads and communal areas on or around the urbanización. You cannot opt out of joining a comunidad and you are legally bound to become a member when buying a property.

You will need to read the regulations and statutes pertaining to the comunidad before you buy the apartment, as they will be binding after your purchase. If they are only available in Spanish – and by law they must be set out in Spanish – you must get them translated into English and have them explained in detail.

Properties that are part of a comunidad de propietarios pay less property tax than detached villas or houses as the tax is on the urbanización or apartment block as a whole rather than on individuals. Maintenance of the communal areas will be taken care of for you. However, there will be rules and regulations that you may well feel to be intrusive and unnecessary and being part of a community of strangers may not suit everyone. Talk to other owners before committing to buy a community property.

Retirement Villages

The over-55 age group make up over 50% of the total number of foreign owners of property in Spain. However, this fact is not reflected in the number of retirement homes being built in the country. Top end retirement complexes however, arrived in Europe more than a decade ago. One of the first was the Colina Club in Calpe (Costa Blanca), which offered apartments on long-term rentals to mainly British residents, with shared leisure facilities, organised social events, a 20-bed nursing home and 24-hour access to an English-speaking doctor.

These days the market is mushrooming and Spanish developers now provide 'designer' retirement homes at reasonable prices. These developments are particularly prevalent along the Costa del Sol around Marbella and along the Costa Blanca. Both the British Consulate and Age Concern España advise people to look ahead when considering where to buy their retirement home. Although none of us like to think about the possibility of ill health in our later years, it is always prudent to consider the future.

Retirement villages offer wonderful facilities – swimming pools, restaurants, a medical block, shopping centre, gym etc., and as with urbanizaciónes there are additional service charges payable (around €30-€80 per month) on top of the purchase price of the flat. The difference is that there is 24-hour security and medical care on site, as well as home cleaning services, room-service food, and a laundry and grocery service.

The majority of these residential developments have all of the luxuries expected from an urbanización, but being age-specific they have the added advantage that residents will be surrounded by people with similar interests. Many of these developments organise cultural and sporting activities for their residents including arts and crafts, music, languages, computer courses, bridge, chess, walking and so on.

Depending on what you are looking for – whether you are happy to live out your last years away from your family back home – nursing costs in Spain are likely to be lower and residential nursing homes far more appealing than those in, for instance, the UK.

Retirement Homes in Spain

KEI Homes: ☎966-795229; or from the UK: ☎0870-011 5065. Brand new resort near Santa Pola, Alicante. Properties range from €125,000 to €225,000 with average service charges of €150 per month.

Palazzo Vivaldi: ☎0845-430 9337; www.wpml.co.uk/palazzovivaldi/. Retirement resort in Roquetas de Mar, Costa del Sol.

Sol Andalusí: ☎952 963 096; www.solandalusi.com. Residential resort home with 24-hour medical service on the Costa del Sol.

Sanyres: ☎957 475 676; www.sanyres.es or www.grupoprasa.es. 10 residential developments already open in the provinces of Córdoba, Madrid, A Coruña, La Rioja, Málaga, Alicante, and Léon, and fifteen more centres planned by 2007.

Sensara: ☎(UK) 0870-240 3258; www.sensara.com. New development near to Benalmádena (Costa del Sol). Apartments to rent or buy. Sensara plan to have five such facilities up and running between Nerja and Sotogrande within the next three years.

Self-Build

Buying a plot of land in order to build your ideal home is a dream held by many expats. Unfortunately it can be a lengthy and complex process – there are a number of bureaucratic hoops to be jumped through and it can take a year or more to be granted the necessary licences. Finding a site can also be very difficult, and finding land to buy is practically impossible in the Balearic Islands since an embargo on the erection of new property has come into force.

Actions you Should Take Before Buying a Plot of Land

o The ratio of build to plot is determined by local planning authorities and should be checked with them. If you are buying the plot through an estate agent then he or she should already know what type and size of property would be allowable.

o Get a lawyer, an architect and a surveyor to check over the plot before you buy and get price ranges for the area in which you are interested.

o You should also run checks on the general status of the land:

  o Is it in a conservation area where there will be tight regulations on planning permission?

  o Are there public rights of way over it, by-laws pertaining to water, hunting, grazing, harvesting rights?

  o Are there likely to be objections to the building schemes that you may have?

  o How costly will it be to install services such as sewerage, a telephone, electricity, or a water supply?

  o Are the ground and resources suitable should you want to put in a swimming pool or tennis court?

o Consult the town plan (*plan general de ordenación urbana*) at the local town hall. This should tell you the areas that have already been given over to development (where planning permission should be relatively easy and straightforward to obtain). The town plan will also tell you at a glance whether the piece of land you are interested in developing has major restrictions imposed on the size or height of proposed building projects.

o Check the details of the separate plots around the one that you are interested in. Are they set for further development? Is the view of the sea or spectacular mountain scenery from your planned home liable to be blocked by an urbanización planned for completion a few years down the line?

o Check that the vendor is in possession of the *escritura* (title deeds).

o Firm up descriptions of the land bordering neighbouring property. A casually waved arm pointing over towards a row of olive trees and the words 'Your land stops over there' really isn't good enough and is likely to lead to problems in the future. Get the boundaries marked on the escritura if they aren't already. The land should be surveyed either by an independent surveyor or through the *Catastro* (Land Registry) which holds plans marking boundaries of plots (*parcelas*) of land.

Only when all of the above points have been satisfied should you consider signing the escritura. You will then need to apply for a building permit (*Permiso de Obra*). To obtain this you have to submit the plans for the building to the Town Hall. It is likely to take at least two months for plans of the building project to be ready for submission to the authorities.

Building Plans. To get a plan for your house you will need to get in touch with a firm of builders or an architect. If you are buying a plot on an *urbanización* then the developers will be able to give you details of local builders, or you can enquire locally. A builder will be able to provide you with details of the type of houses he could build for you and together you can work out any variations you may want, interior designs etc.

Alternatively you can find an architect and work together to come up with an original design that will answer your needs and pass the building regulations. An architect's fee is typically 6% but may run to as much as 9% of the total cost of the build, which means that they will be in no hurry to design you a cheap house. Once you and the architect have finalised the plans, building specifications (*memoria*) are prepared. These include such things as the type of materials to be used, the specification of window and door frames, guttering, tiles etc., and are submitted to the Town Hall. Once approved, a building licence will be issued and a fee will be due (around 3-4% of the total cost of the project, depending on the region).

Keep in mind that things rarely go exactly to plan – for instance there may be rock where the footings should go and blasting this out of the way will increase the labour cost, or you may decide that you want changes made to the original designs. It is therefore a good idea to factor in at least 10%-30% on top of the original estimate. Building costs are likely to come in at £1,000 per square metre.

Builders. With planning permission granted you can now look for a build-er to take on the contract to build your house. Get several estimates. The builders will look at the plans, the *memoria* and tell you how much they think it'll cost them to complete the job. Estimates will vary – both for the time it will take to complete the job and the price they will. Having decided upon a builder, get your lawyer to look over the contract and make sure that any changes and amendments that arise over the course of the building work (there may be quite a few) are added to the contract and signed by both parties. This will avoid any problems when it comes to the reappraisal of the initial estimate and the final demand for payment.

As with all purchases it is advisable to use the services of a solicitor who speaks fluent English and get all documentation completely translated into English. Don't just settle for a précis or summary of contracts. The process of buying a plot of land will involve obtaining one escritura while the building of a property on that land will necessitate obtaining a second.

Tips for the Building Process

○ Builders everywhere can occasionally be unreliable. Try to be on site as often as possible or at least find someone to keep an eye on things.

○ Check the plans. Make sure that the footings are laid correctly – it would be a great shame if your house ended up facing the wrong way for example – and check on type and costings of materials. This is your house and you will want to be on hand to choose materials and fixtures and fittings.

○ Stagger payment to the builder and negotiate to hold back a final payment until a specified date after completion so that should cracks in walls appear, or there be problems with drainage, plumbing, electrics, etc., you will have some clout should you need to call the builders back in to repair defects.

○ Depending on the size and design expect a wait of about a year before being able to gaze upon your dream house. Even after completion it could take an additional year or two to knock the garden and surrounding land into shape.

On Completion. Once the house has been built the final instalment of the architect's fees will need to be paid, but only after he has signed the completion of construction certificate (*certificado final de obra*). You will need to make a 'Declaration of the New Building' (*declaración de la obra nueva*), which will allow you to add the new building to the original *escritura* relating to the purchase of the land. You will also need to take the *permiso de obra* (building licence), the *certificado final de obra* (completion of construction certificate) issued by the architect and the *licencia de primera ocupación* (licence of first occupation) to the local town hall. To register the building for real estate taxes (*Impuesto sobre Bienes Inmeubles* – IBI) refer to the chapter on *Housing Finance*.

Because so many foreigners are interested in self-builds there are a lot more clued up agents and developers these days, buying up plots of land, often with services and permiso de obra already obtained, to sell on to clients. Property developers also sell plots on their housing schemes (parcelas) for buyers to build their own house on.

A prospective self-builder should look into ways to minimise the amount that will need to be paid in VAT and municipal taxes over the period of the project from its inception to its completion and the registration of the property. There may also be tax saving ways to finance the building project, whether through funds held in Spain, at home or in an offshore account. Be aware that IVA (Spain's equivalent to VAT) will need to be paid on building land at 16 percent; IVA at a rate of 7% will be added on to building costs.

Useful Contacts

Househam Henderson Architects: ☎(UK) 01962-835500; ☎(Spain)913-081 555; www.hharchitects.co.uk. UK architectural practice with a Spanish office.

Punta de Lanza: ☎619-641635; www.puntadelanza.com. One stop shop architectural service in Andalucía.

Altasur Ingeneria y Proyectors S.L.: ☎952-414765.

BUYING IN THE VALENCIA REGION: THE LRAU

Those planning on buying property in the Valencian autonomous community should be very careful. Over the last few years an obscure planning law in the region has been hitting the headlines for forcing homeowners to hand over their property to local developers with barely any compensation. As many as 15,000 people who have bought property as holiday or retirement homes in Valencia have had up to 75% of their legally owned land taken from them by developers, and have even been charged up to £100,000 for the privilege. Dubbed the 'Spanish Acquisition' by the newspapers, this phenomenon has been described as one of the biggest illegal land grabs in Europe since the Second World War.

The *Ley Reguladora de la Actividad Urbanistica* (LRAU) was introduced by Valencia's socialist government in 1994 with the aim of making land available for low-cost social housing and to provide space for major public works. Unfortunately the wording of the LRAU is so complex and ambiguous that it is being exploited by property developers, who are using it as carte blanche for a massive land grab. Any property developer in the area can submit a planning application for a piece of land whether they own it or not. If no competing plan is submitted, or the town hall does not object, or respond within six months, then the developer can proceed with his plan and the owner must cede part of his land to the town hall, often receiving as little as 10% of the value of the property as compensation. Worse still, owners may also be assessed as liable for a proportion of the cost of the infrastructure of the new development (construction of roads, drains, lighting and other urban development costs). Reports have shown that these ruthless developers are unlikely to build the kind of low-cost houses that the law supposedly requires. The idea of LRAU is to provide houses for Spanish people who cannot afford to buy now that Northern European property prices have hit the area. In fact, developers are building anything they like, including expensive luxury housing. As long as the town hall agrees it to be in the public interest, then there is little that can be done.

Those affected by the law should be notified in writing when a planning application is lodged, but often the town hall's information is out of date and does not include many non-resident owners. If the owner wishes to object, they have just fifteen days in which to submit a counter proposal, for which they must obtain the agreement of the majority of property owners in their zone, but even if they do so, the probability is that the plans will be accepted.

Risk to property here is such that Spain is the only western European country where it is impossible to get any form of 'clear title' insurance that would either cover legal costs or pay some reimbursement in situations where good titles (deeds, escrituras, etc.) can mean little or nothing in the face of land grabs.

An organisation known as *Abusos Urbanísticos No* (www.abusos-no.org), backed by more than 30,000 people (including many Britons) is pushing the issue, writing petitions and helping to bring individual lawsuits against the local government. The law is also being challenged in both Spanish and European courts.

In early 2006 a new law known as the LUV (*Ley Urbanística Valenciana*) replaced the LRAU for all but those projects already under way. However, according to Charles Svoboda, President of *Abusos Urbanisticos No,* the new law is just as pernicious:

The new law will fix nothing in terms of what property owners had to fear from the LRAU. In some ways things will be worse. Because of pressures from the promoters, developers and builders, almost all of the promised concessions vanished in the final version of the LUV.

Until the situation has been resolved it is very important when buying property here to check all future developments at the town hall. According to a report in *The Times,* estate agents selling properties in this area are aware of the 'land grabs' but are not legally obliged to warn their clients (and therefore do not). Prospective purchasers should take professional advice from a lawyer who can help with the necessary investigation. Further information on the new LUV can be found, in English, at www.abusos-no.org.

FEES CONTRACTS AND CONVEYANCING

Overview
The ins and outs of the buying process are described in some detail below, but it is useful to begin with a simple step-by-step guide to property purchase in Spain:

Step 1 – Find an estate agent, consult a lawyer and find your ideal property. Estate agents are dealt with in some detail in the chapter *Finding Properties for Sale*. Nevertheless, it is worth reiterating the importance of finding a reputable agent. It is a very good idea to have a lawyer on board as early as possible. You can then ensure that they are well-prepared and ready to carry out checks right from the start. The importance of finding a reliable and impartial lawyer is covered below. Whether you choose a UK-based lawyer, or a local lawyer specialising in property transactions, you should make sure that they are fluent in both Spanish and English, and are fully versed in the legal and tax implications in both countries.

Step 2 – Make an offer. Having found the property and decided how you will pay for it you should make a verbal offer via the agent to the property vendor. When the offer is accepted, some buyers will sign a reservation contract and put down a deposit (often non-refundable). The property is then taken off the market.

Step 3 – Signing the contracts. For an existing re-sale property, your lawyer should next negotiate a full preliminary contract (*contrato privado de compraventa*). Before this agreement is signed any surveys and necessary legal checks should be carried out. On signing the contract, the buyer will transfer a deposit (usually

10% of the price) for which a receipt is issued. The date of completion should be agreed in this contract. If the buyer pulls out after signing this agreement they will lose the deposit.

If you are buying an off-plan property, you will have to sign a reservation contract, agreeing to make stage payments as building work advances. Ensure that you have the full building specification for the property translated into English and copies of the agreements you have signed.

Step 4 – Signing the title deeds. This is the last step and will give you possession of the property. The deeds must be signed before a notary, and prior arrangements for the transfer of the balance of the cost of the property must have been made. The deeds will then be registered with the land registry. It is the buyer's responsibility to ensure that this has been done.

TYPICAL COSTS INVOLVED IN CONVEYANCING

o Notary Fee: for preparation of the title deed (around €300-€600).

o Land Registry Fee: dependent on the value of property (around €300).

o *Plus Valia* Tax: paid to the municipality on the transfer of property. It is dependent on the value of the land on which the property sits. The vendor should pay this, but contracts of sale often try to impose the fee on the buyer. It can come to several thousand pounds and is usually around 0.5% on a property.

o VAT/Transfer Tax/Stamp Duty: depends on the value of the property, the type of property and where the property is situated. Usually around 7% of the purchase price on new property.

o Registration with the Spanish Tax Authorities and obtaining a foreigners' identification number (NIE): This can be done by your solicitor for a fee.

Fees

Total inclusive costs (lawyers, land registry, *notario*, taxes, bank charges, associates fees etc.) bring the overall costs of conveyancing to around 10% of the cost price of a resale property in mainland Spain, and between 7-9% on such properties in the Canary Islands. Tax on new property in mainland Spain is 7%, to which must be added 4% additional fees; in the Canary Islands tax on new property is 4%, with another 4% to pay in additional fees. The cheaper the property, the greater the likelihood of that percentage rising due to the minimum charges imposed by lawyers and others involved in the conveyancing.

EXAMPLE OF COSTS ON THE PURCHASE OF A €125,000 PROPERTY		
Notary Fees	Preparation of *escritura*, registering of ownership, stamp duty	€1,950
Legal Fees	Making searches on registries, preparation of *escritura*, translation of contracts, etc	€1,250
Plus Valia	Capital Gains Tax levied by the Town Hall on increased value of land since last sold	€120
VAT (IVA) 7%	Payable on the declared value of the property	€8,750
Connection Charges	Water, electricity, gas, drainage, telephone	€425
	TOTAL	**€12,495**
(Fees exclusive of VAT)		

Lawyers

When buying property, it is very important to employ an *abogado* to look after your personal interests. An independent lawyer should be either a specialist lawyer from home or an English-speaking Spanish abogado.

The lawyer will be able to:

- Advise a client whose name should be registered as the owner of a property as ownership will have knock-on effects with regards to taxation.
- Advise on how to pay for the property – whether through a mortgage, re-mortgaging, forming a company, cash, etc., and how to minimise costs.
- Arrange for Power of Attorney should it be necessary.
- Arrange for the signing of the *escritura* and making purchase payments, and may also be able to organise currency exchange and the transferral of funds from a buyer's home bank account into Spain.
- Check that there are no cases pending against the property with regards to planning permission not having been obtained when the property was originally built.

- Draw up the contract for the sale of the property or between a builder, architect and client.
- Guide a client through the legal processes involved in buying property in Spain.
- Look after the conveyancing procedures.
- Make payments for the conveyancing costs, taxes etc, on behalf of the buyer.
- Obtain an NIE number on behalf of the client.
- Recommend local tradesmen, surveyors, agents, mortgage brokers and banks that will suit a client's needs.

Should you use a Spanish lawyer, even if they speak fluent English, they may be unfamiliar with UK law and the ramifications that buying a property overseas may have on your tax or legal situation back home. Also, bear in mind that Spanish lawyers tend to specialise in individual areas of law, so you should make sure that you hire a lawyer who is an expert in property law, and has a good working knowledge of the kind of market where you intend to buy. For example a lawyer who is only used to dealing with properties on the costas, may not have the same expertise in inland properties.

Be wary of using the services of a lawyer recommended by the vendor or their estate agent, as their impartiality may be compromised. According to Mark Stucklin of www.spanishpropertyinsight.com: *'Those who use lawyers recommended by the estate agent or developer they are buying from run the risk of hiring the very lawyers they need protection from'*. It is certainly the case that lawyers who are not fully independent may be overly tempted to draw up contracts in the interests of the company, and not wholeheartedly fight your corner should a dispute arise.

If your grasp of Spanish is shaky then you should definitely find a lawyer who speaks English. In the major Spanish coastal resorts this will not be a problem. Lawyers in these areas will be used to dealing with foreigners looking to buy property in their locality and may well advertise their services in local free sheets and the English-language press. They will be well aware of potential areas of conflicting interests and will be able to smooth your way to the best of their ability within the confines of Spanish law.

If you are hoping to buy property with land attached in a rural part of Spain then your lawyer will be useful in finding out about what the planning restrictions are in the area and if there are local bylaws in force with regards to water, grazing or hunting and access rights on the land. You will also want your lawyer to check out where property boundaries end and begin as these may differ from what has been written in the *escritura*, what the owners of the property believe, and what is registered in the Land Registry. If you are buying into an *urbanización* or an apartment block where you will be part of the *comunidad de propietarios* you will also want the rules and regulations checked by a lawyer.

You should get your lawyer to check everything that is put on the table by the agents before signing anything. Don't rely on a notary to do the work that a lawyer would normally do. Another good reason for getting a lawyer is that they may well be able to advise you on the most financially beneficial way to deal with the conveyancing process, saving you money by guiding you through the taxation systems of Spain and the UK.

It is a good idea to find a lawyer and get their advice before even starting on the house-hunt in Spain. They will be able to give you pointers and tell you about the possible pitfalls. They will also be ready to look at contracts before you sign – you may be able to fax them over while you are in Spain and wait for their appraisal before going ahead and signing and committing yourself to something that you may later regret. Remember that you will need to find either a lawyer from home versed in international law and the laws pertaining to Spanish property in particular, or an English-speaking Spanish lawyer versed in the taxation system of your home country. Without this knowledge a lawyer may not be able to organise your affairs to your best advantage.

Fees. The fees charged by a lawyer for their work on buying a new or resale property are likely to be about 1%-1.5% of the price of the property. Some lawyers will agree a percentage at the outset, whereas others charge on an hourly basis or take a flat fee. There are a number of variables here, so it is always best to start by asking for an explanation of the fees and an estimate of the hours involved. You will need to be aware that apart from the basic fee, should additional negotiations need to be undertaken on your behalf you will be charged. For example there may need to be further clauses added to a contract, or negotiations over the price of a property; if there are irregularities in the *escritura* these will need to be corrected before change of title can take place. There will also be correspondence generated between the solicitors and a mortgage company if you are taking out a mortgage and all these matters will incur further fees.

It is fairly common to be asked for a provision of funds of around €1000 or up to 50% of the fee when your lawyer starts working for you, and the remainder will be due on completion of the purchase. Always keep receipts of any payments.

For properties that have not yet been built, lawyers will generally charge around 1% of the property value plus an hourly rate on work done on your behalf while the construction continues. Because, as in the way of all things, there can never be a 100% definite completion date, more work may need to be done on your behalf as projects and the legalities involved unfold. The solicitor should give you an estimate of the likely charges to be incurred once they have seen the existing paperwork relating to the project.

Changing lawyers. Most people find that they are able to establish a good working relationship with their lawyer, based on trust. Nevertheless, it is essential to keep copies of all important documents and keep records of any conversations that you have with your lawyer. If, at any point, you begin to doubt the competence or impartiality of your lawyer, then you have the right to change to a different lawyer. Buyers should not be afraid to make such a move. With the right lawyer, you are running far lower risks when purchasing properties.

The procedure for changing lawyers is fairly simple. Simply send a letter or fax informing your current lawyer of the decision to dispense with their services and give them instructions to pass on your file to a new lawyer, making sure to specify a date for the changeover. If these instructions are ignored, then make clear your intention to go to the *colegio de abogados* with your grievance and, as a last resort, do so. Those who change lawyers during the purchase procedure need only pay for the work provided up to that date.

Finding a Lawyer in Spain

It is best to find an abogado through a personal recommendation. Failing that there are a number of alternatives. In the UK the *Law Society* (☎020-7242 1222; www.lawsoc.org.uk) holds lists of registered English-speaking lawyers in Spain. The website allows you to search for a list of lawyers in Spain who specialise in residential conveyancing. Consulates and embassies in Spain will also hold lists of English-speaking lawyers in your locality (000 *Boolóo*). You may also contact the

General Council of Spanish Lawyers for further guidance (*Consejo General de la Abogacia Española:* ☎915-232593; www.cgae.es).

UK-Based Spanish and English Lawyers

Bennett & Co. Solicitors: 144 Knutsford Road, Wilmslow, Cheshire SK9 6JP; ☎01625-586937; fax 01625-585362; www.Bennett-and-co.com.

Cornish & Co: Lex House, 1/7 Hainault Street, Ilford, Essex IG1 4EL; ☎020-8478 3300; fax 020-8552 3418; www.cornishco.com. Spanish office: ☎952 866 830.

Fernando Scornik Gerstein: Holborn Hall, 193-197 High Holborn, London WC1V 7BD; ☎020-7404 8400; fax 020-7404 8500; e-mail cedillo@fscornik.co.uk.

Florez Valcarcel: Lawyer and Notario: 130 King Street, Hammersmith, London W6 0QU; tel/fax 020-8741 4867.

Javier de Juan: 36 Greyhound Road, London W6 8NX; ☎020-7381 0470; fax 020-7381-4155; www.spanishlaw.org.uk.

John Howell & Co: The Old Glass Works, 22 Endell Street, Covent Garden, London WC2H 9AD; tel 020-7420 0400; fax 020-7836 3626; e-mail info@europelaw.com; www.europelaw.com.

The International Property Law Centre: Suffolk House, 21 Silver Street, Hull HU1 1JG; (☎0870 800 4565; fax 0870 800 4567; e-mail; internationalproperty@maxgold.com; www.internationalpropertylaw.com. Specialists in the purchase and sale of property and businesses in Spain, with in-house foreign lawyers. Fixed quote and no VAT payable. Contact Antonio Guillen, Abogado at ☎0870 800 4589 and e-mail antoniog@maxgold.com or Manuel Riguera, Legal Assistant, at manuelr@maxgold.com.

English-Speaking Spanish-Based Lawyers

Anderson & Asociados Abogados: Centro Dona Pepa Local 1-2 Urb Reserva de Marbella, Ctra. Nac. 340, km. 193,6 Marbella 29600; ☎952 932 997; fax 952 934 902; www.andersonabogados.com.

Buño Leon: Pintor Lorenzo Casanova, 66, 1ºA, 03003 Alicante; ☎965 921 853; fax 965 921 450; www.cbleon-abogados.com/ingles; e-mail bufeteba@terra.es.

De Cotta McKenna y Santafé Abogado: Centro Commercial Valdepinos 1 y 3A, Urbanización Calypsoi, 2964 Mijas-Costa; ☎952 931 781; fax ☎952 933 547; e-mail cottalaw@cybonline.com, and another office at C/. Diputación, 6-2ºA Nerja, 29780 Malaga; ☎952 527 014; fax 952 523 428.

Euro-Abogados Costa Blanca S.L.: Calle Apolo 88, 30 B, 03180 Torrevieja, Alicante; ☎966 703 202.

Inspections and Surveys

It wouldn't be prudent to buy a property in your native country without having it checked over by a qualified surveyor, so it makes sense therefore to get a property in Spain surveyed. That said, the surveying of property before purchasing is not a typical Spanish trait and many buy on sight. However, there are always horror stories of people who have bought a flat that looked 'okay' only to find that during the winter months it became flooded; or the hairline crack that they were told wasn't anything structurally damaging, worsened year on year. The old adage, 'when in Rome do as the Romans do...' shouldn't apply when it comes to something as financially risky as buying a house.

If you are buying a property on a mortgage, the lenders may well require a survey, even if it is only to provide an appraisal of the purchase price. Nevertheless, Ashley Clark, Director of *Need An Adviser.com,* offers these words of warning:

There have been accusations of surveyors linked with unscrupulous estate agents or builders actually inflating the value of properties to achieve greater purchase prices for increased commissions or to ensure that a mortgage be obtained. The simple answer is to always engage your own independent surveyor.

> For new properties, and property that is less than ten years old the structure will have been guaranteed by the original builders or developers as all builders must guarantee their work against major structural defects for a decade. However, should you buy an older resale property, or even a derelict building that you are hoping to renovate, you would be wise to get a survey done.

When you initially view a property that you are interested in, give it the amateur eye and check for any signs of subsidence, bowing walls, damp patches or strange smells. Check for dry rot (stick a knife into windowsills and other likely areas where damp may have struck), a leaking roof (stains on the ceilings), cracks or fractures in the walls. You will want to make sure that all plumbing, electrics, and water heating systems are in good working order, as well as the drainage and water provision. Be on the look out for any signs of rising damp or signs of condensation/humidity. While viewing a property take your time and get the feel of the place – you will usually be able to tell if there are any *major* structural problems.

Expert Opinions. Both estate agents (other than the ones selling the property) and builders will be able to give you their 'expert' opinions on whether your desired property is sound or not but they are unlikely to be backed up by a professional report. A trained surveyor on the other hand will be able to cast a professional eye over the property and give you a full and detailed report on it. Such a survey will cost you perhaps £1,000-£1,500 depending on the surveyor and size of property. Spanish surveyors tend to concentrate on different aspects than their British equivalents, although those who are used to dealing with foreigners are likely to provide you with a report similar to what you would expect to get back home. Be sure to get any report that is presented to you in Spanish translated into English.

Because of the differences in surveying criteria between the UK and Spanish systems you should make sure that *you* know what should be checked and discuss this with the surveyor. Note that most vendors will not sign any contract of sale with a 'subject to survey' clause. They are more likely to demand that you arrange a survey (at your own expense) before they sign anything. Should another interested party come along and sign a contract with the vendor before you have been able to satisfy yourself as to the soundness of the property, you will have lost out on the chance to buy.

Finding a Surveyor

The Royal Institute of Chartered Surveyors website has a directory (www.ricsfirms. com) of 47 member organisations in Spain. Search by location to find the company nearest to you. Alternatively English-language newspapers will offer a selection of English-speaking surveyors, advertising in the Classifieds section.

Conveyancing

Once you have found the right property, you will probably have to act swiftly to ensure that you get it, although you should remember that as the property boom slows down, Spain is becoming more and more a buyers' market. Never sign anything without having first sought independent legal advice. Contracts are often short, containing the details of the vendor and purchaser, the purchase price, a legal description of the property, the date set for completion and possession of the property and the type of payment involved in the sale.

Purchase Contracts for Resale/New Properties. There are three differing types of contract that you may be asked to sign at this stage:

- ○ *Offer to Buy:* A formal offer to buy the property at a fixed price – the contract being valid for a set period of time. Should the vendor accept your offer then a non-returnable, negotiable deposit will be payable and the contract will become binding between the two parties.
- ○ *Reservation Contract:* An agreement between the potential buyer of a property and the vendor or estate agent. This type of contract dictates that the property is taken off the market for a set period of time. A reservation fee is paid by the potential buyer, which, if a full contract to buy is signed within the set period, will count towards the full price of the property to be paid. If problems concerning the property are unearthed during the reservation period (such as the vendor not being the named owner on the *escritura*) and the potential buyer decides to pull out then the reservation fee will be lost. The clauses in this type of contract, therefore, need to be carefully checked.
- ○ *Private Purchase Contract:* A full and binding contract to buy. You will pay a negotiable deposit of around 10% of the purchase price, the balance to be paid on the signing of the *escritura*. Obviously, before signing such a contract you will want to get your lawyer to check it.

The contract will be prepared by either an estate agent or developer or, if you decide to buy privately from an individual, by the vendor's lawyer. Whichever contract is offered to you, have it presented to you in your mother tongue as well as in Spanish, and make sure that you have your lawyer check it before you sign. There may well be clauses that either you or the vendor will not accept and these will need to be negotiated, as will the purchase price and the amount of deposit payable.

There are strict conditions relating to the repayment of deposits. Make sure that you are informed of these by your lawyer. When paying a deposit ensure that the money is kept by the estate agent or legal representative of the vendor in a bonded account until the sale has gone through. This will guard against a crooked vendor, or estate agent, taking your deposit and then deciding to sell the property to another instead.

Purchase Contracts for Off-plan Properties. For properties that are still under construction at the time of purchase, stage payments will be required during the construction period. It may be possible to arrange the payment schedule to suit the purchaser's individual needs and a typical payment schedule could be as follows:

- On the signing of the contract: a deposit of 20% payable by bankers draft, personal cheque, cash, traveller's cheques or credit card.
- After a set period, or on completion of a certain phase in the building work (e.g. completion of the exterior walls and roof): 25% of the agreed purchase price.
- After a set period, or on completion of another phase in the building work (e.g. completion of interior, fitting of interior furniture and windows and doors): Another 25% of the agreed purchase price – the timing of this payment may vary and is generally dependent upon the building project completion date.
- On completion or signing of the *escritura*: Outstanding balance payable.

With such contracts it is advisable to negotiate a clause in the contract that allows you to withhold a certain percentage of the cost price – say 10% – for a certain period after you have moved into the property as a guarantee against possible defects. This will ensure that the builders will come back to rectify any problems that crop up, and a good firm should be happy to provide this type of insurance. You may also want to alter the specifications of fixtures and fittings, type and style of tiles, etc., that have been specified by the builders/developers. If you do alter specifications, changes will need to be made to the price structure and also to the completion date. Make sure that the developer is the legal owner of the land, has obtained the required building regulations and that the required payments are held in a bonded account until completion.

Checks That Should Be Made On A Property Before Completion
Resale Properties
- Are fittings and/or furniture included in the purchase price?
- Are there any planning restrictions pertaining to the property and/or location which will affect your plans should you wish to build on or alter the property?

- Are there community charges to be paid on the property? Do you understand the statutes of the *comunidad de propietarios*, and are you happy to comply with them?
- Are there restrictions on the uses that can be made of the property?
- Boundaries, access, and public right of way bylaws should be clearly defined and understood.
- Check the *Plan General de Ordenación Urbana* at the town hall to see whether there are going to be future developments (e.g. new lines of communication/building projects, etc.) that may affect the value/view of the property at a later date.
- Check the description of the property in the Land Registry and the Property Registry.
- Check the property is free of any debts or charges; that all utility and community bills, and taxes (including the IBI tax) have been paid up to date. Remember that debts on a property are 'inherited' by the new owner.
- Has there been a completion of a survey to your satisfaction?
- Has there been any alteration done to the property that has not been registered with the authorities?
- How much are the local taxes and charges?
- Is there adequate water, drainage, electricity and telecommunication provision?
- The vendor is the legal registered owner of the property.

Additional checks that should be made on off-plan and new build property
- A full breakdown of the materials, fixtures and fittings used in the building of the property.
- Be clear what you are paying for. What are the finishings? Will the surrounding land be landscaped? What will the property look like (have you seen a show home to gauge this)?
- Make sure that all completion licences (*certificado de fin de obra, licencia de primera ocupación,* and the *boletin de instalación*) have been obtained.
- Make sure that the developers or builders have obtained the necessary planning permissions to build upon the land.
- Make sure that the payment schedule and completion date are clear.
- Make sure the developers or builders are the legal owners of the land they are developing.
- Protect yourself against the possibility of the developer or builders going bankrupt before completing the property.

○ The property has been registered with the local authorities for real estate taxes.

Additional checks that should be made on the purchase of plots of land for self-build projects
○ Will you be given a permit to build (*permiso de obra*) from the town hall?
○ How much will it cost to build on the land and can you afford the costs. Get quotes from architects and builders?

Registries. The Land Registry (*Catastro*) contains details of the physical and topographical details of a property as well as a valuation, while the Property Registry (*Registro de la Propiedad*) only holds the details of ownership and title. These two registries may have differing details of the same property and a potential buyer should check that the description of a property in the contract tallies with that in both the Property and Land Registries. It may take a month or so for the Land Registry to provide a *certificado catastral* outlining the boundaries and measurements of a property so you should ask for it as soon as you have found the property of your choice.

The Notary. The Spanish Notary Public – the *notario* – although a lawyer, does not give legal advice to either the vendor or the purchaser of a property. The job of the *notario* is to witness the signing of the title deeds (*escritura*) in his or her office located in the area where the property is being purchased and to deal with other administrative matters. Once the *escritura* has been signed, the purchase price of the property is then handed over to the vendor, or the vendor confirms that payment has already been received. Proof of payment is then noted down in the *escritura*, which is then registered in the local Property Register. Before preparing the *escritura* a *notario* will ensure that the purchaser has received the property as stated on the contract and that the vendor has received the correct purchase price. The *notario* will also advise on taxes that are due on the property.

Notaries collect their fees from the vendor and the purchaser and these fees are charged in accordance with a sliding scale of charges set by the Spanish government. These will vary depending on the price of a property and the amount of work the *notario* has done on behalf of the two parties in preparing documents. Note that not all notaries will speak English and you may therefore need to be accompanied to meetings by a Spanish speaker.

Power of Attorney. The person buying or selling a property does not necessarily have to be present when the title deeds are signed in front of the *notario* and, for a fee, a Power of Attorney can be granted which will allow another person to attend on the vendor's behalf instead. If a Power of Attorney has been arranged outside Spain, it will need to be witnessed and stamped by a *notario* in Spain.

The Signing of the Escritura

The date of the signing of the *escritura* will have been fixed in the contact to buy, though in reality the date may slip a little depending on the status of the checks on the property made by your lawyer. It should normally take place two to three months after signing the contract to buy a resale or new property but will take longer if you are buying off-plan. If there are problems such as sorting out ownership of the property or outstanding taxes on the property then this can obviously hold matters up.

When the *notario* has received all the documentation he or she needs to complete the *escritura* you should receive a draft copy, which it is advisable to have scrutinised by your lawyer to check that all is as should be. Though a notary is a trained lawyer who has taken further exams to qualify for the post of notary, it is not a requirement of the job to do the work of a lawyer. Make a last check on the property to see that everything is in order and that what was agreed as included in the purchase price in the contract of sale remains in or with the property (e.g. fixtures and fittings).

Once everything has been settled the vendor and the purchaser meet at the *notario's* office. The notary will read through the *escritura* after which the two parties will sign the document.

For properties that are ready for immediate occupation, full payment is made before signing the *escritura*. It may be that the money paid for a property is to be transferred to wherever in the world the vendor wishes to receive it. However, if the purchase price is paid into a Spanish account, then the importation of currency will need to be registered with the Spanish authorities and your solicitor should deal with this for you. Many people hand over a banker's draft at this point as it can be witnessed by the *notario* there and then, but other methods of payment are available. At the same time the notary will collect his fee and inform the purchaser of any taxes payable on the transfer of property. If the vendor is a non-resident there will be 5% withheld from the purchase price, which will be paid to the Spanish Tax Agency on the vendor's behalf due to Capital Gains Tax liabilities.

After the signing of the *escritura*, the payment of the purchase price and all fees, the notary will pass the purchaser a copy (*copia simple*) of the *escritura* and the keys to the property. The original (*primera copia*) will be sent to the Property Register and the new owner's name registered. It can take several months for the process of registering the change of title deeds as all taxes and fees must be paid before a property can be registered in the new owner's name. Once a certificate has been issued stating that the name of the owner of the property has been registered, the purchaser's lawyer should collect it and forward it on to the new owner.

RENOVATING A PROPERTY

Buying an old *finca* in need of a certain amount of renovation, should be approached with as much caution as when buying a resale property that is ready to move into. You need to ask yourself whether you have the know-how to renovate a tumbledown property or if you have the necessary funds to hire builders who do. Depending on the amount of work involved in renovating a property, new build often tends to work out cheaper, by up to a third, than renovation. When you have found a property that you are interested in, get a survey done.

Licence for Renovation

If you are going to be carrying out major building work, whether erecting a new building or renovating the existing property, you will need to get a building permit (*licencia de obra*) from the town hall. Before buying a property in need of renovation, make sure that the vendor and *notario* are aware that you will only buy subject to the planning permission and building licence being granted. Building permits (*licencia de obra*), if granted by the town hall, will cost around 4% of the cost of the build.

Once everything has been checked out by your lawyer to your satisfaction you can go ahead, buy the land and sign for it at the office of the *notario*. The registration of the land or property can be left to your lawyer, together with the paying of taxes due.

Before starting on any major renovation work, employ an architect. Shop around and get several quotes as these will vary a lot, and will depend on the size of the property, or the planned building work, and perhaps on how *au fait* you are with Spain and your ability to negotiate in Spanish. A registered architect, like a builder, must guarantee their plans and the instructions given to the builder for a period of ten years. Even though it may seem easier to deal with an architect from home, or someone whose mother tongue is English, a Spanish architect familiar with local building rules and regulations, and the local climate, is likely to more helpful to you in the long run.

An architect's fees will include plans (make sure that you are completely satisfied with them) and the supervision of the building project. The fee will also include the copies of the plans necessary for approval by the College of Architects before you can obtain the building permit and should also include the cost of preparing the *memoria*, or building specification. This states such things as the quantity and sizes of tiles, bricks, pipes etc, that are needed for the project, the type of concrete and cement needed, and the rest of the building materials to be used. It is likely that you will want to be involved in deciding on the type of electrical and bathroom fixtures and fittings. Windows and doors and the kitchen units can all be discussed with the architect or builder while the *memoria* is being compiled.

Once the *memoria* is complete it is then given to the builder/s in order to get a quote for the cost of the building work involved. This quote will obviously be given after having taken into consideration all the materials listed in the *memoria*, and though it may change a bit as work proceeds, any alterations that you make to it later on will cost you extra – and you will need to amend the contract that you have with your builder accordingly. Sift through several quotes from builders who you have found through recommendation. Recommendation really is the only way to 'vet' a builder, though make sure that such praise comes from independent parties. Ask around among locals and expats and if a builder comes highly recommended then meet him and ask to be shown some of his work. Quotes that come in will vary and the highest quote will not necessarily guarantee the best results, just as a low quote doesn't necessarily mean that the work or materials will be second-rate. Also be advised that there are plenty of expats living in Spain who are looking for work without having registered with the Spanish tax authorities. If you employ such a person and the authorities find out, you and your employee may both face heavy fines.

When you sign a contract with the builder get your lawyer to check it to see whether there are any clauses included that may work to your detriment. The contract should include the *memoria*, the total price for the job with payment schedule and work to be carried out. The cost of the job will need to be negotiated with the builder. Builders will often ask to be paid 50% before they start work with the balance payable in stages as the work progresses. Try and negotiate with them and if possible include a clause in the contract whereby you hold back 10% of the total for a period to insure against possible building flaws or defects. Such things may not be evident until the house has managed to 'settle'.

Builders

Any builder you employ should be covered by an insurance policy so that if they go bankrupt while in the middle of working on your house you will be able to claim compensation. By law, a builder in Spain must guarantee any work carried out for a period of ten years. Arrange to pay builders by instalments, never in one lump sum, all in one go. It is also advisable to remain, if possible, *in situ* or nearby, while the builders are at your property. This isn't to say that you should be on hand to continually interfere and 'direct' operations, but to check that the builders are actually turning up for work and doing the hours that you are getting billed for. Also being aware of what is going on will ensure that the architect's original plans are being adhered to and that the fixtures and fittings are those that were originally agreed upon.

There are good and bad, reliable and unreliable people all over the world, but if you are trusting someone with a hefty investment of your time and money you need to make sure that your investment is safe in their hands. Because of the amount of continued construction work going on in Spain, skilled tradesmen are in short supply. Builders often contract to take on several jobs at a time so that should interruptions occur on one project they can turn to the next. Be sure to get several quotes on any major job that you need doing.

DIY

For basics such as nuts and bolts and screws, wire, nails, etc., the local *ferretería* (hardware store/ironmongers') is going to be a useful resource. Additionally, on the outskirts of towns and cities are large industrial estates where you will find workshops and wholesalers who will often be in the building trade. There are also DIY superstores such as *Akí* and *Leroy Merlin*, which sell all the kit that you will need to knock up anything from a garden shed to a villa with pool.

Retired Expat Ian Adams has done most of the renovation work on his property himself:

> *I bought our property cheaply and have been lucky enough to have the time to do a lot of the renovation work on the place. You need to be careful as Spanish materials are very different from British materials, but I have taught myself how to bricklay, plaster, do the electrics and plumbing. Essentially I have knocked all of the internal walls out and started again – restructuring the inside completely. Building materials are extremely cheap here, and it has been an enjoyable project.*

For projects that need a professional touch, plumbers (*fontaneros*), carpenters (*carpinteros*), bricklayers (albañiles) etc., will be listed in the local yellow pages (*las páginas amarillas*) or found through talking to neighbours. The best way to find tradesmen is by recommendation, as Ian Adams warns:

> *You have to be careful with tradesmen, and it is best to only employ those that you have heard good things about. British tradesmen out here will often try to charge British prices, and Spanish tradesmen tend to assume that the British have a lot of money and will put the price up accordingly.*

Swimming Pools

Most people thinking about buying property in Spain will also be dreaming about how great it will be to have their own swimming pool. With the amount of sunshine that Spain enjoys, owning a home without a pool seems a tragedy. Swimming is incredibly good for physical fitness and keeping the heart healthy. Unfortunately, swimming pools aren't cheap either to install or to maintain. The cost of installing an average sized pool of, say, 8 x 4 metres, is likely to come in at around €20,000. This price excludes the cost of heating. Even if you buy a property with an existing pool you will need to consider the costs involved in its upkeep and maintenance.

Those who wish to build a swimming pool in the grounds of their house will first have to apply for planning permission from the town hall (*ayuntamiento*). In some areas, especially those where water shortages are a frequent problem, this can be quite an obstacle.

Once you have permission, one of the most important issues is the position of the pool. Clearly it must be in the sun, otherwise it will never heat up, and the ground must be as flat as possible. If pools built on a slope are not properly anchored they can move. Anchoring can only be safely carried out by a professional pool builder. As always, take recommendations before committing yourself to a builder.

○ There are several popular means of building a pool in Spain: using reinforced concrete, block construction; or an excavated hole, which is plastered and then PVC lined. The differences in design are reflected in a difference in cost. The cheapest option is to install an above ground, prefabricated pool. Obviously a pool needs a regular supply of clean water and this is something that you will need to plan for.

○ Sanitising pools once a week with chlorine will prevent water-born viruses and bacteria. There are many ways to do this. Chlorine is by far and away the most popular and the risk of overdosing or under-dosing is now greatly reduced by the use of automatic computerised dosing equipment. Other, non-chemical forms of sanitation include ultra-violet light and ionisation.

○ To keep a swimming pool in good condition, i.e. clean, warm and pure, it is necessary to remove the total body of water from the pool several times a day, pass it through filters and sanitise it. Filters remove the dirt, drowned wasps, crumbs etc., from the water, while a sanitiser kills any bacteria that may lurk. The time required for all the pool water to pass through the filters etc. is called the 'pool turnover' time. In the case of a domestic pool a turnover time of 6-8 hours is quite sufficient, because usage is generally very low.

○ Because electricity in Spain is relatively expensive (and about three times the price of gas or oil) should you want to heat your swimming pool it may be an option to go for a heater that is fired by gas or oil or, even better, through solar panelling. Solar panels are more expensive to install but cheaper to run, and they will usually allow you one month's extra swimming either side of the season.

THE RENTAL SCENE

There are thousands of apartments and villas for rent in Spain, available both through commercial agents and through private owners. For those hunting around for property to buy and who intend to live in Spain permanently it is always a good idea to initially rent for a while. Renting property means a less permanent commitment and will allow you time to make up your mind about where you want to live, to see if you like the area, the climate and the amenities and decide what kind of property will suit your needs. If you are thinking about buying a holiday villa or apartment remember that such properties are mainly purpose-built for summer only residence, and that even in the south of Spain winter can still be chilly. Marble floors can be unpleasantly cold on the feet over the winter months, the walls not particularly thick, and anyone considering buying one of these holiday properties with an idea to moving in permanently should spend a winter renting such a property first before buying.

The disadvantage of Spanish rentals generally is that, price-wise, they can be fairly exorbitant. This is largely because the actual market for long-term, good quality rented property remains relatively small compared to many other European countries.

In 2005 the Spanish government announced the creation of a new agency aimed at encouraging people to rent more (*La Sociedad Publica de Alquiler*). The government aims to create a pool of 25,500 properties to rent in Spain over the next four years, and to offer them at a lower monthly rent than is currently available. Hopefully this will help to reduce rent across the board in the future.

Currently prices in sought-after locations such as Mallorca start at a minimum of €800 per month. Rents in Madrid and San Sebastián are uniformly expensive, and to live in one of the more affluent suburbs of Barcelona you would be looking at about €4,500 a month or more for a spacious two or three-bedroom house. Prices will depend on the size of the property, the time of year, and the location – beach and golf properties command premium rates and as elsewhere the cheapest rents are to be found in the smaller towns and villages inland away from the coasts. Rents on short term accommodation will be at their highest in July and August (and often over Christmas and Easter), and at their lowest in late autumn and over the winter.

Finding Rented Accommodation

The best way to start looking for rental accommodation in Spain is by reading the classified sections of local newspapers. Alternatively you can visit local estate agents, but the disadvantage with this is that they charge a finders fee of around a month's rent. This means that you will have to pay three months rent upon signing the contract – the deposit, the agency fee and the first month's rent. Many websites list accommodation for rent in Spain and more and more people are using the internet to advertise their properties.

Tenancy Laws

Spanish renting and letting laws were extensively updated with the enforcement of regulations passed in 1985. These were revised in the Rent Law of January 1995. These regulations have ended some very strict forms of tenant protection, which included what was in effect the tenant's right to an indefinitely extendable rental contract. This situation was regarded as unfair to landlords and made many owners think twice about renting out their property. Rents in some circumstances can now be raised by more than the cost of living index. However, there are still some third-generation Spanish families in Madrid paying these low protected rents for central apartments.

The new legislation means that the rights of tenants are very similar to those in Britain, with some additional protection that stops landlords raising the rent unfairly. When a rental contract specifies that the rental period ends, for example, in July, it means just that. All tenants now have the right to renew their tenancy for an initial minimum period of five years and if a tenant fails to vacate the property when the temporary contract expires, the owner does not have the right to evict if a renewal has been sought. Therefore, a landlord must offer a tenant a new contract, which can either be temporary or long-term. It used to be that landlords could raise the rent as much as they liked in the process, however, the present situation is that most annual rent rises are in line with inflation and the Consumer Price Index (IPC), which is rarely more than 3% to 4%.

There is provision for a tenant to pay a deposit of one month's rent for unfurnished accommodation, or two months for furnished accommodation. This would be lodged with the local Autonomous Community. Additional guarantees may also be negotiated.

The Rental Contract

A rental contract is a prerequisite to renting any kind of property in Spain and you will find that both short- and long-term lets are available. Short-term leases (for a period of six months or less) are known as *por temporada*, while long lets, which generally give tenants more rights, are known as *viviendas*. Longer-term contracts often require tenants living in blocks of flats to pay *comunidad* fees. However, if these charges are not mentioned in the contract then they are wholly the landlord's responsibility and the tenant is under no obligation to pay them or to have them imposed subsequently.

All long-term tenants are legally required to take out house insurance on the property they are renting. The choice of which insurance company to take out a policy with is entirely his or her own decision and cannot be dictated by the landlord.

Contracts are drawn up through the standard, state-sponsored tenant/landlord agreements which are available from street kiosks and *estancos*: it is really your responsibility as the tenant to obtain one of these and to make sure the contract type matches the rent you will be paying, as contracts vary. A contract will include personal details of the tenant and the landlord together with information about the property (location, size, and inventory of furnishings, fittings etc.), the terms of the lease and payment and expenses details. It is advisable to have the contract checked by a solicitor or someone who really knows about rentals before signing. The written contract should clearly state the amount of rent payable and when the tenant should pay it (usually within the first five days of every month). Many rental contracts ask for rent to be paid by direct debit into the landlord's bank account.

When you sign a contract for a long-term let you will usually need to pay between one and three month's rent as a deposit or bond to cover damages to the property. When the contract is terminated the deposit is returned in full or in part depending on the state of the property. Sometimes the tenant and landlord may agree to use up the deposit in lieu of rent at the end of a lease. You will need to agree on whether the landlord or tenant pays rates, the property tax (IBI) and community fees and you will almost certainly have to pay the bills for electricity, water, gas and the telephone. It is advisable to ask to see previous bills for the property to give you an idea of how much you will need to pay each month and also to make sure that all utility charges have been paid up to date.

The landlord's obligations include maintaining the property in good order and offering the services stated in the contract. Anyone who feels that they have a complaint to make regarding their rental contract can – surprisingly – apply to the local tourist office. This is more suitable for those in short-lets, while semi-permanent and permanent tenants will do better to enquire at the nearest OMIC (*Oficina Municipal de Información al Consumidor*) – the consumer information office run by the local government or Autonomous Community. Although the OMIC's function is primarily to deal with consumer problems, they will be able to put you in contact with the most effective place to register a formal rental complaint.

UTILITIES

It is essential to understand that although all public utility services are widely available in Spain, and that the service in question will always be provided in the end, how long it will take to arrive is far less certain.

Electricity, telephone and water bills have a payment term of between 15 days and a month, after which a reminder notice will be sent to the occupant. If payment is still not made then the telephone line, water supply or electricity supply will be cut off and a reconnection fee charged. It is therefore important to give the utility companies notice of a second address should you have one, or set up a standing order from your bank account so that you remain in credit with the utility service companies at all times. You will also need to notify the local Town Hall (*ayuntamiento*) that you own property within their jurisdiction, and register with the municipality for local rates (*Impuestos sobre los Bienes Inmuebles (IBI)*). Make sure that all bills have been paid up to date before you move into a property. If the previous owner has left without paying them then you will be responsible for clearing the debt.

Electricity

Electricity is supplied by the electricity supply company (*la compañía de electricidad*) that operates in your area through the overhead lines of an extensive grid system linking the hydroelectric and atomic power stations with cities, towns and villages throughout the country. It is essential to organise meter installation or reconnection through your regional branch of the electricity company well in advance, as the waiting lists for both services can be very long. New owners of a previously occupied property will need to present to the electricity company the deeds of the property (*escritura*), a Spanish bank account number to pay by standing order, and some form of identification document. The *compañia de electricidad* will come and inspect the electrics on the property and if they need updating you will need to have this done before you can transfer the contract for electricity from the previous owners into your name. Owners of new property that isn't already connected to the electricity grid will need to register with their local electricity company and arrange to have a meter installed.

Electricity is priced on the international system of a small standing charge and a further charge per kilowatt-hour consumed, the rate for which diminishes as consumption increases. Bills are issued bi-monthly and VAT (IVA) at the standard rate is added. Currently the standard rate is approximately €10 per month, plus 9.6c per KWh including tax.

Gas

The use of butane gas (*butano*) is not as common in Spain as in Northern Europe and, except in the larger cities and perhaps on urbanizaciónes, there tends to be no piped household supply. However, readily available bottled gas (supplied in cylinders known as *bombonas*) is cheap (a large 12.5kg cylinder will cost approximately £5) and commonly used for cooking and heating in most homes. *Bombonas* can be easily re-filled through the butane home delivery service that operates in most areas. Those in more secluded areas may have to collect their gas supplies from the local depot. As with electricity, if you are in an area where piped gas is provided you will need to sign up with the gas company and arrange to pay the standing charge and gas bills by standing order. The gas companies are likely to come and inspect your appliances for safety every few years. Gas bills (for piped gas) are rendered bi-monthly and VAT (IVA) is added.

Because gas is generally a cheaper form of energy than electricity many properties run as many household appliances as possible on it. There are safety issues when using gas so make sure that the property has adequate ventilation, that pipes are checked regularly to ensure that they haven't perished and that regulator valves are in good order. Bottled gas has a tendency to run out at the most inopportune times and so it pays to always make sure that you have an adequate supply ready for such eventualities.

Water

Spanish water is perfectly safe to drink in almost all urban areas as government regulations require public water supplies to be treated with anti-pollutants. However, for this same reason the water can have an unpleasant taste and most expats and visitors to Spain follow the example of the Spanish and drink bottled mineral water instead. This is cheap, of good quality and sold at practically every corner shop in Spain – *con gas* means carbonated and *sin gas*, non-carbonated.

Although there is surplus rainfall in the north that provides an adequate natural water supply, water shortages can often occur over the summer months along the Mediterranean coast and in the Balearic Islands. The problem mainly arises because the municipalities individually control the supply of water and plans to lay national pipelines are continually frustrated by local political issues. The provision of desalination plants, purification plants and the sinking of wells are common topics of discussion in local politics. The Canary Islands, in particular, have a problem with sourcing enough water for the local populace.

The mains water piped to private premises is metered, with charges calculated per cubic metre used. To have a water meter installed, you will need to apply to the local water company office with your passport, the *escritura*, a copy of a previous water bill for the property if you have one, and the number of your Spanish bank account. A deposit is payable, and there is a charge made for installing (or repairing) a water meter. Bills are usually issued quarterly. Depending on the hardness of the water it may pay to have filters installed, preferably within the system (as opposed to just on the outlets), to prevent the furring up of pipes, radiators etc.

Heating and Air Conditioning

With the notable exception of northern and central areas of Spain, the provision of heating is not of major importance throughout most of the year. Winters (December, January and February) all over Spain will have their cold days and evenings will be cooler after sunset during these months. Rest assured though, this is nothing compared to a northern European winter.

Bear in mind that if you decide to live in a purpose-built summer holiday villa through the winter months your heating bill is going to be substantially higher than if you reside in a well-insulated house. Older properties in Spain may not be too well insulated and it will be well worth the investment to insulate your property as well as possible – it will keep the place cooler in the summer, and warmer in the winter.

Often the cheapest options of heating, if you live near a ready supply of logs, is to install a wood-burning stove, which can also be used as a water heater and from which radiators can be run. Alternatively portable gas or electric heaters can be used. Surprisingly solar heating is not that common, although it is beoming more so in most areas of Spain. Apartment blocks may have central heating systems running through the building, the cost of which is paid for by the community charges.

Many modern air-conditioning units will also incorporate warm air heating systems. If you can't afford air conditioning, then installing either fans on the ceilings or portable fans is a good idea, especially in the hotter parts of Spain such as Almería, and on the Canary Islands.

Foreign Exchange... How to get the most from your money

When you start to plan your retirement to Spain there are lots of things that you need to consider to make sure that your new life is a happy one. Currencies Direct explain how one of the most important things that you need to consider, and often one of the most overlooked, is foreign exchange.

If you're retiring to Spain you will no doubt have to change your hard earned money from sterling into euros. Whether it's to buy a new house or simply to transfer your savings to live off, foreign exchange can't be avoided. Unfortunately, no one can predict the exchange rate as many economic and political factors constantly affect the strength of the pound. Exchange rates are constantly moving and there is no guarantee that they will be in your favour when you need your money, so it is vital that you protect yourself against these movements. A lack of proper forward planning could potentially cost you thousands of pounds and reduce your spending power abroad.

For example, the affect the exchange rate can have on the cost of a new house can be seen if you look at what happened to the euro during 2005. Sterling against the euro was as high as 1.5124 and as low as 1.4086. This means that if you were buying a house worth €200,000 it could have cost you as little as £132,240 or as much as £141,984, a difference of almost £10,000.

However, it is possible to avoid this pitfall by buying and fixing a rate for your currency ahead of time through a **forward contract**. This is the *Buy now, Pay later* option and is ideal if you still have some time to wait before your money is due in Spain or if you are waiting for the proceeds from the sale of your UK property. Usually a small deposit will secure you a rate for anywhere up to 2 years in advance and by doing so you will have the security of having the currency you need at a guaranteed cost and knowing exactly how much money you are taking with you.

Another option available to you if you have time on your side is a **limit** order. This is used when you want to achieve a rate that is currently not available. You set the rate that you want and the market is then monitored. As soon as that rate is achieved the currency is purchased for you. You can also set a 'lower' level or 'stop' to protect yourself should the rate drastically fall. This is ideal for when you don't have to make an immediate payment and you have a specific budget available.

If however you need to act swiftly and your capital is readily available then it is most likely that you will use a **spot transaction**. This is the *Buy now, Pay now* option where you get the most competitive rate on the day.

It is however fair to admit that many of us do not have the time or sufficient knowledge of these options to be in a position to confidently gauge when the foreign currency rates are at their most favourable, and this is where a foreign exchange specialist can help. As an alternative to your bank, foreign exchange specialists are able to offer you extremely competitive exchange rates, no commission charges and lower transfer fees. This can mean considerable savings on your transfer when compared to using a bank.

It is also very easy to use a foreign exchange specialist. The first thing you will need to do is register with them as a client. This is usually very straightforward and requires you to complete a registration form and provide two forms of identification, usually a copy of your passport and a recent utility bill. Once you are registered you are then able to trade. Your dealer will talk you through the different options that are available to you and help you to decide which one is right for you depending on your timing, circumstances and foreign currency needs. Once you have decided which option is best for you and agreed a rate you will then need to send your money. With clearance times at each end some companies can complete the transfer for you in as little as a week.

Even once you have retired to Spain you may find yourself in the position where you need to regularly transfer funds from your UK bank account to Spain. This may be because you are still receiving a pension in the UK or perhaps you have decided to rent out your house until you settle and so are receiving rental income. If this is the case using a reputable foreign exchange specialist to do the transfers for you can make sure that you get more of your money each time, even on small amounts. This is because unlike your bank they will offer you competitive exchange rates on these smaller amounts plus they won't charge you commission and transfers are often free.

Currencies Direct is a leading commercial foreign exchange company; offering superior rates of exchange and a personalised service they meet the needs of thousands of private and corporate clients every year.

With offices in the UK, Spain, Australia, South Africa and India, Currencies Direct is always on hand to help you. For more information about their services, please contact one of their dealers who will be happy to discuss your currency requirements with you.

UK Head Office: 0845 389 0906
Email: info@currenciesdirect.com
Web: www.currenciesdirect.com

Housing Finance

CHAPTER SUMMARY

- One of the most important considerations is whether or not to sell your UK residence in order to fund the move abroad. Around 20% of those who retire to Spain retain their UK base as insurance against things going wrong.

- If you take out a mortgage you will need to decide between opting for a UK based or euro mortgage. Generally Spanish mortgages entail higher set up charges, but interest rates are higher in the UK, so it is best to consult a mortgage advisor.

- The average running costs per year of a property, including local council taxes, community fees and general upkeep amounts to around 3-4% of the cost of the property.

- IBI is an annual property tax calculated at around 0.5% of the official rateable value of the property. The percentage varies from region to region.

- If you are part of a *Comunidad de Propietarios*, then you will have to pay an annual community fee, which covers maintenance costs for communal areas.

- Capital Gains Tax in Spain is calculated at 15% for residents. For non-residents it is 35%, discriminating heavily against second-home owners. You should always declare the full purchase price of a property in the escritura to avoid high CGT when you come to sell.

- You can save thousands of pounds by using the services of a currency dealer to pay for your property, rather than using a high street bank.

- There are advantages to insuring your property in Spain through a UK company. For example, insurance premium tax is lower in the UK, and any claims will be processed in English.

AFFORDING THE MOVE

Deciding What To Do With Your UK Property

Before departing for Spain, deciding what you are going to do with your UK home is a vitally important consideration. The decision will vary depending on individual financial situations. The majority of people sell their UK home and use the funds to buy a property in Spain and provide enough additional funds to live on during their retirement. However, those who can afford it, tend to hang on to their UK property as security against things going wrong in Spain and as a source of income. Indeed, around 20% of those who have retired to Spain retain their base in the UK. The pros and cons of these two solutions are discussed below. There is however, a third way: sell your main property in the UK and use the proceeds to buy a small apartment in both the UK and Spain. This was the choice that expats David and Liz Austen made:

We put our house on the market and bought an apartment down in Eastbourne. Then we came out to Spain and found an apartment here. Buying the two cheaper properties was an insurance against things going wrong, but it also gave us the chance to look around and find exactly the right property in Spain. We knew where we wanted to buy and we waited a year for the right property to become available. We were then able to sell the Eastbourne flat, and the apartment here and move into our dream villa.

Retaining a home in the UK. Those expats who retain their UK base, do so for a number of good reasons. First and foremost property in the UK is generally a good investment, as Ian Adams, an expat in Oliva has found:

Whilst the housing market is slowing down in the UK, prices are still going up. Our house has risen in value by thirty per cent, just in the time we have been out here (4 years). So I want to hang on to the property for as long as possible. Hopefully it will continue to provide me with a pension when I'm old and grey.

Others who retain their UK property do so in order to ease the uncertainty of making such a dramatic move. If you still have a home in the UK then you can spend part of your retirement back in Britain, visiting friends and family. More importantly you will always have a fallback position should things go wrong, as Mac and Meryl Macdonald, expats in Javea point out:

We didn't want to cut our ties with the UK completely. We thought if we sold up completely and then in 5 years time found that we didn't like it, then it would be far more difficult to reassemble our lives in the UK and indeed get back into the housing market. So we have kept that option open. We have a foot in both camps, at least while we can financially, although I'm sure the day will come where we may have to make a final decision.

A major disadvantage in owning two properties is the tax on profits. When UK resident (see *Personal Finance*), your main home in the UK is free from Capital Gains Tax on any increase in value when you sell it and move under Private Residence Relief rules. If you remain a UK resident for tax purposes and buy a second home in Spain you are liable to Capital Gains Tax in the UK on any growth in the value of your second home when you sell it, with allowances made for Spanish taxes. If you become a Spanish resident, you are then liable to a range of wealth and other taxes in Spain on both your Spanish and UK homes. The timing of when to buy and sell existing or second homes is crucial to a lower tax bill. This area is complex and you should seek professional tax planning advice before making any purchase.

Unless you have a large amount of ready cash at your disposal, you may think that you simply cannot afford to retain your UK base and buy a new home in Spain. However, there are a number of ways in which your UK property may be used to help finance your new life. The most obvious way is to take out a second mortgage on your UK property in order to finance the Spanish purchase. This is discussed under *Mortgages* below.

Alternatively you could rent out your UK property in order to help pay the mortgage on the new house in Spain or simply to provide you with an income, as Ian Adams does:

I've still got a house in England, but it's not home anymore – it's a business. I rent it out and that helps to keep us out here as it gives us a monthly income. We have a letting agent that deals with it and they take a commission but pay me the rent and deal with all the hassles.

Whilst rental income received may be subject to income tax, the added advantage of renting is that houses that are left empty tend to deteriorate quite rapidly and there is always the danger of a burglary. Empty houses also command a much higher insurance premium . If you do decide to rent the property out, be sure to draw up tenancy agreements that will allow you to regain possession of the property fairly quickly, should you ever decide to return to the UK.

Selling Up. Selling up completely has the enormous advantage of releasing a large amount of capital that can then be put towards finding the perfect home in Spain. As property tends to be so much cheaper in Spain, it is likely that you will also have a lump sum left over which can either be rein-vested or used to supplement your retirement income once in Spain. However, there are a number of disadvantages to selling up. For one thing, the recent slowdown in the UK property market has meant that it may take you much longer to sell your UK property. If your UK property is the main source of funding, then you should never commit to buy in Spain unless you have exchanged contracts in the UK. This could prove very frustrating and hold up your dreams indefinitely. Nevertheless, it is possible to rent out the UK property whilst you are waiting for a buyer. This will allow you to rent in Spain and give you time to find the right property.

As mentioned above, selling your UK base precludes the possibility of rushing home, should life in Spain not turn out as you had imagined. It may also cause problems in the long term. If at any point in the future you are forced to return home then it may be very difficult to get back on the property ladder. The amount that you raise from selling your Spanish property is unlikely to fund the purchase of a similar sized property in the UK.

MORTGAGES

An enormous number of banks and financial institutions both in Spain and the UK are prepared to lend money for residential property purchase in Spain. It is advised that you begin the mortgage process prior to searching for your property, so that you are aware of all of the options available to you. Mortgage brokers will also offer you a 'mortgage offer in principle', which will avoid wasting time looking at properties you simply cannot afford.

The first thing to decide is whether to opt for a mortgage based in the

UK, or a euro mortgage. There are advantages and disadvantages to both depending on your personal circumstances, so it is always best to speak to a professional mortgage adviser (see *Personal Finance*). Generally speaking, with a Spanish mortgage you will incur higher set-up charges compared to the UK, but this is offset by the fact that interest rates are higher in the UK. One of the main reasons for choosing a euro mortgage however is that it protects you against currency fluctuations. If your mortgage and property are both in euros, any movement in the currency is irrelevant because the value of the property and the size of the debt will go up or down in tandem. However, if the debt is in sterling and the euro falls against the pound, the value of the property will drop when converted into sterling, but the debt will stay the same and therefore account for a higher proportion of the value of the property.

Sometimes a fixed UK mortgage will be a better bet, and is usually quite easy to organise. It is easier to borrow money at home and be a cash buyer abroad. If you use your home as equity to fund buying a property in Spain you won't have to deal with overseas lenders and brokers and won't have to worry about the mortgage increasing should the euro appreciate against the pound.

If you are thinking of taking a mortgage with a lender in Spain remember that there are fewer fixed, capped and discounted schemes operated in Europe and terms can be more restrictive than those offered in the UK – a high deposit and repayment periods are generally for fifteen years or less. Euro mortgage rates are about 3.75% in Spain, although they can be as low as 2.95%. You will find that the cheaper interest rates and special deals on offer usually only apply to more high-value properties of between £100,000 and £200,000 and not to the more modest end of the property market.

UK Mortgages

These days it is possible to approach the banks for a sterling loan secured on the property in Spain. If you are considering borrowing in the UK, then the method of calculating the amount that may be borrowed is worked out at between two and a half, or three and a half, times your primary income plus any secondary income you may have, less any capital amount already borrowed on the mortgage. Your credit history will also be checked to assess whether you will be able to manage increased mortgage payments.

A number of people planning to buy second homes in Spain arrange loans in the UK – taking out a second mortgage on their UK property and then buying with cash in Spain. There are advantages to using your UK property as security for financing your Spanish home. For example, it allows you to obtain the finance independently of the property value (if you had sufficient equity in your UK property and sufficient income, you could borrow 100% or more of the total cost of buying your Spanish property). Also, you could use a re-mortgage to finance the purchase of a restoration property, which may not be suitable security for a Spanish mortgage. Loans are normally based on salary multiples of 3.5 times the larger income plus 1x the second income, or 2.75 times joint incomes. The maximum loan can be as much as 90% of the property value.

If you are going to take out a second mortgage with your existing mortgage lender then a second charge would be taken by the mortgage company. Note that some lending institutions charge a higher rate for a loan to cover a second property. You should ensure that if a loan is arranged in the UK then all of the details of this are included in the Spanish property contract deeds (*escritura*). The typical costs of re-mortgaging a property are around £650 (solicitors fee of £250, legal disbursements of £150, and a valuation fee of around £250), but some fees may be paid by the lender.

Spanish Mortgages

Many Spanish banks offer euro mortgages both within Spain and through branches in the UK. The conditions relating to Spanish mortgages differ from those in the UK in that a deposit of at least 30% is usually required, with a maximum of 80% of the property value being provided as a loan, unlike the 95% or even 100% available from UK lenders. This figure is a maximum guideline set by the Bank of Spain, so it is very unusual to borrow more than this and in many cases the ratio is 66% or less. Those deemed to be non-resident in Spain sometimes have a lower limit of borrowing (although some lenders such as *Solbank* offer 70% or more) imposed by the lender, and the mortgage repayment period is often shorter, although it could well be up to thirty years. The buyer must be less than 70 years old by the completion date of the mortgage repayment. Fixed rate loans usually run for periods of up to 20 years (10-12 year deals are commonplace) and early redemption penalties may apply. These loans also carry introductory commissions of between 1% and 2.5%. Spanish mortgage companies peg their rates to a number of different indexes, offering an index-linked rate plus the company's percentage. You will need to provide the mortgage company with identification, a fiscal identification number, evidence of income and details of your financial situation and, if married, your spouse's consent may be required.

In Spain the method used to assess your mortgage is also a little different from that in the UK. You will have to put all your UK and, if you have any, your Spanish earnings and income forward, and get references from your UK bank. Any other borrowing you have will also be assessed. Although repayment mortgages still predominate, there are endowment and pension-linked options as well. The self-employed must have held such status for a minimum of three years and be able to show fully audited accounts of earnings.

Spanish mortgages generally offer fixed or variable interest rate mortgages, mixed interest rate mortgages and fixed repayment instalment mortgages. Interest rates may be lower than at home but there will be additional costs incurred, related to the registering charge on property in Spain. Acquisition, construction and renovation mortgages are available. Mortgages are on a capital and interest repayment basis, and security will be taken on the property. Most Spanish mortgage lenders work on the basis of repayments being made at a third of the borrower's net income.

Those buying a new (off-plan) property should be aware that mortgages cannot be granted until the property has been completed and registered. Therefore it is not possible to use a mortgage to finance stage payments during the construction period, although the full amount can be paid out once the property is completed and registered. Those purchasing a country property or a restoration property should be aware that the banks may not consider such a property to be suitable security for a mortgage, and even if they do, they may offer a far lower maximum borrowing amount.

Remember that if you take out a Spanish mortgage you will need to have the currency available in your Spanish bank account to meet the monthly mortgage repayments. There are likely to be tax implications and you will need to ensure that your lawyer explains the legalities in both countries to you. Mortgage lenders deciding how much to advance a potential buyer, both in the UK and in Spain, will not take into consideration any possible income derived from renting out the property.

However, in truth it may be possible to offset the cost of the mortgage against the income received from renting out a property and so reducing tax demands. And in effect the rental value on a property should repay the mortgage if problems occur.

Barclays offers euro mortgages through its Spanish subsidiary and other overseas mortgage companies include *Banco Banesto; Banco Halifax; Citibank Espana, Deutsche Bank* and *Banco Atlantico.* Spanish banks are not interested whether you have an existing mortgage in the UK.

Taking a Spanish mortgage can help to reduce inheritance tax liability according to Ashley Clark, Director of Need An Adviser.com

An indirect advantage of a Spanish mortgage, is the potential reduction of inheritance taxes. Spanish Succession Tax (see Personal Finance) is payable by residents and non-residents alike on assets that are in Spain. In the UK, if you are married or in a civil partnership, no inheritance tax is payable on inheritance gifts between partners on death for UK or worldwide assets. Tax may only be payable after the second death. In Spain, succession tax (in some cases up to 82%) is payable on the transfer of assets on the first death. Many couples are faced with huge succession tax bills on the death of their partner. However, if you have a Spanish mortgage on the property, the net value of your assets in Spain on death is therefore lower. This means a much lower succession tax bill. Many people who have retired to Spain are now trying to raise capital and indeed increase their debts in Spain by considering Spanish Equity Release Mortgages (see below).

Equity Release Mortgages

This is a relatively new market in Spain and is still developing. Capital is released by raising a mortgage on the Spanish property. This creates a debt and reduces your asset estate value in Spain for succession tax. Generally, this money is then invested outside Spain in offshore investments. The investment returns are used to pay the interest on the debt. If the investment returns are greater than the interest due on the mortgage, you receive this as an income. Problems arise if the investment returns are not great enough to cover the mortgage payments and you will have to make up the difference. Equity Release is extremely high risk and specialist advice should be sought before entering into such a scheme.

REAL ESTATE TAXES AND FEES

Buying property is an expensive business. There are all sorts of additional payments that have to be made to various individuals and institutions. These payments (taxes, stamp duties, lawyers' fees, notary fees) are likely to add another 10% onto the purchase price of your chosen property. The fees payable on a brand new property in Spain will be slightly (1.5%) higher than those for a resale property. The figures for the individual services involved in buying property in Spain break down as follows:

- Transfer tax on a resale property: 6%
- *or* IVA (VAT) on a new property: 7%
- Stamp duty (if buying a new property): 0.5%
- Plus valia (local municipal) tax: 0.5%
- Legal (lawyers') fees: 1%
- Notary fees: 0.5%
- Property Registry fees: 0.5%

In addition there may be extra fees payable for the services of a surveyor, for the connection of utilities (electricity, telephone, water, gas, etc.) and for the property agent.

Most of these fees (with the possible exception of the *plus valia* tax) will be paid by the purchaser. Make sure that you are clear on which fees are payable by the buyer and which are payable by the vendor. There is no law in Spain that states one or other of the parties must pay a particular tax or fee, however, the majority of contracts will state that the buyer is liable for *todos los gastos* (all expenses). These fees and taxes are calculated as a percentage of the value of the property as declared in the *escritura*.

Traditionally the price declared in the escritura was often much lower than the actual price paid for a property (the difference being discreetly handed over to the vendor in a brown envelope). However, these days the local councils value properties in their area and therefore have accounts of the rateable value (valor catastral) of properties. If it is found that the declared value of a property is far below the valor catastral a surcharge of 6% (plus costs) on the difference will be levied on the buyer by the authorities, and if the declared value if ridiculously under-valued, by say 50%, then the authorities have the right to buy the property from the new owner at the declared value within a period of two years. Under-declaring the price of a property is illegal. Doing so will also mean that if you decide to sell the property at a later date the increase in value of the property will be disproportionately large and you will then have to pay a large Capital Gains Tax bill. The majority of the fees and taxes (with the exception of the plus valia tax) listed above must be paid within 28 days of the signing of the escritura at the notary's office. Penalties will be incurred for late payment.

It is quite common for a prospective buyer to deposit 10% of the purchase price declared in the *escritura* with the lawyers dealing with the conveyancing so that they can make the payments on the buyer's behalf. The lawyers must give you the receipts of payment for these costs and should not charge you extra for this service.

Impuesto Sobre Transmisiones Patrimoniales (ITP). This is a property transfer tax payable on the purchase, from a private owner, of property or land. (If you buy a new property from a developer you will be liable for IVA (VAT) instead – see below). The ITP is usually charged at a rate of 6% of the value of a property as declared on the *escritura*, although the rate varies between autonomous communities.

Impuesto sobre el Valor Añadido (IVA). IVA is the equivalent of Value Added Tax (VAT) and is paid instead of ITP (see above) if you buy a new property from a development company rather than a resale property from an individual. IVA on the construction of a building is charged at a rate of 7% of the purchase price. If you buy a house *and* a plot of land at the same time you will be charged the 7% IVA on both purchases.

Note that in the Canary Islands, Ceuta and Melilla there is no IVA. In the Canaries a regional tax (Canarian Indirect General Tax – IGIC) is charged instead at a rate of 5%.

Impuesto sobre Actos Jurídicos Documentados (AJD). Stamp duty is paid at a rate of 0.5% of the purchase price of a new property (property bought from a developer). If you are buying a resale property stamp duty is included in the transfer tax (ITP). In some *Comunidades Autónomas* the rate of stamp duty is 1% of the purchase price.

Impuesto sobre el Incremento de Valor le los Terrenos de Naturaleza Urbana (Plus Valia Tax). This is a municipal Capital Gains Tax based on the value of urban land. It is a tax on the increased value of the land since the last sale, and is not a tax on the increase in value of any *buildings* on the land. It is only payable on urban land, not on rural land. The tax is payable on both new and resale property and will vary depending on how long the property has been in the hands of the vendor, the amount of land being sold and its value as a building plot. Although this tax should, in theory, be paid by the vendor (who has, after all, made the profit) it is more than likely that the purchaser will pay this tax unless a clause is added to the contract of sale and a sum is withheld for the payment of the tax. If and when you come to sell you will need to make sure that the purchaser of your property also pays this tax or you will end up paying it twice over. The local municipal tax office will be able to tell you before you sign a contract of sale what the *plus valia* tax will be on the property concerned.

Impuesto sobre Bienes Inmeubles – IBI. The *Impuesto sobre Bienes Inmeubles* is an annual local property tax calculated on the official rateable value of a property, *valor catastral,* (this is usually around 70% of market value). It is payable by both residents and non-residents. The percentage of the property value charged as tax will vary depending on the region/province and takes into consideration such things as the level of local leisure facilities provided, emergency services, population and local services and infrastructure. The tax rate is usually no more than 0.5% of the valor catastral.

IBI is raised annually in line with inflation and will be higher in a resort town or city than in a small inland village. Make sure before buying a resale property that all IBI taxes due on the property have been paid to date. Ask to see IBI receipts for the preceding five years if possible. If these charges have not been paid you will inherit any back taxes and penalties liable on the property. If the property that you are buying is new, it is up to you to register it with the town hall within two months. Failure to do so, and late payment, will incur a penalty charge. Payment deadlines of IBI will vary from region to region and from year to year and your fiscal representative should keep you informed of pertinent dates so that you can arrange to pay by standing order.

The IBI receipt will show the *catastral* reference number as well as the *valor catastral* of the property – both of which will be asked for by the notary before a sale of property can go through. The *catastral* reference number refers to details of the property kept at the *Catastro* office.

Legal Fees. These will depend on the amount of work carried out by the lawyer (or *abogado*) on the buyer's behalf, though there will be a minimum charge imposed. Expect to be billed for about 1% of the purchase price. Each party will pay the fees of the legal representatives acting on their behalf.

Notary Fees. These are dependent on the declared value of the property and the number of pages of the *escritura*, but generally amount to around 0.5% of the value of the property and could be anything between €300 and €700. The fee is calculated using an official sliding scale but there may be further fees applicable depending on the amount of work carried out and the number of documents prepared on your behalf by the notary. Note that if you are buying a plot of land and then having a dwelling constructed on the land you will have to visit the notary (*notario*), and pay his fees, twice. The costs of granting the first copy of the *escritura* are payable by the vendor while the costs for the second copy are payable by the buyer.

Property Registry Fees. Fees for registering a new property with the Spanish authorities in the Property Register (*Registro de la Propriedad*) vary depending on the size, value and locality of a property. The cost is likely to amount to the same as that payable to the notary (around 0.5% of the purchase price of a property). The initial fee payable is a deposit, and you may get a refund should it be discovered that you have been charged too much.

Other Fees and Charges Likely to be Applicable.

- The agent's fee will almost certainly be included in the purchase price and will be between 2% and 10%. However, if the selling agent is a member of the Federation of Overseas Property Developers, Agents and Consultants (www.fopdac.com), the maximum fee will be 3%. If there have been negotiations carried out by an agent's representative back home the fee for this should be included in the agent's fee. Check the contract.
- Surveyors' fees will vary depending on the type of survey carried out (valuation only, or full structural survey, etc).
- Utility fees will need to be paid if a new property is without water, electricity or telephone and gas connections. There may also be charges incurred when changing the names in utility bill contracts.
- Mortgage and mortgage arrangement costs.
- Insurance – both contents and building insurance will need to be paid for.
- If you have hired a tax consultant, their fees will depend on the complexity of your tax affairs. It is worth finding out the most advantageous way to manage your tax affairs in the matter of buying a property abroad.
- Bank charges relating to the transfer of funds from your bank account at home to your bank account in Spain.
- A 5% tax deposit. If the property is bought from a non-resident then 5% of the declared purchase price is deposited with the Tax Agency as a guarantee against Capital Gains Tax payable on the sale of a property in Spain. In such cases the buyer pays the vendor 95% of the purchase price and the other 5% to the Tax Agency. A notary will need to see proof that the 5% has been received by the tax authorities. This 5% will be included in the purchase price and is not an additional cost – the vendor therefore receives 95% of the agreed purchase price of the property.

Tasas y Cargas

Some, though not all municipalities charge a certain amount for services such as rubbish collection and drainage maintenance etc (*basura y alcantarillado*). This is an annual tax that must be paid by both resident and non-resident property owners, although it is sometimes included in IBI rates (see above), and comes to around €150 per year.

Day to day running costs of property in Spain will include local council taxes, rates, the annual Wealth Tax, tax relating to the letting of property, community fees if you are part of a *comunidad de proprietarios*, garden and pool maintenance, fees for a financial consultant or fiscal representative, standing charges for utilities, and caretaker or property management fees.

The average running costs per year for a property amount to around 3%-4% of the cost of the property, but will depend on size and opulence.

CAPITAL GAINS TAX (IMPUESTO SOBRE EL PATRIMONIO)

Every time a property changes hands in Spain, taxes and fees are incurred. Capital Gains Tax is calculated on the net gain in the declared (as shown in the *escritura*) purchase price of a property when bought, and the price that it fetches when it is subsequently sold. There are certain allowances available on this tax for the cost of conveyancing and any improvements made to the property. Those resident for tax purposes in Spain will need to include the Capital Gains in the tax return of the year in which the gain occurred. Capital Gains Tax is calculated at 15% for residents. Residents who sell their property within the first year of ownership must include this as a capital gain within their income tax return – a break that is not available to non-residents.

Non-residents with assets in Spain must pay Capital Gains Tax on the sale of a property at 35%. Whereas Spanish residents are able to rollover CGT to a new property, this is not allowed for non-residents. Currently the CGT situation discriminates heavily against foreigners, who are forced to pay a far higher rate, and do not benefit from the progressive discounts on capital gains that are available to Spaniards and residents if they sell a property within the first year of ownership. However, in July 2005, the European Commission called for Spain to reduce tax for non-residents selling property there. According to the EC: *'the difference in the tax treatment of the two categories of taxpayers constitutes indirect discrimination on the grounds of nationality prohibited by the treaty [of Rome]'*. The Spanish government has yet to comment, but observers believe that ending the discriminatory rate would fit in with its policy of attacking the country's large black economy with lower, more transparent taxes. It seems likely that a fairer rate for foreigners would lead to increased revenues as house vendors might be encouraged to stay within the letter of the law when declaring house sale prices for tax purposes.

It is always best to declare in the escritura the full purchase price when you buy in order not to have to pay a high Capital Gains Tax when you sell. If you own a property through a company and the property has not risen in value when you come to sell it is possible to change the ownership structure without incurring a large Capital Gains Tax bill.

Capital Gains is generally paid via the buyer of the property, who retains 5% of the agreed purchase price and pays this to the Tax Agency on account of the vendor's Capital Gains Tax liability. The purchaser therefore only pays 95% of the purchase price to the vendor. The declaration should be made on Form 211 and presented to the Spanish tax authorities within 30 days of the transaction in order to ensure that they will not be held liable for any additional CGT that the vendor may owe. The vendor should also be supplied with a copy of this form so that he/she may request a tax refund once the sale has gone through.

There are several circumstances where the vendor of a property is exempt from paying Capital Gains Tax and is not subject to the 5% tax deposit:

O Those 65 years of age or over, who are resident in Spain and whose property has been the principal residence of the individual for at least three years pay no Capital Gains Tax on the sale of the property.

O If a resident of Spain sells his or her principal residence in Spain of at least three years and reinvests all of the proceeds of the sale into another property that will become his or her principal residence, s/he is exempt from paying Capital Gains Tax.

O Residents and non-residents who bought the property which they are selling before 31 December 1986 will not have to pay Capital Gains Tax.

O If a resident is 65 years old or over and sells his or her principal residence to a company in exchange for the right to reside in the property till death and a monthly payment there will be no Capital Gains Tax to pay.

There are several circumstances where the vendor of a property in Spain has partial exemption from paying Capital Gains Tax:

O If a resident of Spain sells his or her principal residence in Spain of at least three years, and reinvests part of the proceeds of the sale into another property that will become his or her principal residence s/he will be entitled to tax relief on a proportion of the proceeds.

○ Anyone who bought a property in Spain between 1987 and 1994 has the right to a reduction of 11.11% per year, beginning from two years after the purchase up until 1996.

○ Those who bought property after 1996 can apply an inflation correction factor that saves them a certain amount of money on Capital Gains Tax liabilities.

TRANSFERRING MONEY

Once you have found the property that you want to buy in Spain you will of course need to pay for it. As it will be priced in euros, at some point during the buying process you will need to exchange your money and transfer it to Spain. When working out your finances you need to be aware that because of fluctuating exchange rates you may find that your home could cost you more (or less) than you originally thought. You also need to make sure that you take into account all the additional costs of buying a property including conveyancing costs, builders, architects and surveyors fees, comunidad de propietarios etc.

The effect that fluctuating exchange rates can have on the cost of your property can be seen if you look at the period between late December 2004 and mid-June 2005, the cost of a €200,000 house could have been as little as £133,431.18 or as much as £142,156.51. This is a difference of £8,725.33, so it is imperative that you minimise the cost by considering your options carefully.

There are a number of options open to you when transferring money to Spain. Many people transfer funds by obtaining a banker's draft from their home bank. This is a cheque guaranteed by the bank, which can be deposited into your bank account in Spain or anywhere in the world (depending on the currency it is made out in). When making the final payment on the purchase of a property at the notary's office it is advisable to hand over a banker's draft made payable to the vendor. You can also transfer money directly from your bank in the UK by SWIFT electronic bank transfer. This procedure can take several days and most of the time you will not know what exchange rate you are getting until the money arrives in your bank in Spain. You also need to be aware that Spanish banks often charge a fee of 0.6% to receive your funds.

There are alternatives to using your bank, in the form of specialist foreign exchange providers such as Currencies Direct (☎0845-389 0906; www.currenciesdirect.com). They can help in a number of ways, depending on your circumstances, timing and currency requirements. As an alternative to the bank, they offer more competitive exchange rates, no commission and lower transfer fees. They also give you the possibility of 'forward buying' – agreeing on the rate that you will pay at a fixed date in the future; or buying with a limit order, which involves waiting until your specified rate is reached. For those who prefer to know exactly how much money they have available for their property purchase, forward buying is the best solution, since you no longer have to worry about the movement of the pound against the euro working to your detriment. Payments can be made in one lump sum or on a regular basis.

Don't forget that even when you have purchased your property you may still need to transfer money to Spain for things such as mortgage payments, pensions and living expenses. Specialist foreign exchange providers can handle these regular payments for you and will make sure that you get a more competitive exchange rate than through your bank. Also be aware that money left sitting in a Spanish bank account attracts little interest and it is therefore advisable to only take into Spain the money that you need and leave the rest offshore or, if you live on or near the Costa del Sol, perhaps open a non-resident account in Gibraltar.

Remember that if the vendors of the property are non-resident in Spain they are likely to want the purchase price paid in their home currency.

INSURANCE

Some considerations that need to be taken into account while looking for an insurance policy on your new property include:

- Is your villa or flat covered by insurance in the event of your letting the property to someone who accidentally burns the place to the ground/ floods the bathroom and locks a dog in before vacating the premises?
- Is the property covered for insurance purposes even if it remains empty for part of the year?
- Does the insurance policy allow for new-for-old replacements or are there deductions for wear-and-tear?

It is always a good idea to shop around to see what options and premiums are available. Ask neighbours in Spain for recommendations and remember to always, *always*, read the small print on any contract before signing. Do not under-insure property and remember that insurance will also be needed if a property is being built to order by a developer or builder.

It may be better to go with a large insurance company than a small independent company that may be less amenable when it comes to paying out on a claim. Most companies will anyway demand that any claim must be backed by a police report, which may need to be made within a specific time limit after the incident. If such an event takes place while the house is empty this may be impossible: one of the reasons why you should check the small print carefully on all contracts.

In areas where there are earthquakes, heavy flooding or forest fires each year, premiums will be much higher than back home and may not be as comprehensive. Additionally, buying cover from a Spanish company while in Spain is likely to cost a lot more than taking it from an insurance company back home. Insurance premiums will be cheaper in rural areas than in the larger towns and cities and, wherever your property, you may be required by the company to install certain security arrangements which will need to have been in place should a claim be made.

Insurance premium tax in the UK for instance is about 5% while in Spain it is around 6.5%. Some high street companies will ensure a second home abroad if you are already insured with them. *Norwich Union* (www.norwichunion.co.uk), for instance, place a premium on the value of a prospective client's main home, while Saga (www.saga.co.uk) has special premiums for those over 50 (£2 million liability for property, loss of rent provision, full cover of 60 days for untenanted properties, emergency accommodation cover, etc.) The head office addresses of several major British insurance companies that have operations in Spain are given below; these may be worth contacting on arrival.

Insuring through a company back home with representatives in Spain will mean that claims will be processed in English rather than Spanish which can be a great help and will also mean that reading the small print will present no problems. Premiums vary depending on the size, location and age of the property, in addition to other factors such as security arrangements, the amount of time it will be occupied over a period of a year, the value of the contents, distance from emergency services, etc.

Most insurers prefer a multi-risk policy covering theft, damage by fire, vandalism, etc. If you have bought into a development, it may well turn out that the building as a whole is already covered. It is advisable to check this before taking out an individual policy. In any event, it is unlikely that the existing cover will include the private property of individual inhabitants.

Anyone who has purchased a resale property may find that the seller's insurance may be carried on by the next owner. However, the new owner will have to check whether the policy is transferable.

Useful Contacts

Axa Seguros e Inversiones: ☎915-551700; www.axa.es.

Direct Seguros: ☎902-404025; www.directseguros.es.

Hiscox: ☎0845-450 4011.

Insurance for Homes Abroad: ☎01934-424040.

Jennifer Cunningham Consultancy: ☎966-461690.

Knight Insurance: ☎952 660 535; www.knight-insurance.com.

Linda Rowland Insurance Brokers: ☎966 880 190.

La Unión Española de Entidades Aseguradoras y Reaseguradoras *(Spanish Union of Insurance and Reinsurance Companies)*: ☎917 451 530; www.unespa.es.

Saga: ☎020-8282 0330/0800-015 0751; www.saga.co.uk/finance/holidayhome/.

Schofields Insurance: ☎01204-365080; www.schofields.ltd.uk.

Part three

A New Life
in Spain

Adapting to Your New life

Quality of Life

Personal Finance

Healthcare

Crime, Security & the Police

Returning Home

Adapting to Your New Life

CHAPTER SUMMARY

O **Shopping.** Open air markets held in streets and squares throughout Spain are still very much part of Spanish life and the best place to buy the freshest, most desirable local produce.

  O The best purchases in Spain are local handicrafts (*artesanía*), although prices are not as cheap as they once were.

O The Spanish take their food very seriously and you will find great loyalty towards traditional regional cuisine.

  O Eating out is an important part of Spanish culture. Around 70% of Spaniards will eat in a restaurant at the weekend.

O The Spanish are a nation of telly addicts, preferring it to all other forms of media. There are several options available for obtaining British channels.

O **Motoring.** The Spanish are renowned for their hair-raising driving style, but traffic police are becoming increasingly vigilant.

  O It is more convenient and safer to have a left-hand drive car in Spain. Brand new cars are slightly cheaper in Spain, but second-hand cars retain their value for much longer.

  O The Spanish equivalent of the MOT is the ITV. All cars over 4 years old must take the ITV every 2 years; all cars over 10 years old must take it annually.

O Spain is divided into 17 autonomous communities, although the definition of 'autonomy' is different in each region. The Basques and the Catalans have the most pronounced independence from the central government.

O British residents may vote in local and European elections (although not national ones).

SHOPPING

It is worth remembering that although the low cost of living in Spain a couple of decades ago was one of the foremost reasons why Brits chose to move out there, especially in retirement, this situation has changed. Prices have risen with inflation, while salaries have not. However, markets and small villages still offer bargains and these are the areas to explore in order to get a flavour of the country, and to live more economically.

Cultural Differences

Although shopping centres and hypermarkets have begun to spring up in Spain, as a rule shopping is a much more personal and sociable pursuit than we are accustomed to in the UK. The majority of Spanish shops are small family run affairs and you will find that in small communities, shop-keepers will soon know your name (and possibly much more besides!)

Whilst the Spanish can be very good business-people, you will generally find that they are rarely pushy salesmen. Indeed they often display a remarkably laissez-faire attitude towards making money. Joanne Kitching, used to the cut-throat business arena of Hong Kong, was astonished when she attempted to place an order for a considerable amount of furniture for her new villa, and was told to come back four hours later because it was nearly siesta time. Although this may at times be frustrating, it is certainly refreshing to live in a culture where relaxation is regarded as a higher priority than wealth.

There is also a different attitude to queuing. The British will often insist on attempting to form queues where it is clear that no such structure exists, and will then become irritated when the Spanish bustle past them and get served immediately, simply by shouting at the shop-keeper for assistance. Unless there is an obvious queue, then treat it like a busy pub and jostle for position with everyone else. If there is a queue (*la cola*), enquire as to who is the last (*la ultima*) and join it. However, do not be surprised if the Spanish natural capacity for gossip means you are left waiting for some time. Jane, an expat living in Xativa explains this.

The Spanish attitude to customer service is very different. You can be in a ferreteria (DIY shop) queueing up with €50 worth of items and the person in front of you will be looking for just one particular screw – and they will spend as much time with that person as they need. The difference is that the person they are serving is the most important, regardless of how much money they are spending. Once you get to the front of the queue, you then become the most important person and will have their undivided attention.

Markets

Open-air *mercados* held in the streets and squares of Spain remain extremely popular both as a means of buying local produce at a good price and of exchanging local news and gossip. They offer a real and rare insight into Spanish, small-town life and are not to be missed. The markets cater for an enormous range of goods and articles. There are arts and crafts markets, antiques and bric-a-brac markets and markets selling locally produced fruit and vegetables. At some of the larger markets, you can buy just about everything, and usually very cheaply; especially if you are prepared to haggle. One of the most famous open air markets is the Rastro Market in the centre of Madrid, which is well worth a visit, but there are similar local markets everywhere. Markets tend to be open from 9am to 2pm, although those in the tourist areas may go on all day. Remember that markets can get very crowded, so it is best to get there early, and to be on the lookout for pickpockets.

Part of the attraction of living in Spain is the availability of fresh, healthy Mediterranean cuisine, and the markets are a wonderful source of the most desirable local produce including fruits and vegetables, a huge variety of cheeses, bread and meat. Becoming a devotee of the *mercados* is also a great way to improve your Spanish as well as becoming accepted by the locals.

Many of the cities and larger towns also have permanent indoor markets, such as the Mercat Sant Josep in Barcelona, and the Mercado Central in Valencia. Both of these offer local produce including great piles of fruit and vegetables, herbs, cured meats, and a variety of fish and seafood. The indoor markets are generally open all day Monday to Saturday.

The larger flea markets selling crafts and second hand goods are known as *rastros* or *mercadillos* and are generally held on a specific day each week. Your local Spanish Tourist Office (www.spain.info) will be very helpful in advising on local markets and where and when they are held.

Artesanía (handicrafts)

Although there are fewer artisans in Spain today than a few decades ago, the best purchases in Spain are undoubtedly the country's diverse handicrafts. Catalonian textiles are famous around the world. Handmade wooden furniture is one of the traditional products of Valencia and fine rugs and carpets can be found in markets and shops in the south. Spain also has an ample supply of high quality leather and leather goods, including handbags, jackets, belts and shoes. Leather shoes, produced mainly in Alicante and the Balearic islands offer very good value. Prices are not as low as they once were so it is best to shop around. Pottery thrives in Andalucia where gaudy, brightly coloured pots are proudly displayed on most balconies. Most forms of ceramics are fairly cheap in Spain and very functional. The Andalucian style has a very attractive Moorish influence, which can be seen most obviously in the intertwining patterns on the regions ubiquitous floor and wall tiles.

Many areas of Spain are renowned for the quality of their intricate lace and linen. Other hand-made products of high quality throughout Spain include embroidery, paintings, porcelain and carved woodwork. Good quality jewellery, cultured pearls, trinkets, ironwork, cutlery and glassware can also be found.

Those looking to buy a high-quality hand-made nylon string guitar will be in their element in Spain. This is the one craft industry which refuses to be beaten into submission by modern factory-production techniques. Artisan guitar-makers, known as *luthiers,* exist in their thousands throughout Spain, supplying an enormous domestic demand. Each guitar is lovingly hand-made to produce the finest sound, which by far surpasses the sound created on the Far Eastern imports that dominate the classical guitar market in other countries. Hand-made Spanish guitars are also much cheaper, with student guitars selling for under €150.

Necessities

Clothes. The Spanish fashion industry has come on in leaps and bounds over the last few decades and the Spanish do take pride in their appearance, from the sober elegance of the north to the vibrant colours of the south. National chains offering reasonably priced clothes include Zara (now a massive multi-national company), Mango, Pull & Bear, Blanco, Massimo

Dutti and Oysho. International chains are also well represented in Spain, for example C&A, Benetton and Topshop. Buying very cheap clothes is more difficult than in the UK or USA as there are very few bargain, second hand, or charity shops. However, Spain's numerous markets, complete with fake brands, offer a variety of clothes at knock-down prices (though the quality varies enormously). At the other end of the scale Madrid, Barcelona, Galicia and Seville have no end of designer boutiques.

Consumer Durables, such as refrigerators, washing machines, electronic and electrical equipment and cameras, tend to be slightly more expensive in Spain than they are in the UK, but prices are falling. It is probably still advisable to buy electrical appliances (*electrodomésticos*) locally as not only will this save on haulage costs, but the appliances will be compatible with the Spanish power supply, and it will be easier to get local goods serviced or repaired. British bought televisions and videos tend not to work in Spain.

Furniture (*muebles*) should also be bought locally as there are good quality, hardwearing products available all over Spain. IKEA has five stores in Spain, near to Barcelona, Madrid and Seville, and there are three more on the islands. Alternatively you could source items online and then ship them directly to Spain. Oka Direct (☎0870-1606 002; www.okadirect.com) has a large collection of furnishings, china and cutlery, including sofas tables, chairs and beds. John Lewis (☎0845-604 9049; www.johnlewis.com) will also deliver abroad. For all household items, the hypermarkets offer very competitive prices.

Home Comforts

Spain's thriving import market means that many of the international brands of canned and frozen foods and drinks are also available in Spain. All large towns have modern, self-service supermarkets which, as well as stocking usual supermarket items, also carry a wide variety of goods as diverse as tableware, clothes, toiletries and hardware. Supermarkets still tend to close for the afternoon siesta (from 2pm-5pm) but then re-open from 5pm-8pm every day except Sunday.

If you live in a major city or on the costas, then finding your favourite British food brands will certainly not be a problem. Bear in mind though that there is a hefty mark up on the price, and it is fairly foolish not to go for the local equivalents where they are available. Those who cannot find their favourite British foods (which is fairly unlikely unless you are living in a rural area) have a number of internet options open to them. Websites such as www.britbuys.com; www.expatshopping.com and www.expatdirect. co.uk will ship your favourite foods direct to your door, wherever you are in the world, at fairly reasonable prices. Those who simply cannot live without their Heinz baked beans should try www.heinz-direct.co.uk.

Shop Opening Hours

Opening hours are strictly regulated in Spain and vary depending on the area, type of shop and the time of year. Most general stores are open Monday to Friday from 10am to 1.30-2pm and then again from 4.30-5pm to 7.30-8pm and on Saturday mornings. In the larger towns and cities many shops also stay open on Saturday afternoons. In the south of Spain during the height of summer, some shops may not open up again in the afternoon until 6pm – staying open until 9pm or later. In some places, particularly in small towns and villages, there's often one day or afternoon a week when all shops are closed.

Most shopping centres and department stores are open continually (without closing) from 9.30am until 9.30pm or later Monday to Saturday.

FOOD AND DRINK

One of the great pulls of Spain, in addition to the cheap cost of property, the sunshine, the warm seas and the low price of alcohol and cigarettes, is, without a shadow of doubt, its cuisine. In terms of both quality and variety, very few, if any, European countries can beat it. Indeed a recent report in the *New York Times* claimed that Spanish gastronomical supremacy has displaced even France. It is a country replete with dishes influenced by the climate and the local way of life of each region; the occupation of the Moors, as well as imports from abroad such as the potato, tomato, sweet potato, vanilla, chocolate, many varieties of beans, and the pepper.

Without exception the retirees interviewed in the process of researching this book listed Spanish cuisine as a key influence on their decision to move to Spain. Valerie Mash, a retiree on the Costa Blanca describes her love affair with Spanish food:

I have always loved Spanish cuisine, and I love cooking, so I am really in my seventh heaven here. I get all of my ingredients from the market, it's just so fresh and it tastes wonderful. Living on the coast I eat lots of fresh fish, often cooked outside on the barbecue, and served with a glass of wine. The selection of good wines here is so huge that I have started to need a list when I go to the supermarket, so that I can remember which ones I have tried and which are the best. My diet is so much healthier here than it was in the UK, and it gives me an enormous amount of energy.

A fresh Mediterranean diet complete with olive oil and red wine is indeed very healthy and is one of the factors consistently used to explain the longevity of the Spanish people – not that you will need an excuse to try as many Spanish delicacies as you can!

Food in Spain is taken very seriously. Dining is an important ingredient in the country's social lifestyle. A light breakfast may be taken at 8am followed by a mid-morning snack at 11am and tapas at 1pm. Lunch (*la comida*) is the big meal of the day and is generally served between 2pm and 4pm. A snack may follow at 6pm; then an evening tapas at 8pm. Dinner (*la cena)* is traditionally served late, between 9pm and 11pm. Restaurants are rated by vertical forks (from one to five) on a plaque outside the entrance. Prices must be listed both inside and outside the establishment.

Regional Specialities

It is difficult to generalise about Spanish food. Just as each autonomous region of Spain has its own government, music, culture and often language, it also has its own style of cuisine. There are certainly similarities between the regions. Some of the staples include lentils (*lentejas*) and chickpeas (*garbanzas*), and pork (*cerdo*) is the most widely eaten meat. And throughout Spain you should expect to find an abudance of garlic and olive oil, the universal *jamon serrano* (dried, cured ham that is considered a delicacy) and huge amounts of fish (*pescado*) and seafood (*mariscos*). Nevertheless every region has its speciality. These are considered below.

Mediterranean Cuisine. The food in **Andalucia** is heavily influenced by the region's proximity to the sea, the climate and its Moorish heritage. Traditional dishes include *gazpacho* (chilled soup – often tomato-based but also almond-based), *calamares* (squid), *Pescadito frito* (fried fish) – often *sardinas* and *boquerones* (anchovies), cured ham, and bean stews that were common when the region was at its poorest.

Catalonian cuisine is considered to be one of the most elaborate and prestigious of all Spain, offering a wide range of fish dishes. Particularly recommended are the Catalonian sausages (*butifarra*) which are less spicy than *chorizo* found in the south.

Valencia is the home of one of Spain's most famous dishes *paella* – saffron flavoured rice cooked with vegetables and seafood or chicken (although traditionally it should be served with rabbit and broad beans. Valencia is also famed for its sweet *turrón* (similar to nougat – made with almonds and honey).

Meseta Cuisine. The food served in the central plateau (the *meseta*) of Spain differs greatly from other regions of this big country. In **Castilla-León** cooking is based on vegetables, haricot beans (*la bañeza* and *el barco*), chickpeas (*fuentesaúco*) and lentils (*la armuña*). Pork (raised on acorns and chestnuts) is flavoursome, and game is used in *botillo* (mountain sausage from León), savoury *morcilla* from Burgos, and the red Segovian sausage known as *cantimpalo*.

Ham and pork are also staples of **Extremaduran** cuisine. Specialities include *calderetas* (stews) and *cochifritos* (lamb seasoned, garnished and casseroled in an earthenware dish), cold *escabeches* (marinades), wild mushrooms, cardoons and leeks and cheeses.

Castilla-La Mancha has its saffron, *la alcarria* honey and *manchego* (ewe's milk cheese). Another speciality is *duelos y quebrantos* (a cattle-drover's and shepherds' dish of a fry-up of eggs, bacon and brains). Country cuisine includes *morteruelos* (chopped pig's liver braised with seasoning and breadcrumbs) and roast lamb and kid. Sweets include varieties of the Moorish-inspired marzipan of Toledo.

Madrid's traditional dishes include *cocido madrileño* (broth followed by the soup-meat, chick-peas, potatoes and greens), cod and *callos* (tripe). Sticky *torrijas* (sweet fritters), desserts and sweetmeats complete a pretty tableau.

Northern Cuisine. The north is a wet verdant region renowned for its meat and fish dishes. The **Basque Country** has local specialities such as *txangurro* (clams and spider crab) and the city of San Sebastián has a tremendous concentration of five-fork restaurants serving some of the finest food in Europe. **Asturias** has a similar cuisine, with its own local dishes such as the *fabada* (haricot bean and pork stew), regional cheeses and cider. **Cantabria** meanwhile offers beef, anchovies and dairy products and **Galicia** has the *pote* (a soup made with ham, haricot beans and turnips), *pulpo* (octopus), a wide variety of fresh shellfish, from scallops and mussels, dairy products and pastries as well as the famed Albariño and Ribeiro wines.

The fertile valleys across **Aragón**, **La Rioja** and **Navarre** produce fruit and vegetables – asparagus, peppers, borage, cardoon, peaches and pears, potatoes, cabbage hearts, pochas and trout. Specialities include meat marinades (*chilindrones*) and *confits*. Desserts include cheeses, milk puddings and fruit (fresh, chocolate-coated or preserved in syrup).

Tapas

Spain's greatest gastronomic legacy may well be *tapas* – small portions of regional specialties served in restaurants and bars and accompanied by a glass of wine or beer. In the good old days tapas, known as *pinchos* or *pintxos* in northern Spain, were served free with a beer in *cervecerías* and *tabernas*. These days you generally have to pay for them, although there are certain places where they are still complementary (such as the chain of bars: *Tapas y Cañas*). Away from the costas however, they tend to be no more than €2-€3 per portion, giving you the opportunity to experiment with a selection of tapas, especially if you are out in a large group. Often tapas bars and restaurants will offer a choice of tapas or *raciones* – these are simply larger plates of the same, and are intended for sharing or as a light meal. Raciones cost around €6-€10 per dish. In bars and on market stalls, the tapas are often displayed at the counter, giving you the chance to see exactly what you are ordering.

There is an enormous range of tapas, and the selection varies dramatically depending on the specialities of the region. Some of the staples however are *patatas bravas* (fried potatoes in a spicy sauce), *tortilla española* (potato omelette), *aceitunas* (olives), *chorizo* (spicy sausage), *carne en salsa* (meat in tomato sauce), and *jamon serrano* (dried ham). On the costas you should expect an array of seafood based tapas including *boquerones* (anchovies), *calamares* (squid), *gambas* (prawns), *mejillones* (mussels), *navajas* (clams), *pulpo* (octopus) and *sepia* (cuttlefish). Wherever you go for tapas, it is always advisable to watch what dishes the locals are ordering, and to go for the local special.

Eating Out

Eating out is a vitally important part of Spanish culture. Every weekend around 70% of Spaniards have lunch or dinner outside the home in one of Spain's 68,000 plus restaurants. Spain offers a huge variety of places to eat including *comedores,* which serve cheap but substantial lunch time meals, roadside inns known as *ventas,* that offer country cooking at bargain prices, *marisquerías,* which serve only seafood, *cafeterías* and *restaurantes.*

The Spanish take their food very seriously. Eating is very much a social occasion and it is common for Spaniards to entertain their friends and family at a restaurant rather than at home. The strong food culture and the Spanish loyalty to traditional regional cuisine have severely hampered the penetration of fast food into Spanish eating habits and the majority of restaurants are independent family-run affairs. The Spanish do not tend to have lunch before 2pm or dinner before 9pm but most restaurants are open for both, with the exception of comedores, which are often closed in the evenings.

Many establishments offer a *menu del dia,* or a *menu de la casa,* which are usually three courses plus wine and bread for a very reasonable price. More expensive restaurants often offer a *menu de degustación* – a sampler meal at a fixed price. Bars and cafeterias tend to serve *platos combinados* (combined plates) of things like egg and chips. Restaurants are designated between one and five forks, but these are a guide to the price and the facilities rather than the quality of the food. The best food is very often found in inexpensive restaurants.

Vegetarians

The Spanish are, as a rule, utterly bewildered by vegetarianism, and tend to give you a very odd look if you say *'soy vegetariano/a'* (I'm a vegetarian) as expats Mac and Meryl Macdonald have found: *'Sourcing vegetarian restaurants is very, very difficult. That is the one thing which we think is better in the UK: if you go to a restaurant there are always 2 or 3 choices for you, whereas in Spain, if you say you are vegetarian they think you're mad. They are not used to it at all.'.*

The few vegetarian restaurants there are tend to be in the larger cities (for a list of vegetarian and vegan restaurants visit www.happycow.net/europe/spain/). In the majority of restaurants you will be faced with a very limited selection and may very quickly become sick of tortilla (omelette). Nevertheless the situation is slowly improving and bear in mind that the markets and supermarkets have a wonderful selection of fresh produce.

If you have a great meal in a restaurant, or the service is superb then it is common to leave about 10% as a tip (*propina*). Often however, a service charge is already included in the bill (*la cuenta*) so be sure to check before leaving a tip. IVA at 7% is also included on the bill.

Alcoholic drinks

Until the 1980s, the wines of Spain were better known for their quantity and low price than for their quality, but in recent years Spain has shed its cheap plonk reputation and earned international recognition. Indeed, the harvests of 1994 and 1995 produced some of the highest quality wines in Rioja and the Ribera del Duero and the 1994 harvest is considered the best vintage of the century.

Spain has over fifty per cent of the European Union's vineyards. There are over 5,400 square miles of vineyards producing a range of both young and aged reds, crisp whites and rosés. The best red wines (*vino tinto*) come from Rioja, Navarra and Ribera del Duero, and the best whites (*vino blanco*) hail from Galicia and rueda and Penedés in Catalonia. *Cava* (Spain's champagne) is produced mainly in Catalonia and is incredibly cheap. For a detailed analysis of Spain's different wine growing regions, visit www.filewine.es/english/default.htm.

Spanish Wine – The Ageing Process

The terms related to the ageing process will help you to select and appreciate the best wines on offer.

Crianza: wines which have a minimum of two years ageing before going on sale.

Reserva: applies to red wines only. Reservas must be aged for at least two years and at least one of these years should be in oak barrels

Gran Reserva (red): at least two years oak ageing and three in the bottle.

Gran Reserva (white): five years of ageing, of which six months must be in oak.

Sherry (vino de Jerez) comes from the area around the Andalucían town of Jerez de la Frontera. There are many different types of sherry but the main distinction is between *fino* or *seco* (dry sherry), amontillado (*medium dry*) and *dulce* or *oloroso* (sweet). Other sherry like drinks include Montilla, which is produced in Córdoba, and Manzanilla, produced in Sanlúcar de Barrameda.

Spanish beer (*cerveza*) is light and refreshing, and there are many good local brands to try, although the most famous are San Miguel, Mahou and Cruz Campo. The Spanish tend not to drink beer with meals, but will often wash down tapas with a *caña* (small draught beer). Cider is not common, except in Asturías where the distinctive *sidra* is produced. *Sangría* (wine and fruit punch) is usually only served at fiestas and in the tourist areas.

MEDIA

Spanish Television

The Spanish are a nation of telly-addicts; after the British they watch more television than any other country in Europe. Nearly every Spanish household contains at least one television set, sometimes where the household lacks several more essential facilities, and approximately 90% of Spaniards over the age of 14 watch television every day. The influence that the television has as a media form is intensified by the fact that the Spanish do not read newspapers with the same avidity as the British or Americans.

Television Española (TVE), the main Spanish television station, set up as a state monopoly in 1956, was subject to heavy censorship under Franco's regime. This censorship continued well into the 1980s and had the effect of lowering the general quality of the programmes aired. TVE's two channels are called TVE1 and TVE2 and despite being a public service, funded by tax-payers, they still run commercials. The first is directed to a more general public. TVE2 has a flexible programming which lends special attention to sports broadcasts and live broadcasts of important cultural events. Its television coverage and audience have grown considerably, however, TVE1 has the larger audience with more than 20 million viewers.

At the beginning of the 1990s two new national channels started broadcasting, Antena 3 and TeleCinco. There is also a subscription channel, Canal+ (still available as analogue, but the recent merger of Canal+ Digital and Via Digital has led to the new Digital+ service) and various regional television channels also exist in Catalonia, the Basque Country, Galicia, Andalusia, Madrid and Valencia. Added to this, today there are satellite networks, with more than 700 local channels serving the different cities and towns. Cable TV is very much a rarity in Spain however

Traditionally light entertainment did not enjoy the same popularity among the Spaniards as it does with most other viewing publics and the audience figures reflected an interest in current affairs and serious discussion programmes. However, in recent years, Spanish television has been increasingly dumbed down and the newspaper *El País* recently demanded, *'How much deeper can gossip programmes plunge, with their libel-ridden, rumour-mongering, humiliation and lying?'* It is true that Spain's three main broadcasters pump out an average of 13 hours a day of *programas de corazón*: a blend of scurrility, plunging neck-lines and shouting. However, documentaries are still very popular, as are TVE's two main current affairs programmes, *Informe Semanal* on TVE1 and *La Clave* on TVE2.

All Spanish channels are technically commercially run and this means an unfortunate average of 8-10 minutes for advert breaks. Also bear in mind that, although it is improving, advertised programme start times should be treated as no more than a rough estimate.

IPTV - Imagenio

In 2004 Telefonica, the Spanish telecoms giant launched a new digital interactive service known as *Imagenio* (or IPTV), which allows access to 48 TV channels, 15 audio channels and a video on demand service in both Spanish and English. In order to obtain IPTV it is necessary to rent a set-top box for around €7 per month, and the signal is delivered via ADSL broadband. The advantage of this service is that it has an extensive video library and also that it allows you to rewind, fast-forward and pause programmes as you would with a video. The disadvantage is the limited coverage so far. By the end of 2005 the service was only available in all Spanish cities with more than 100,000 inhabitants. However, Telefonica are investing €8 billion (2005-2008) in order to extend their broadband services. Further information is available from www.telefonica.es/tol/imagenio.html.

Access to British Television

'You tend to find that there is one major topic of conversation amongst expats' says David Kitching, President of the Gandía International Club, *'satellite television'*. Some such as Valerie Mash, an expat on the Costa Blanca claim to be so busy and active in their retirement that they have 'thrown away' their aerial. Most expats however enjoy their home comfort television and like nothing more than a good argument about the cheapest method of

obtaining the greatest number of English-language channels.

One possibility is the Digital Plus service, which offers films in both the original language (*versión original*) and dubbed Spanish, and it is also possible to watch English Premier League football for around €45 per month.

It is possible, however, to obtain far more English-language programming by obtaining a Freesat card from Sky in the UK. It is not illegal to do this, but it is Sky's company policy to only subscribe to UK and Ireland residents and it is therefore necessary to subscribe from a UK address. In areas where there are large numbers of British expats, there are often companies (usually advertising in the local English-language press) who will provide and install Sky Digital without the need for a UK address.

All satellite systems require the installation of a dish on the roof. In the case of those living as part of a *comunidad de propietarios* the community president must be advised of the intent to install a dish. If, after a period of three months a community dish isn't installed then permission cannot be denied to an individual to install a dish.

The first step is to obtain an information pack from Sky. The Freesat card is valid for 3 years and costs £20. Sky will only send it to a UK address and you will also need to give a UK phone number. You should not tell Sky that you are abroad. The company www.insatinternational.com can obtain a Sky digibox and Freesat card for you, or you could ask a friend. UK company Satalogue can supply a digital satellite system that will receive all of the Sky Astra Satellite and Radio channels plus normal UK television channels anywhere in Europe. Another great advantage of having satellite TV is that it enables you to pick up British radio stations, without the bother of accessing them over the internet.

The Decoder. You will need to obtain a decoder, which costs in the region of £250. The rest of the equipment will cost around £70, and there is still the cost of €200-300 for someone to do the actual installation. If you are technically minded you could buy the decoder for far less on eBay. Where there are large communities of Britons, you will be able to obtain assistance more cheaply. There are numerous British-owned companies who will provide the complete package; they advertise in the local English language press.

Satellite Television Providers	
Digital+	www.plus.es
Sky	www.sky.com; ☎08702-404040
Insatinternational	www.insatinterntional.com; ☎020 8886 7155
Satalogue	www.satalogue.com; ☎01332-812588

Radio

Spanish radio has a reputation for high-quality and entertaining programming and its audience is greater than that in any other European country. The most popular radio networks include *SER*, which has three different stations, *Los 40 principales*, directed mainly at young people, *Radio Minuto* which alternates music and news, and *Radio Corazón* which is aimed primarily at housewives. COPE (*Cadena de Ondas Populares Españolas*) is the second-largest system of private stations and is owned by the Church. Antenna 3 is a national network and groups together a number of FM stations, which appeared after the concession of new licences in the 1980's. Most of the stations and networks are now on FM rather than medium wave (Spain has no long wave stations); and many, like the newspapers and TV channels, also have their own political stance and alignments as well.

Listening to local radio is a very good way to improve your Spanish, and many of the stations seem to offer continuous discussions and phone-ins. Those who wish to listen to the radio in English will find that in areas where there are large numbers of expats, there are a number of English language local stations. Try, for example, Octopus FM (98.3FM), Central FM (98.6FM), Spectrum (105.5FM) and Radio Gibraltar (91.3FM) on the Costa del Sol. It is also possible to get the BBC World Service on short wave, although the frequency can change. To check the frequency visit http://www.bbc.co.uk/worldservice/schedules/frequencies/index.shtml. Nearly all radio stations can of course be listened to over the internet if you have a broadband connection. A great portal for finding internet radio stations is www.radio-locator.com, which currently offers 364 UK stations.

Newspapers

Freedom of the press was not established in Spain until 1978, in the aftermath of thirty years of censorship under the Francoist dictatorship. However, the removal of the censorship laws have not changed what can only be described as the apathy of the Spanish towards newspaper reading, at least compared to their more voracious British and American cousins. The circulation of the daily press is far lower than in most other European countries; the only countries in Europe with a lower newspaper readership than Spain are Greece, Portugal and allegedly Albania. The most popular daily newspaper in Spain is *El País* (www.elpais.es), which has a reputation for liberalism and for being supportive of more 'leftwing' causes; it is one of very few Spanish national newspapers to offer any serious political analysis and competent foreign news coverage.

El País has an average daily circulation of about 400,000 – which compares not too unfavourably with the most widely read quality newspaper in Britain *The Daily Telegraph*, which has a daily circulation figure of just under a million. Apathy towards politics is another reason for the mixed popularity that newspapers as a media form receive throughout the country. Only eight papers in Spain sell more than 100,000 copies a day. The statistic that only one Spaniard in every ten buys a daily newspaper is also fairly staggering. However, as newspapers in Spain tend to be handed around and read second, third and fourth hand, this statistic is based only on sales figures and is thus not wholly accurate as to readership.

The second biggest selling daily in Spain is *El Mundo,* (www.elmundo.es), which became increasingly critical of the PP in the run up to the last general elections. *ABC* is the other leading daily newspaper of national circulation; similarly to *El País*, this is published in Madrid, with regional editions in some of the Autonomous Communities. This, however, is where the similarity ends as *ABC* is aligned very definitely right of centre in its politics as well as in its stringent moral dictums. Other leading national papers include *La Vanguardia Española*, *El Periódico* (published in Barcelona and read mostly in Catalonia and to a much lesser extent in other parts of Spain) and *AS* and *Marca* – both of which are dedicated to sports coverage. In Spain the newspapers circulated in the week are also published on Sunday; Sunday sales are generally 50-100% higher than those for the rest of the week.

Shocking though it may seem to those whose literary staple diet is *The Sun* or *The Daily Mail*, Spain has no real equivalent of our tabloid newspapers. Instead, national curiosity tends to be aroused, not by the latest on the royals, but by current affairs of a rather less frivolous nature, and by sport. The Spanish popular newspapers do cover the lives of the rich and famous, but these articles are left to the back pages rather than taking the role of lead stories as often happens in the UK.

Keeping up with News from Home

For those to whom a British newspaper is an indispensable commodity, even when abroad, British newspapers and the *International Herald Tribune* are available in most of the larger Spanish cities. *The Guardian Weekly* subscription rates for Europe are currently €66 from Spain for six months (€89 for a year) available from *The Guardian Weekly*, 164 Deansgate, Manchester M3 3GG; ☎0870-066 0510; e-mail gwsubs@guardian.co.uk. *The Weekly Telegraph* is a similar digest of news culled from *The Daily Telegraph*. A year's subscription currently costs £89. The Telegraph also has a section of its website devoted entirely to people living abroad: www.expat.telegraph.co.uk (it is also possible to subscribe to the Weekly Telegraph here).

These days many expats keep up with the news via the internet. The BBC and all of the major UK newspapers allow access to news stories that are updated day and night via their websites. Those who wish to read British newspapers and magazines should visit the following portal, offering 800 free online editions: www.wrx.zen.co.uk.

English Language Publications in Spain

Spain is well served for English-language publications. *SUR in English* is one of the best-known English-language newspapers in the country. It is distributed on Fridays through outlets such as supermarkets, bars, travel agencies, banks etc. and is published by *Prensa Malagueña*, in Málaga. The quality of these newspapers and magazines varies enormously, but they are useful for keeping up with expat news and for finding accommodation, clubs and social activities, and services:

Absolute Marbella: www.absolutemarbella.com; ☎902-301130.
Barcelona Connect: www.barcelonaconnect.com; ☎902-200701.
Barcelona Metropolitan: www.barcelona-metropolitan.com; ☎934-514486.
The Broadsheet: www.tbs.com; ☎915-237480.
Catalunya Lifestyle: www.catalanlife.com; ☎972-327311.

The CB Friday: www.cbfriday.com; ☎ 966-477275.

Costa Blanca News: www.costablanca-news.com; ☎ 965-855286.

Costa del Sol News: www.costadelsolnews.es; ☎ 952-448730.

Essential Marbella: www.essentialmagazine.com; ☎ 952-766344.

Estepona Magazine: www.esteponamagazine.com; ☎ 952-798208.

Euro Weekly: http://euroweeklynews.com; ☎ 952-561245.

Inland Magazine: www.inlandmagazine.com; ☎ 952-596346.

In Madrid: www.in-madrid.com; ☎ 915-226780.

Island Connections: www.ic-web.com; ☎ 922-750609.

La Chispa: www.lachispa.net.

Living Tenerife: www.livingtenerife.com; ☎ 922-394244.

Madrid Connect: www.madridconnect.com.

Majorca Daily Bulletin: www.majorcadailybulletin.es; ☎ 971-788400.

Sur in English: www.surinenglish.com; ☎ 952-649600.

The Paper: www.thepaper.net; ☎ 922-735659.

Tenerife News: www.tennews.com; ☎ 922-346000.

The Town Crier: www.towncrier.es; ☎ 952-455185.

Valencia Life: www.valencialife.net.

Magazines

As none of the Spanish newspapers has an equivalent of the social diaries or gossip columns that are found in such abundance in British and American papers, the Spanish magazine market has successfully exploited this gap in the market. There are now countless glossy and profitable women's magazines devoted to the lives and loves of the famous; a few of the most well known include, *Hola!* (which spawned *Hello!* magazine in the UK); *Pronto*; *Diez Minutos*; *Lecturas*; *Semana*; and *Garbo*. These magazines are known as the *Prensa del Corazón* (Press of the Heart) and account for six of the ten most popular magazines in Spain.

Before leaving for Spain there are numerous magazines to whet your appetite. The British property buying boom in Spain and the interest in the country in general has led to a rise in the number of publications dealing exclusively with life in Spain, aimed at expatriates and those who dream of moving to Spain.

British Magazines About Life in Spain

A Place in the Sun's Everything Spain: ☎01342-828700; www.everythingspain
   mag.co.uk.

Homes Overseas: ☎020-7939 9888; www.blendoncom.com.

Living Spain: ☎01234-710992; www.livingspain.co.uk.

Spain Magazine: ☎0131-226 7766; www.spainmagazine.info.

Spanish Homes Magazine: ☎01225-442244; www.spanishhomesmagazine.com.

Spanish Magazine: ☎01225-786857; www.merricksmedia.co.uk.

Books in English

English-language libraries and bookshops are scattered along the costas
and in the larger cities. Book fairs are often held in town squares. These are
good opportunities to buy books on a wide range of subjects and languages
at reasonable prices.

All of the Spain-related English magazines listed above offer reviews of
the latest books about Spain and life in Spain and some of them have their
own book-clubs, from which the latest releases can be ordered overseas.
Santana Books (☎952-485838; www.santanabooks.com) based in Málaga
publish a wide range of English language books about various aspects of
life in Spain. Another good contact is the Spanish Book Shop (☎01962-
773792; www.thespanishbookshop.com) who have a wide range of mail-
order books relating to all things Spanish.

CARS AND MOTORING

Driving

Since the mid 1980s there has been a huge amount of investment in Spanish roads. The extensions and improvements have taken place at a pace
that matches Spain's rapid modernisation. The ongoing road revision programme also includes widening roads, to introduce special lanes for heavy
traffic, improving traffic signs and road markings, and to build town by-
passes around the most built-up areas.

Tolls are required on all motorways except urban ones; a useful map
of all the Spanish toll points is available, free of charge, from ASETA,
(*Asociación de Sociedades Españoles Concesionarias de Autopistas, Túneles,*

Puentes y Vías de Peaje; www.aseta.es) or may be supplied by local tourist offices. Current Spanish toll rates can be obtained from www.dgt.es.

The Spanish are known for their hair-raising driving style, but according to expats David and Liz Austen, *'Spanish drivers are not really much worse than English drivers. The only thing to look out for is the kids on scooters. In the summer the roads are packed with them, and many do not wear helmets.'*

Spanish Driving Regulations

The Spanish traffic police have become increasingly vigilant in recent years, and it is a foolish expat who considers themselves above the law. As Valerie Mash, an expat on the Costa Blanca points out:

The police have become a lot stricter than they used to be here. In the summer months there are a lot of tourists on the roads, and the number of accidents has steadily been increasing, so they have had to crack down. They are particularly intolerant of those who speed, and of drink-drivers, but they are also very fair.

Basic Rules
- The minimum driving age in Spain is 18.
- Drivers and front and back seat passengers are required by law to wear seat belts at all times. Children under 12 may not travel in the front.
- The speed limits in Spain are 120km/h on motorways (*autopistas*), 100km/h on dual carriageways (*autovías*), 90km/h on main roads (*carreteras*) and 50km/h through towns (*via urbanas*). Speed traps are fairly common.
- There is a €1053 fine and a suspension of the driver's licence for up to a year for using a mobile phone while driving, driving without a proper licence or driving an unregistered vehicle.
- Always indicate before overtaking on a motorway and before returning to your lane.
- Spain's drink-driving laws are strictly enforced and only allow 0.5mg of alcohol per mm of blood (in the UK this is higher at 0.8mg). Recently passed drivers may only have 0.1mg.
- Fines from €302 to €602 and suspension of licence for up to

> three months may be enforced for driving under the influence of alcohol or drugs, refusing to take the breathalyser test, exceeding the speed limit by 50%, reckless driving, racing or carrying 50% more passengers than there are seats.
> o Always carry spare bulbs and two warning triangles.
> o It is now a legal requirement to also carry at least one 'visibility vest' (a luminous yellow jacket) in your vehicle and in the event of a breakdown, it is mandatory that this should be worn.

Documents to Keep with You

Anyone driving in Spain should carry the following documents, just in case they are stopped by the traffic police as failure to produce them can result in a €90 fine:

o Driving licence.
o Spanish vehicle tax (paid annually at the *ayuntamiento*).
o *Permiso de Circulación* – car registration document.
o *ITV* certificate: the Spanish equivalent of the MOT.
o Insurance documents proving that your insurance is paid and up-to-date.

Should any of these documents be invalid or out of date then you could face an on-the-spot fine of €300. If you are unable to pay, the police can impound your car.

Parking – Basic Rules

Yellow Lines: No parking. Police will either clamp or impound your car.

Blue Lines: Metred parking. Spanish meters are located at the side of the road and allow you to pay for the amount of time you require. Failure to obtain a ticket, or overstaying the time period can result in fines, or even being towed away by the police.

Supermarkets: Many supermarkets offer free parking, but you must remember to ask at the checkout for a *ficha* to raise the barrier in order to leave the car park.

Parking Fines: In some areas, if you receive a fine (*multa*) in a metred area, you may find a form and envelope allowing you to pay a reduced fine at the metre. The metre will print you a receipt which must then be posted, along with the form in the envelope provided.

Driving Licences

All licences issued in the EU are valid in any other EU country. This means if you got your licence in France, Britain, Ireland etc. you no longer have to exchange if for a Spanish one if you decide to take up residence in Spain. Nevertheless, after six months you will need to have your licence validated and stamped at your local Provincial Traffic Headquarters – *Jefatura Provincial de Tráfico* (usually based within the police station). The process is very quick and simple. In order to get your licence validated you should take the following documents:

- Your UK or EU driving licence. If you have the new licence photo card, you should bring a photocopy of both sides.
- A copy of your NIE.
- Your passport and one photocopy.
- Two passport photographs.

If you are in Spain for a long time, or you originate from outside the EU then you may wish to get a Spanish licence, available from the Jefatura de Tráfico of your province. You will need your present licence and a copy, your residence card and one photograph. This exchange procedure, known as *canje*, only takes a few hours and costs around €18.

Note that licences in Spain are not sacrosanct until the driver reaches the age of 70 as in Britain. Instead they have to be renewed according to your age and the type of licence held. A car licence is usually granted for ten years if the driver is under 45, and for five years if he or she is between 45 and 70. Drivers over 70 years old must renew their licence each year.

Importing a Car

Anyone thinking of importing a foreign-registered car into Spain should first of all consider carefully the drawbacks: the inconvenience and safety concerns of having a right-hand drive car in a country which drives on the right and the inevitable tortuous red tape that the import procedure gives rise to.

A UK or Irish citizen who feels that they cannot possibly part with their UK car and decides to import this permanently into Spain does not need to apply for authorisation to use the vehicle for a period of up to six months.

Legally the car may be retained in Spain indefinitely as long as the UK road tax, insurance and MOT are kept up to date. However, Spanish law states that you may not use a foreign registered vehicle for more than six months in any one calendar year. If you intend to move your vehicle permanently to Spain it is therefore best to register it there. Indeed, if you take out a residence permit in Spain, then your vehicle must be Spanish registered.

In order to import the car and register it in Spain, Britons should surrender their registration document to the DVLA and in return obtain a Certificate of Permanent Export (V561). You will also require a roadworthiness certificate, known as the ITV in Spain (*Inspección Técnica de Vehiculos*). The procedures are fairly complex, and the bureaucracy fairly convoluted, however, advice and information is available from RACE (*Real Automobile Club de España*, www.race.es; ☎914-473200). Residents of Spain are exempt from the Spanish 12% import tax. Once in Spain, the vehicle must be registered with the Department of Transport, and an application for Spanish number plates must be made within thirty days.

Buying a Car in Spain

As importing your car into Spain brings with it a number of problems, many people choose to simply buy a new car once in Spain. Brand new cars are cheaper in Spain than in the UK. However, second-hand cars can often be quite expensive, as expatriate resident of Oliva and retired mechanic Ian Adams explains:

> *Whereas in the UK the depreciation in value of new cars begins as soon as you have bought it, cars in Spain hold their value for much longer, and so are much more expensive here than in the UK. For example we recently bought a second-hand car for around €12,750 (around £8,700) and I know that in the UK we could have picked up the same model for around £5,000.*

This is partly just a cultural difference, although Spain's good weather does mean that cars tend to last for longer. Many of the used cars available along the costas are ex-hire cars, which are generally sold on by the hire-car companies after two years and it is occasionally possible to find bargains.

As in the UK, it is possible to buy cars on an instalment plan, although dealers may be less likely to offer credit to those who have recently arrived in Spain and do not yet own property.

When buying a second-hand car, remember that it is necessary to transfer the car's ownership. Many dealers will do this for you for a small fee, but if you buy privately then it may be necessary to employ the services of a *gestor*.

In many ways, selling a UK car and simply buying another one in Spain, with Spanish registration plates and with the steering wheel on the left, saves a lot of paperwork and bother.

ITV – Technical Inspection

The Spanish equivalent of the UK MOT is known as the ITV (*Inspección Técnica de Vehículos*). All cars over four years old must take the test, which costs around €40, in an authorised station every two years. All cars over ten years old must have an annual test. If the car passes, you will receive a sticker which should be displayed on the right-hand side of the windscreen. You should also keep the paperwork with you in the car.

Insurance

The basic legal requirement for Spanish car insurance is third party only (*terceros*); thus drivers are insured for claims made against them, but not for any accident which may befall driver or car. This type of insurance can cost as little as €400 a year and covers third party claims for bodily harm and collateral damage. Anyone who feels that they don't have enough security with only third party insurance can take out more comprehensive insurance which either raises the limit on the amount the insurance company will pay out on third party insurance, or insures the car owner, his or her family and the car. Coverage can also be bought against fire, theft and damage.

Fully comprehensive car insurance, known as *todo riesgo* policy will cost more (between €1,200 and €1,800 per year). As in the UK, policy holders are entitled to a no-claims bonus – a discount on their insurance premiums if there have been no claims against the policy.

In the case of an accident, either party must bring charges within two months. This simply involves going to the local police station, making a statement (you must know at least the registration number of the other car involved) and then letting the insurance companies on either side battle it out. However, if it comes to a court case then you may have to wait, literally, for years as the Spanish judicial system heaves its way towards justice.

Breakdown Insurance

Spanish breakdown insurance policies (*seguro de asistencia en carretera*) are provided by Spanish car insurance companies and Spanish motoring organisations such as RACE (*Real Automobile Club de España*, ☎914-473200; www.race.es). Membership of RACE is round €30 (registration fee), plus an annual fee of around €98. Their services are very similar to those of the AA or RAC in the UK.

LOCAL GOVERNMENT ADMINISTRATION

'Autonomy' is a difficult word in a political context. The heady, near neurotic drive for local home rule which gripped Spain as the years of Franco's repressive dictatorship drew to a close was to cause years of political controversy, unrest and negotiation. The result of these troubled years (which climaxed in the failed military coup of 1981, the military's response to the seemingly all-embracing move to a federal Spain) was the carving up of the country into seventeen Autonomous Communities. The devolution of power to the regions was the outstanding innovation of the 1978 Constitution although this was not effectively achieved until 1983.

The definition of 'autonomy' is also tricky, as some of the Communities enjoy greater powers of self-rule than others. Although the 1978 Constitution ruled that each Autonomous Community was to have a President, a Governing Council, a Legislative Assembly and a Supreme Court, the central government was still to be exclusively responsible for foreign affairs, external trade, defence, justice, criminal, commercial and labour law, merchant shipping and civil aviation. However, many grey areas, such as education were not allocated specifically to either central or federal government; and this is one issue which is handled differently in different regions.

The Basques and Catalans were the first to achieve autonomy; they were both given control of education in their area and won the right to plan their own economies and set up their own police forces. A difference between the two is that in the Basque country the regional government collects taxes and hands them over to the central government, retaining what it needs for its own purposes, whereas in the Catalan provinces, as in the rest of the country, the central government collects the money and then gives the regional government its share.

Many of the regions now feel that the statutes drawn up in the early 1980s are out of date and need to be re-examined. In Catalonia and the Basque region particularly, there are strong calls for further autonomy.

The Ayuntamiento

Although all of Spain is now divided into Autonomous Communities, and each of these enjoys a varying degree of autonomy, the concept of self-rule has come to have very little direct effect on the man in the street. Locals and expatriates often find that power is really devolved further in Spain, down to the city administration; and to get things done you will find a visit to the *ayuntamiento* (town hall) more useful. The town hall functions as part of the regional administration; and will answer queries on local taxes, and dispense advice on both central and federal government matters.

Voting in Spain

British residents may vote in local and European elections. They can also stand as candidates, and in areas of expatriate predominance many foreigners have become heavily involved in local politics. In order to register to vote, it is necessary to appear on the municipal register (*padron municipal*) at the local ayuntamiento. The British Embassy in Spain points out that legally all residents of Spain are required to do this, but in fact many do not get around to it. Enrolling on the local electoral register (*empadronamiento*) requires you to present your residence card and evidence that you reside in that particular area (such as your title deeds or rental contract). It is also necessary that you make clear your desire to be able to vote. Whilst you cannot vote without appearing on the municipal register, registration does not automatically allow you to vote. Further information is available from the Spanish Ministry of the Interior (☎900-101900; www.mir.es).

RETAINING YOUR RIGHT TO VOTE IN UK NATIONAL AND EUROPEAN ELECTIONS

If you are a British citizen living abroad you can apply to be an overseas voter in UK Parliamentary and European elections. You have to have appeared on the electoral register in the UK within the previous 15 years.

You can register as soon as you move abroad by completing an Overseas Elector's Declaration form from your nearest British consular or diplomatic mission. For more information contact www.aboutmyvote.co.uk or for Northern Ireland www.electoralofficeni.gov.uk.

RELIGION

The Catholic Church in Spain has a long and rich, if sometimes intolerant history, which reaches far back to the Church's spearheading of the Counter Reformation. The years of the Inquisition resulted in the virtual elimination for a time of Protestantism in Spain (and forced Jews and Muslims to convert). The right to worship freely and of freedom of conscience was not granted to other religious denominations until as recently as 1978; and even then the centuries of power and influence which the Catholic Church had enjoyed through its close association with the state (particularly in the early Franco years) persisted, meaning that by this time there were few strongholds of any other religious denomination left.

The lay religious order, Opus Dei, was primarily responsible for the influence over the secular authorities which some would say the Catholic Church still wields in the twenty-first century. Founded in 1928 by José María Escrivá Balaguer, this semi-secret organisation succeeded in infiltrating Spanish society at many professional levels, in schools, government and business, and became tremendously powerful in the 1960s. A tax scandal exposed in 1969 by a government official succeeded in reducing but not extinguishing the rather sinister power of this group.

However, Catholicism in Spain has been forced to adapt to a modern secular society since the 1978 constitution, and changes in Spanish society such as legal divorce, contraception and abortion have forced the church to re-think its approach. Spanish society has become markedly more liberal in the last few decades, a change that has been most visibly demonstrated to an international audience by the success of Pedro Almodóvar's films dealing with issues such as relaxed sexual morality, drugs, prostitution, homosexuality and transsexuals. Under Aznar and the PP, there was an attempt to restore some of the church's influence on public life, especially in education, where religious instruction was controversially restored to the state curriculum. However, under Zapatero and a far more liberal government, and with the influence of a massive influx of immigrants, creating a far more multi-cultural society, the extent to which the Catholic Church will maintain its influence remains to be seen.

Unsurprisingly, newly fledged Spanish residents will find themselves immersed in Roman Catholicism in almost every town in the country. Notices of services are posted not only outside the churches, but at strategic viewing points throughout the town to attract as many churchgoers as possible. There are many festivals and holy days which are popular with visitors and locals, as in Seville. In fact, the effect of Catholicism in Spain is not only to be felt in the church (with the number of churchgoers now in sharp decline); its culture and values are an integral part of many social attitudes within the country. Even those Spaniards who claim agnosticism have the Catholic culture as part of their heritage.

Christianity in Spain is all but synonymous with Catholicism. There are a mere 350,000 Protestants in the country; while 94% of the population is Catholic. However, there are resident Anglican clergy in a number of tourist and retirement areas and many Anglican services take place throughout Spain which are attended by expatriates and visitors. These are usually listed in the local paper. Such services often take place in buildings borrowed from other denominations or in schools or church halls, even in hotels. There are also synagogues in the main towns and cities.

Useful Addresses – International Churches

British Embassy Church of St. George: C/ Nuñez de Balboa 43, 28001 Madrid; ☎915-765109; e-mail stgeorgemadrid@telefonica.net.

Community Church of Madrid: C/ Viña 3, 28014 Madrid; ☎915-712136.

Immanuel Baptist Church: C. Hernandez de Tejada 4, 28027 Madrid; ☎914-074 347; email info@ibcmadrid.com; www.ibcmadrid.com.

Mountainview International Church: C/Playa de Sangenjo 26, 28230 (Las Rozas), Madrid; ☎916-305137; e-mail richard@mountainview-church.com; www.mountainview-church.com.

Our Lady of Mercy Catholic Church: Avenida de Alfonso XIII 165, 28016 Madrid; ☎914-169009; e-mail ourladyofmercy@terra.es; www.ourladyofmercy. info/.

Synagogue: C/ Balmés 3, 28010 Madrid; ☎915-913131.

St. George's Church (C of E): Calle Horacio 38, Bonanova, 08022 Barcelona; ☎934-178867; e-mail stgeorges@wanadoo.es; www.st-georges-church.com.

St. John's Church (C of E): Formentera; ☎971-322769.

The English-Speaking Church of Ibiza: ☎971-343383; e-mail chaplainibiza@ ya.com

Quality of Life

CHAPTER SUMMARY

- Seniors and retirees in Spain are eligible for a range of concessions including free entry to state museums and galleries and reduced fares on trains and buses.
- **Sports and leisure pursuits.** Spain has over 7,000km of disused railway lines, many of which have been recovered for the enjoyment of cyclists and ramblers.
  - Green fees tend to be more expensive in Spain, but most of the golf courses are brand new and pristinely maintained.
  - Scuba diving is well established in Spain and there are some stunning underwater worlds to be discovered such as the marine reserve at las Islas Medias, a tiny archipelago just off the Costa Brava.
  - The Sierra Nevada ski resort is the most southerly resort in Europe, where it is possible to ski in the mornings and sunbathe on the beach in the afternoons.
- Many of the Spanish public universities offer free courses for people aged over 55. The English-language University of the Third Age offers free courses on a range of subjects.
- Internal air travel is a growing market In Spain. There are over 40 no-frills carriers flying in and out of Spain to a range of European destinations.
- Spain is famous for the number of fiestas, festivals, ferias and general celebrations that it has. There are hundreds of local celebrations with ancestral rites that have been preserved for centuries, and many new ones are created each year.
- Keeping in touch with friends and family back home is now incredibly easy and remarkably cheap, especially with the development of phone calls via the internet.
- Retirement is no longer a period of total inactivity and many retirees fill their days with part time jobs or volunteer work, and others start their own businesses

Ian Adams, aged 44. Retired mechanic on the Costa Valencia.
I retired early because I was fed up with the rat race, fed up worrying about overheads and dealing with whinging customers. I am in a position now where I don't really need to work full-time and I have re-evaluated my priorities. These days I would much rather have a better quality of life and less money in my pocket than loads of money and no time to enjoy it.

WHERE TO GET INFORMATION

The Ayuntamiento

The first useful port of call for information about what happens in your local community is the town hall or *ayuntamiento*. You should already be familiar with the town hall as all the forms and official business required to regularise your settlement in Spain will have been dealt with there. The ayuntamiento also holds details of everything of interest locally to its citizens, such as local clubs and associations of all types.

IMSERSO

IMSERSO stands for *Instituto de Mayores y Servicios Sociales* (the Institute of Older Persons and Social Services; ☎913-638888; www.seg-social.es/imserso/), part of the Spanish department of Work and Social Security. Part of their function is to disseminate information about programmes available specifically for those aged over 60. Some of these programmes are to do with health and welfare, such as the state run *teleasistencia* service (a 24-hour personal alarm service), but there are other cultural and leisure initiatives aimed at older people living in Spain. The best place to find information about IMSERSO is the *Portal Mayores* website: www.imserso-mayores.csic.es, some of which is in English. This offers information about initiatives run in your local area, from educational courses for retirees to pensioners' discounts and subsidised holidays.

Spanish National Tourist Office

As tourism is so vastly important to the Spanish economy, there has been huge investment in upgrading tourist facilities, and the network of Spanish tourist offices is vast. Most cities, towns, and areas of interest have their own tourist office, which can supply specific information on the local area. Tourist offices are extremely helpful and their staff speak very good English. For a list of all of the major tourist offices visit www.tourspain.co.uk.

The Institute of Spanish Tourism (☎913-433500; www.tourspain.es) is also an extremely useful source of advice and information about places to visit and things to do in the country as a whole. The Spanish tourism website in English can be found at www.spain.info.

MAKING NEW FRIENDS

Of course most people know how to make new friends and do it instinctively or subconsciously, but moving to another place, in another country with another culture and language can be hard on even the most honed social skills. Making Spanish friends will require having a firm grasp of the language and the desire to throw yourself into a completely new way of life. If you feel that you are ready to start making Spanish friends, a good place to start would be the *Hogar de Pensionistas.*

Hogar de Pensionistas

You will find a pensioners' club (*Hogar de Pensionistas*) conveniently and centrally located in most Spanish towns and villages. Whilst a pensioners club may sound like the last place you would want to visit, they often have extremely good, modern facilities, plus a subsidised bar and café. Many also have their own libraries, television and newspaper facilities, and are generally a good place to meet friends and enjoy a cheap morning coffee. Some are so well organised as to arrange for a local doctor to call on the club, for the convenience of its members. Whilst membership is primarily Spanish, the warmth with which expatriates are received within these clubs is a testament to Spanish hospitality. Anyone over 65 is eligible to join.

Social Clubs

If your Spanish isn't yet up to scratch then a good way to meet people is to join one of the numerous clubs and associations run by expatriates. Although these are more numerous on the coast, you will find English-speaking community organisations dotted throughout the country. The best way to find out about them is via the town hall or the English-language press. For example, the *Costa Blanca News* lists hundreds of English speaking social clubs each week, some of which are designed specifically for newcomers. Most clubs organise any number of activities for their members such as bridge and chess evenings, outings, dances, social events and so on. As expats David and Liz Austen found, social clubs are a great way to meet people and to glean information and advice:

People said we might be bored when we got out here but in fact we're incredibly busy. If you want to join in, there are things to do everyday. We joined the Gandia International Club as soon as we arrived, and we have used that as a base. It has allowed us to meet people and you can find out so much more by talking to people than by simple trial and error.

As well as some of the ad hoc social organisations that have formed amongst the expatriate communities, many well-known UK clubs have been exported to Spain, such as the Lions club, Rotary clubs, the Royal British Legion, the Royal Naval Association and so on. Some of these are listed in the box below. Whatever you want to become involved in, the network of expatriates will help you.

Useful Contacts – Social Clubs

Association of Foreign Property Owners: ☎965-830106; http://afpo.org/. Annual membership €10.

Barcelona Women's Network: www.bcnwomensnetwork.com. Volunteer organisation helping women to adjust to life in Barcelona. Annual membership €55.

British Hispanic Cultural Foundation: ☎913-456344. Cultural & social events.

British Ladies Association: ☎918-034713. Monthly meetings & social activities.

British Society of Catalunya: Tel/fax 972-770517; www.bsce.freeservers.com. Providing channels of information amongst the British community.

Cambridge Club: ☎914-316497. Ex-university members, social activities.

The Good Companions Club: ☎952-471562. Fuengirola based social, cultural and travel charity.

The English Speaking Club of Málaga: ☎952-222144. Provides social evenings and Spanish/English conversation groups.

International Newcomers Club: e-mail info@incmadrid.com; www.incmadrid.com. Provides information about community activities and services.

Madrid Toastmasters Club: ☎615-888634; www.toastmastersmadrid.com.

X-Barcelona Club: www.xbarcelona.com. Free monthly meetings for expatriates.

SENIOR CONCESSIONS

There are the usual range of concessions applicable to retirees in Spain and many of them are well worth having – especially the concessions on public and private transport and cultural spectacles. Most museums, exhibitions, public zoos, and monuments are obliged to provide a discount rate for those aged over 65. Other places of interest, cinemas, theatres, sports clubs etc. frequently also offer cheap rates upon presentation of proof of age.

Trains. RENFE, the Spanish railway company, offers a discount card, the *Tarjeta Dorada* for pensioners and anyone who is over sixty. The card entitles you to a 40% discount on any regional trains. On long distance trains (*Grand Linea – AVE and Talgo*) there is a reduction of 40% from Monday to Thursday, and 25% from Friday to Sunday. This can add up to quite a saving, especially if you are taking the opportunity to do a lot of travelling around the country.

The card, which is valid for a year, costs €5 and is available in train stations and travel agencies. You will need to take proof either that you are over 60 (passport), or proof of your pension. RENFE also specifies that foreign residents will need to provide proof of residence, such as a residence card or certificate of *empadronamiento*.

Buses/Metro. The discounts for pensioners on urban transport such as buses and the metro, and on local buses in rural areas, differ depending on the region that you live in. In Madrid pensioners are able to buy an *abono* (season ticket) *de tercera edad*. These offer enormous discounts on local buses, trains and the metro. It is possible to buy either a monthly or annual abono, from your nearest tobacconists (*estanco*).

In other areas, transport is included in a special discount card for pensioners, provided by the municipal government (see below). The best way to find out what deals are offered on public transport in your area is to enquire at the town hall, or at the bus station. Alternatively the state *Portal Mayores* website has a list of programmes for pensioners (www.imsersomayores.csic.es).

Pensioners' Discount Cards. Some of the regional governments have introduced special cards that entitle older people to an array of discounts.

For example, the *Junta de Andalucía* offers the *Tarjeta Sesentaycinco* to anyone aged over 65, which allows them to enjoy discounts on hotels, cinema tickets, entrance to sports clubs, monuments and theme parks throughout the region. It also entitles them to discounted public transport (50% off urban transport and inter-urban buses that begin their journey within the region) and care in the home (further information: ☎900-200165; www.juntadeandalucia.es).

The *Ayuntamiento de Barcelona* has a similar card, known as the *Tarjeta Rosa*, open to anyone aged over 60 who is registered on the electoral role in Barcelona. Bearers receive free public transport and free or discounted entrance to exhibitions, zoos, municipal sports centre and so on (further information: ☎900-700077).

For similar discounts in your region, enquire at the ayuntamiento.

Museums. All Spanish state museums offer free admission to anyone over 65, as well as having free admission sessions once a week that are open to everyone. State museums include the Prado and the National Archaeological museum in Madrid. Most other museums have concessionary policies, but details must be obtained from the individual museums.

SPORT AND LEISURE PURSUITS

Sport

Sports facilities in Spain are excellent around the main tourist areas, where communal swimming pools and tennis courts are nearly always attached to apartment blocks. Wherever there are large concentrations of Brits and other expatriates, there are numerous rugby, football, cricket and even lawn bowls clubs.

Outdoor sports in Spain are plentiful, largely due to the country's climate and wealth of natural wonders. Hiking, trekking, rock climbing, hunting and fishing are all readily available, as are more adventurous sports such as hang-gliding and bungee-jumping. Spain's miles of coastline also make water sports very accessible and surfers, sailors, windsurfers, water-skiers and scuba-divers will all find plenty to keep them busy.

Less than a century ago if you lived beyond 65 you were regarded as aged. These days, 60 is being touted as the new 40 and increasingly retired people are pursuing sports and living fit and active lives into their 80s and sometimes 90s. Sports are the best way of maintaining a healthy cardiovascular system, good reaction time, agility and hand/eye coordination. You will also receive the unquantifiable benefits of belonging to a club and the social interaction this involves. A recent report highlighted the fact that a sixty-year-old can have a cardio-vascular system as efficient as that of a twenty-year-old; sadly this does not apply to joints as well, so it is essential to know your weaknesses and take suitable precautions and medical advice. Many sports, such as Tai chi, swimming and even weight training are suitable for beginners of any age. Most towns have a selection of sports clubs, details of which can be obtained at the ayuntamiento, or you can contact the The Spanish Sports Council: *Consejo Superior de Deportes* (☎915-896700; www.csd.mec.es). Alternatively you can always contact the national organisation of a particular sport (see below)

National Sports Federations

The Spanish sports federations can provide information on where to practice the sport in your region, plus news on competitions taking place in Spain.

Air Sports: *Deporte Aereo;* ☎915-085480; www.rfae.org.

Archery: *Tiro con Arco;* ☎914-260023; www.federarco.es.

Athletics: *Atletismo*; ☎915-482423; www.rfea.es.

Badminton: *Badminton;* ☎915-428384; www.fesba.com.

Baseball: *Beisbol;* ☎913-552844; www.rfbeisbolsofbol.com.

Basketball: *Baloncesto*; ☎913-832050; www.feb.es.

Billiards *Billar;* ☎963-930626; www.rfeb.org.

Bowling: *Bolos;* ☎915-492370, www.febolos.com.

Boxing: *Boxeo;* ☎915-477758; www.feboxeo.com.

Canoeing: *Piraguismo;* ☎915-064399; www.rfep.es.

Car Racing: *Automovilismo;* ☎917-299430; www.rfeda.es.

Chess: *Ajedrez;* ☎913-552159; www.rfeda.es.

Cycling: *Ciclismo*; ☎915-400841; www.rfec.com.

Fencing: *Esgrima;* ☎915-597400; www.sportec.com/rfee.

Fishing: *Federación Española de Pesca*; ☎915-328352; www.fepyc.es.

Football: *Futbol;* ☎914-959800; www.rfef.es.

Handball: *Balonmano;* ☎915-481355; www.rfebm.com.

Hockey: *Hockey;* ☎913-096830; www.rfeh.com.

Judo: *Judo;* ☎915-411536; www.rfejudo.com.

Karate: *Karate:* ☎916-639232; www.fek-karate.com.

Polo: *Polo;* ☎915-310194; www.rfepolo.org.

Potholing: *Espeleoglogia;* ☎913-093674; www.fedespeleo.com.

Rowing: *Remo;* ☎914-414978; www.federemo.org.

Rugby: *Rugby*; ☎915-414978; www.ferugby.com.

Sailing: *Real Federación Española de Vela:* ☎915-195008; www.rfev.es.

Shooting and Hunting: *Caza;* ☎913-111411; www.fedecaza.com.

Squash: *Squash;* ☎916-587104; www.rfes.es.

Speedboat Racing: *Motonautica*; ☎914-153769; www.rfemotonautica.org.

Swimming: *Natacion*; ☎915-572006; www.rfen.es.

Table Tennis: *Tenis de Mesa;* ☎915-423387; www.rfetm.com.

Tennis: *Tenis*; ☎932-005355; www.rfet.es. Further information available in English at www.playtennisspain.com.

Volleyball: *Voleibol;* ☎917-014090; www.rfevb.com.

Water-Skiing: *Esquí Naútico;* ☎934-520895; www.feen.org.es.

Birdwatching

The enormous variety of bird species in Spain is bound to delight those who were avid birders before retirement, and even draw in a few novices exploring new pursuits in their retirement. Bird tour-guide and author of '*Birdwatching on Spain's Southern Coast'* **John Butler** explains the appeal:

Unlike in the UK, birding in Spain is not carried out from windswept commons or from cold, damp bird hides overlooking dreary, empty lakes. Instead, we have warm Mediterranean climates, vast open areas of undeveloped land, huge estuaries and some of the most colourful birds in Europe.

Nor is Spanish birding the frantic affair that is often the case elsewhere. Here, we can spend our days out at a leisurely pace, enjoying not only the birds and other wildlife, but also stunning scenery and the chance to engage in some gentle exercise – an important factor for the recent retiree.

Here in Spain there are almost 600 recorded bird species. Of these, around 50 species are very scarce or unheard of in some other countries, including five eagle species, three types of vultures and the beautifully multi-coloured Bee-eaters, Rollers, Hoopoes and Glossy Ibis.

There are many excellent areas in this country for pursuing your birdwatching ambitions and Spain is often described as the largest birdwatching site in Europe. Indeed, there are places that are of such great ornithological importance that they should be visited at least once, even by those with only a mild interest. So which are the best birdwatching areas? Although opinions will differ, my top five areas are given below.

Doñana. Situated in the southwestern corner of Spain, the Doñana region is one of the most important wetland and wildlife conservation areas in Europe. It covers an area of over 140,000 square hectares of marshlands and forests and contains many of Europe's scarcest and endangered birds.

Tarifa. This is the shortest sea-crossing between Africa and Europe and is the busiest migration route between the two continents. It is estimated that up to six million birds cross the Strait of Gibraltar each spring and autumn.

Extremadura. Situated in the middle of the western region of the country. An area of vast rolling steppes where Great and Little Bustards, Pin-tailed and Black-bellied Sandgrouse, Spanish Imperial Eagles, Black Storks and Eagle Owls are all common.

The Ebro Delta. This is a vast area of marshes and tidal inlets, midway between Barcelona and Valencia on the southeastern coast.

The Pyrenees mountains. In the northeast of Spain and forming part of the Spanish/French border. The mountains are home to the Lammergeier and the Wallcreeper, two of the scarcest Spanish birds, and many other mountain species.

Birdwatching amongst the Spanish is still very much a minority interest and it is hard to find meaningful information from tourist offices or from regional governments. By far the best way of learning about the birds and the sites to visit is by investing in a good guide book or by employing the services of a good professional local guide.

John Butler's book is available from Santana Books (www.santanabooks. com). He also runs guided bird tours in the Doñana area of Andalucia. For further details visit www.donanabirdtours.com.

Useful Contacts

The Spanish Ornithological Society: Sociedad Española de Ornitologia (SEO); ☎914-340911; www.seo.org.

The Black Stork Ornithological Group: Colectivo Ornitologico Cigüeña Negra; ☎639-859350.

Rare Birds in Spain Website: www.rarebirdspain.net.

Local English-Speaking Guides

John Butler: Donaña National Park, Andalucia; www.donanabirdtours.com

Keith Seville: Álora, Málaga; www.fincalimoneros.com

Jules Sykes: Oliva, Valencia; www.olivaramatours.com

Stephen Christopher: Catalonia; www.catalanbirdtours.com

Peter Jones: Ronda, Málaga; www.spanishbirds.com

Cycling

Cycling is one of the best ways to get off the beaten track, explore Spain's hidden delights and get some exercise. There are hundreds of mountain bike rental companies dotted around the country and thousands of kilometers of tracks that wind up and down mountains and through deep valleys.

Obviously you can cycle wherever you choose, but one of the best ways to explore the country by bike is to travel the *Vias Verdes* (Greenways). Spain has over 7,000 km of disused railway lines, many of which have been recovered for the enjoyment of cyclists and ramblers. These routes are perfect for cycling as they offer safe, accessible routes through areas of natural beauty, and away from roads and traffic. The programme is administered by the Fundación de los Ferrocarriles Españoles – FFE (☎911-511065; www.viasverdes.com). The website, some of which is in English, gives details of all the routes (there are 77 in all covering around 1,500 km), as well as a list of railway stations close to the vias verdes.

Fishing

Angling in Spain can offer access to beautiful and unspoilt rivers and lakes and the rewards, apart from some great angling sport, include relaxation and healthy exercise in a stress free environment year round. Angler *Phil Pembroke,* who has written books on coarse and fly-fishing in Spain, has this to say about Spanish opportunities for practicing the gentle art:

> *You don't have to be the best angler in the world to start catching fish here straight away and many angling destinations are less than one hour's drive from the popular costa resorts.*
>
> *Many of Spain's fish species are found nowhere else. The famous comizo barbel can exceed 40lb on Extremedura's river Guadiana. American*

Largemouth Black bass are new to UK anglers. Officially stocked in many embalses (reservoirs) that are too hot for trout, they are often caught using spinner lures and make fine eating.

The river Ebro in Catalonia is home to the infamous siluro catfish. Many will be familiar with the image of its capture from the front page of UK tabloid newspapers. It was introduced illegally from Germany and grows to more than 6 feet in length and over 200lb.

Licences

Always make sure you have a licence with you on fishing trips. The *Guardia Civil* is charged with patrolling river banks and they are renowned for confiscating equipment from anyone without the correct paperwork. For this reason they have the best equipped angling team in Spain! Licences are obtained from the regional *Agencia Medio Ambiente* office (the local council's environment office) and are easily obtained, except in Andalucia where the requirements are more stringent. If you are applying in Andalucia, producing an English licence may help to persuade the authorities that you are likely to behave on the river bank.

Once you have purchased your angling licence, 99% of waters are free to fish, with the exception of trout and salmon fisheries. The licence costs less than 12 euros per year. However if you are over 65 years of age, it's free and does not need to be renewed. There is no close season, but night fishing is not permitted.

Trout and salmon waters offer some of the best game fishing in Europe. Salamanca's fresh-water Hucho salmon grows to 35lb in the beautiful river Tormes. Cotos de pesca *(game fishing reserves) are publicly operated. To fish them you will require, in addition to the regional angling licence, a cheap day ticket purchased either from the* Medio Ambiente *(in advance) or from local bars (on the day).*

Older Spanish anglers prefer to fish for the pot. By selecting a coto pesca sin muerte *(catch and release fishing reserve) you may have a world-class* tramo *(river stretch) all to yourself.*

Spanish anglers are friendly and very helpful. After all the language of fishing is a universal one. A few words spoken in Spanish on the river bank will go a long way to making new friends and improving your language skills.

Phil Pembroke's *'Pescando en España: The Smooth Guide to Angling in Spain'* and *'Pescando a Mosca: Fly-fishing in Spain'* are available to buy. To order, call or email Phil at: ☎01708-764696; e-mail philippembroke007@hotmail.com.

Useful Contacts

Valencia: *Federación Valenciana de Pesca.* ☎963-559055; www.federacion pescacv.com.

Alicante: Local ex-pat Ted Atkinson runs the *Alcalali Angling Club*, which runs bi-monthly angling matches. ☎966-482268; www.aaangling.com.

Murcia: *Federación Murciana de Pesca* . ☎968-221012; www.fprm.es.

Andalucia: *Federación Andaluza de Pesca.* ☎950-151746; www.fapd.org.

Almería: *Mojacár Angling Club* (founded in 2005 by expats living in Almería) – contact at Beachcomber Bar/Restaurant, Mojacar Playa. ☎950-473099; e-mail beachcomberjohn@gmail.com.

Balearic Islands: *Federación Balear de Pesca.* ☎971-463315; e-mail fbpescaic@telefonica.net.

Canary Islands: *Federación Canaria de Pesca:* ☎922-240219.

Golf

Spain has over 180 golf clubs, most of which are relatively new, well maintained and equipped with modern landscaping and design, varied layout and complementary services such as swimming pools, gyms etc. Golf is particularly popular in Spain because the climate ensures around 300 golfing days a year.

Unfortunately it is only recently that the Spanish have taken up golf and for this reason there are still insufficient courses to satisfy the demand. This shortage, coupled with the fact that most courses are privately, rather than municipally, owned makes the sport relatively expensive, as Mac Macdonald has found:

Green fees are currently around €50-70. If you want to join a club out here, you usually have to buy a share in the company that owns the golf course. Then you have to pay a joining fee and the subscription'

Information about golf courses, clubs and green fees can be found at www.golfspain.com. Alternatively contact the Spanish Golf Federation (☎915-552682; www.golfspainfederacion.com).

Scuba Diving

Diving has been dubbed an 'extreme sport', largely because many of its enthusiasts choose to plunge themselves to extreme depths, or into icy temperatures. However, diving in Spain is one of the most relaxing pastimes around. Those who pursue it are able to glide effortlessly through ethereal underwater worlds and experience colourful, and beautiful displays that are inaccessible to land tourists. The calm, warm waters of Spain's coasts make this an even more pleasant experience.

Scuba diving is open to anyone who is in good health and most diving centres will take complete beginners out for a try dive after just a brief medical check up. After that, it takes just five days to become a fully-fledged PADI (*Professional Association of Diving Instructors*) Open Water Diver, a qualification that allows you to dive anywhere in the world without the need for an instructor.

There are hundreds of dive centres in Spain, and the most popular locations are undoubtedly the warm waters of the Canary Islands (particularly Tenerife), the Balearic Islands, and all along the Mediterranean coast. It is always best to find a centre that is attached to PADI (most centres in Spain are). A full list of affiliated diving schools can be found at www.padi.com.

It is necessary to obtain a permit to dive in certain areas. Further information on diving permits and local facilities should be sought from the relevant regional subaqua federation. A full list of these can be found at www.tourspain.co.uk/sports/diving.htm.

For further information contact the Spanish Subaquatic Federation (*Federación de Actividades Subacuaticas;* ☎ 932-006769; www.fedas.es).

Las Islas Medias – A Diving Haven

This tiny archipelago just a mile off the Costa Brava has been declared a marine reserve and is the natural habitat of some 1,350 classifications of marine life, including octopus, bream, lobster, starfish and occasional dolphins and whale sharks. The islets are well known amongst divers due mainly to the massive population of fish and other plant-life not found anywhere else in Spain. There are also caves and a shipwreck to explore. There are organised dives for all levels.

Further Information: L'Estartit Tourist Office: ☎ 972-751910; www.ajuntament.gi.
Useful Diving Contacts: Medaqua (☎ 972-752043; www.medaqua.com); Calypso Diving (☎ 972-751488); Estación Nautica (☎ 972-750699; www.enestartit.com).

Skiing

Spain may not be the first place that one associates with skiing, but in fact it is the second most mountainous country in Europe (behind Switzerland), and as such offers the skier a surprising number of options. There are 36 ski resorts spread around the country, from the Pyrenees in the north, to the most southerly ski resort in Europe just outside Granada.

Spain's resorts cater for every level, although those looking for the most advanced slopes will be restricted to the Pyrenees. The largest and most popular resort is Baqueira-Beret in the Catalonian Pyrenees, which offers some of the best pistes in Europe for experienced skiers.

The Sierra Nevada ski resort is very unusual. Due to the high altitude (over 3000m), it is possible to ski whilst enjoying warm rays of Mediterranean sunshine, and during certain parts of the season, it is even possible to ski in the mornings and sunbathe on the beach in the afternoon. There are also spectacular views from the Laguna and Veleta pistes, and on a clear day it is possible to see the Rif mountains of Morrocco. Another advantage is that the slopes are just twenty-five minutes from one of Europe's most important monumental cities – Granada, the home of the Alhambra

All of Spain's ski resorts offer lessons for every level. A full list of resorts can be found at www.spain.info. For further information about skiing and snowboarding in Spain contact the Spanish Winter Sports Association (*Real Federación Española de Deportes de Invierno:* www.rfedi.es; ☎913-769930), or visit the following websites: www.ifyouski.com; www.goski.com; www.skicentral.com; www.pyrenees.co.uk.

Pop across the border to Andorra's high slopes and low prices

Andorra is no longer the place for a dirt-cheap skiing holiday, but you can still spend a week in far greater comfort than you would get for the same price in the Alps. The skiing here is varied and two of the main ski resorts, Soldeu and Pas de la Casa have recently joined forces, creating Grandvalira – one of Europe's largest resorts, with 120 miles of pistes. Grandvalira offers perfect slopes for beginners and intermediates, with wide, uncrowded pistes. An adult ski pass for six days, with access to all areas costs €168.50 and a week's course of five lessons with a British instructor costs just £67 (☎00 376-890591). Andorra's duty-free rates on alcohol, cigarettes and electronic goods make it the ideal place for a combined shopping and skiing trip. For further information contact Ski Andorra ☎00 376-890670

Try the following ski operators for deals in Andorra:

Inghams: www.inghams.co.uk; ☎ 020-8780 4433

Neilson: www.neilson.co.uk; ☎ 0870-333 3347

Directski.com: www.directski.com; ☎ 0800-587 0945

Walking

Those living in the crowded resort areas will find that they don't have to travel very far inland to find exciting scenery, wildlife and terrain, and the beauty of Spain's countryside is that it is possible to spend an entire day walking without seeing another soul. Spain has some vast national parks, such as the Picos de Europa in Asturias, where the walking can be as challenging or as relaxing as you choose. It also offers ancient pilgrim trails, such as the world-famous Camino de Santiago, which can be walked all year round. Whether you want to take a walking holiday, camping or staying in *refugios* (refuges), or just spend a day hiking, the wild open spaces of Spain are a delight.

The Best Walks in Spain

Sierra de Gredos. Just a short distance from Madrid lie the Gredos mountains, the most dramatic section of the Sistema Central. Whilst not as high as the Picos de Europa, there are fabulous views across the plains of Salamanca and the bull ranches of Extremadura. The main trails are in good condition and the best walking is to be found in the wooded foot hills and river valleys of La Vera. (www.walksworldwide.com)

Picos de Europa. The Picos are an awe-inspiring range of rugged peaks, 40 km long and 20 km wide and made up of three ranges separated by rivers and deep gorges. The best walking is around the impressive Narajo de Bulnes mountain. This area is also popular with cavers. (www.exodus.co.uk)

The Alpujarras. The foothills of the Sierra Nevada, just 50 km inland from the Mediterranean offer extremely picturesque walks through Moroccan-style villages, dramatic ravines, orchards and woodlands. The GR7 path runs through these hills and is clearly marked out.(www.ramblersholidays.co.uk)

The Pyrenees. 435km of jagged peaks run from the Bay of Biscay to the Med and offer some fantastic hiking terrain. The three areas that stand out for walking are the canyons of the Ordesa National Park, the Hecho Valley, and the lakes and mountains of the Aiguestortes national park. (www.altoaragon.co.uk).

Many retirees in Spain have taken up rambling as a means of staying fit and healthy and of meeting new people. There are English-speaking walking clubs in all of the main expatriate areas, which can be found in the expat press. Some of the regional tourist offices also now offer guided walks and offer maps and leaflets, so go in and enquire. There are also several good regional walking guides published by Santana Books (www.santanabooks. com), Cicerone Press (www.cicerone.co.uk) and Sunflower Books (www. sunflowerbooks.co.uk). Footpaths (*senderos*) exist in mountainous areas, and long distance paths are called *Senderos de Gran Recorrido* (GR) or *Penqueño Recorrido*. There are also 7000kms of disused railway lines in Spain, which have been recovered for hiking and cycling (see *Cycling* above).

Mountain Walking in Retirement – Clodagh and Dick Handscome

Clodagh and Dick took up mountain walking and leading walks when they retired to Spain. We asked them:

What made you take up mountain walking?

Firstly to regain a level of strength and fitness lost in busy working years and secondly, to see Spain in a way that is not possible by car.

How difficult is the walking in Spain?

There's something for everyone, whether they are used to gentle walks in the Cotswolds or more strenuous hikes, but the surfaces of tracks and paths are generally hard and rocky. Rarely is there the luxury of walking on grassly downlands or soft muddy paths. Nevertheless, there are many long distance walks that are suitable for fit retirees, such as the pilgrim route to Santiago de Compostela, and the marked routes from Andorra to Gibraltar and from Valencia to Lisbon.

What was your first experience of long-distance walking in Spain?

We decided to walk across the Pyrenees, with just backpacks and a tent. This was something that we had never done before, but we had our reasons for doing it. Dick wanted to prove that he was fit after two cancer operations and both of us wanted to see whether our emergent relationship was for life. The walk took us 52 days in which we walked some 940 kilometres and climbed up and down 32,000 metres. It was a real roller coaster through wonderful scenery, wildlife and deserted villages. AND the walk worked. We got married shortly afterwards.

Do you have any advice for walking in retirement?

Yes. Wear good boots and use two walking poles to take the strain off your hips, knees and ankles. Don't worry that some people will think you're going skiing!

Useful Contacts

Federació d'Entitats Excursionistes de Catalunya: (Catalonia walking society)
☎934-120777; www.feec.es.

Euskal Mendiazele Federakundea: (Basque) ☎943-743172.

Federación Navarra de Deportes de Montaña: (Navarra) ☎948-427848.

Federacion Territorial Valenciana de Muntanyisme: (Valencia) ☎965-439747.

Federación Aragonesa de Montañismo: (Aragon) ☎976-227971.

Other Sports and Pastimes

Art: If you intend to spend part of your retirement improving your own technique, Spain has some stunning scenery to inspire you. Many towns run art courses, and the best place to find out about them is the local *Casa de Cultura*. Spain is universally recognised as having produced some of the world's greatest and most startlingly original painters: Velasquez, El Greco, Murillo, Ribera, Picasso, Dali and Miro to name but a few. For art enthusiasts there are many museums and galleries in which to while away hours of your retirement. One of the most famous art museums in the world is the Prado in Madrid, which houses works by all the Spanish masters.

Must-See Spanish Galleries and Museums

Prado Museum, Madrid: Open 9am-9pm including fiesta days. Free admission on
   Sundays. http://museoprado.mcu.es.

Catalonian Art Museum, Barcelona: 10am-7pm, closed Mondays. www.mnac.es.

Picasso Museum, Barcelona: Open 10am-8pm. Sundays and holidays 10am-3pm.
   Closed Mondays. www.museupicasso.bcn.es.

Picasso Museum, Malaga: Open 10am-8pm. Closed Mondays. www.musco
   picassomalaga.org.

Dali Museum, Figueras: Open 9am-9pm in Summer. www.salvado-dali.org.

El Greco Museum, Toledo: Open 10am-2pm and 4pm-6pm. Closed Mondays.
   Free entry on Saturday afterbiib and Sunday morning. ☎925-224405.

Guggenheim Museum, Bilbao. Open 10am-8pm. Closed Mondays. www.
   guggenheim-bilbao.es.

National Museum of Abstract Spanish Art, Cuenca. Open 10am-2pm and 4pm-
   7pm. Closed on Mondays. ☎969-213069.

National Museum of Roman Art, Merida. Open 10am-2pm and 4pm 6pm. Closed
   Sunday afternoon and Mondays. Free admission Saturday afternoon and Sunday
   Morning. www.mnar.es.

Ballooning: This is the perfect way to escape the world below and see some of the stunning landscape that Spain has to offer (whilst enjoying a glass of chilled *cava*).

Useful Contacts

Vol de Coloms. Balloon trips from Santa Pau, Catalonia. 90 minute trip including cava and cake costs around €150. ☎972-680255; www.garrotxa.com/voldecoloms.
Baló Tour: Flights over Catalonia. ☎934-144774; www.balotour.com.
Flying Circus: Flights from Madrid, Aranjuez and Segovia. www.flyingcircus.es

Canyon Descending: Also known simply as canyoning, this sport began in the 19th century in Spain and involves abseiling, climbing, hiking, swimming and jumping. It may sound as though you'd have to be a professional athlete to give it a try, but in fact most activities are suitable for anyone who is relatively fit. The advantage of this sport is that it really does offer access to untouched and stunning environments. The best canyoning location in Spain is the Sierra de Guara nature park in the Aragónese Pyrenees, which offers around 60 descents for all levels. One of the most attractive on a sunny day is the Cañon de la Peonara. Descending this gorge involves 8 hours of swimming and jumping through natural pools and cascades. Mallorca and Tenerife also offer good canyoning opportunities. The average price per day is around €50-80, which includes a professional guide, equipment, camping and insurance.

Useful Contacts

Speleo Club Cantabro: www.barrancos.tk
Expediciones: ☎974-343008; www.expediciones-sc.es
Exploramas: ☎952-599000; www.exploramas.com
www.barranquismo.com

Flying: For those interested in recreational flying, Spain has 55 flying clubs located at national and international airports. To find your nearest one, contact the *Real Aero Club de España* (☎914-298534). There are also 46 aerodromes, a few of which have their own flying clubs. In order to obtain flying credentials in Spain, you must have a licence from FENDA – the *Federación Española de Deportes Aereos* (www.rfae.org).

Horse Riding: Spain is a paradise for horse-lovers. The Spanish have a long historical relationship with horses, and they are always in evidence during parades and fiestas. Horse-riding allows you access to untouched areas of beauty and wherever you are in Spain it is likely that there will be stables nearby that offer trekking excursions. For further information throughout Spain contact the *Real Federación de Hipica Española* (☎914-364200; www.rfhe.com).

Hunting: Spain offers some fantastic hunting and shooting opportunities as there are many large, private reserves, stocked with deer, wild boar, chamois, goats, and mouflons. Small game includes red-leg partridges, quails and duck among others. However, all shooting activities are strictly regulated in Spain and permits are required. Weapon licences can be obtained at any police station. As with fishing, permits can be applied for at the *Agencia Medio Ambiente* office (the local council's environment office). They also produce a calendar of the hunting seasons that indicates the zones and time periods that hunting is permitted for specific species.

Useful Contacts

Spanish Hunting Federation: *Federacion Española de Caza;*   ☎915-539017.
www.tourspain.co.uk/Sports/Fising_Hunting.htm (sic): List of autonomous
   regional medio ambiente offices.
Spanish Consulate: ☎020-7589 8989 (for details of importing firearms into Spain).

Theatre and Music: Spain has recently completed a massive construction programme for musical auditoria, which has meant more halls for symphony and chamber orchestras around the country. There are also numerous classical, jazz and pop festivals held in Spain's major cities throughout the summer (see local festivals towards the end of this chapter). For opera fans there are regular seasons in Madrid, Barcelona, Oviedo, Bilbao and other cities. A good source of theatre, ballet, opera and pop music tickets in Spain is www.es.lastminute.com.

Windsurfing and Kite Surfing: Spain's varied coastline offers many windsurfing opportunities for all levels. Although virtually unheard of ten years ago, kitesurfing is one of the most popular and fastest growing water-sports in Spain. It is exactly what it sounds like – a combination of surfing and flying a kite, and is much easier to master than windsurfing, although it can be quite an extreme sport when the wind is up. Tarifa, on the southern-most tip of Spain has become the windsurfing and kitesurfing capital of Europe thanks to its consistent strong winds, and is the best place to go to learn or improve.

Useful Contacts

Kitesurfing Pro Centre: ☎956-681668; www.kitesurfingtarifa.com

Dos Mares Hotel: (has a kitesurfing and windsurfing school attached) ☎956-684035; www.dosmares.com

www.tarifaweb.com

www.windsurfspain.com

TAKING COURSES

The Spanish government is very keen to keep its seniors mentally astute and fully active members of society as this contributes greatly to their quality of life in retirement. There are many courses on offer for the older student, so there is every chance you can find one that interests you or develops an earlier interest that you have not had time to pursue in more depth.

For those whose Spanish is up to it, many of the Spanish public universities offer free courses for people aged over 55, under a programme known as *Programa Universidad para Mayores*. The courses may vary according to the university, but as well as the standard courses, most offer a diploma created specifically for older people. These can be quite challenging courses, lasting 450 hours, spread over three academic terms from October to June. In order to find more information about the courses run specifically for *mayores* at your local university visit www.aepumayores.org, the website of Spain's National Association of University Programmes for Older Adults (AEPUM).

There are also other regional government funded classes, for example there are many courses run for older people, that concentrate on *Informatica* – computers, the internet, e-mail etc. However, as education is thoroughly devolved in Spain it is very difficult to generalise about what is available. The best way to find out is to visit the following website: www. imsersomayores.csic.es/programas/ccaa.html, and choose your region.

Public Universities Offering Courses Specifically for Older Students

A Coruña: www.udc.es	**La Rioja:** www.umh.es
Alicante: www.ua.es/upua	**Las Palmas (Gran Canaria):** www.ulpgc.es
Avila: www.ucavila.es	
Balearic Islands: www.uib.es/uom	**Lleida:** www.ice.udl.es/uas
Barcelona: www.blues.uab.es	**Madrid:** www.uam.es
Barcelona: www.ub.es	**Madrid:** www.ucm.es/info/umayores
Basque Country: www.ehu.es/aulas experiencia	**Madrid:** www.fundacion.uc3m.es
	Madrid: www.upco.es
Cadiz: www.uca.es	**Madrid:** www.ceu.es
Cantabria: www.unate.org	**Málaga:** www.uma.es
Castilla la Mancha: www.ulcm.es/universidadmayores/	**Murcia:** www.um.es/promoedu/aulade mayores
Córdoba: www.uco.es	**Navarra:** www.unavarra.es
Extremadura: http://mayors.unex.es	**Santiago de Compostela:** www.usc.es
Extremadura: www.ice.unex.es	**Valencia:** www.vupa.upv.es
Granada: www.ugr.es	**Valencia:** www.uv.es
Huelva: www.uhu.es	**Valladolid:** www.uva.es
Jaén: www.ujaen.es	**Vigo:** www.apv.uvigo.es
La Laguna: www.ull.es	**Zaragoza:** www.unizar.es

Local governments typically sponsor a wide variety of educational activities for people of all ages. In order to find out about courses in your area, enquire at the town hall (*ayuntamiento*). Most towns have a *Casa de Cultura,* which is municipally sponsored and offers inexpensive courses in all sorts of Spanish arts and crafts and traditions such as pottery, weaving, and flamenco. If your interests lie in music then the ayuntamiento will direct you to the nearest public conservatory, where, even if you do not find public classes, a simple enquiry will certainly find you a private teacher. Those interested in more vigorous pursuits will be directed to the municipally sponsored *polideportivo* which typically offers classes in yoga, tai chi, aerobics etc.

Courses in English are provided by the University of the Third Age (see below) and privately. Take a look at the classifieds in the English-language press, where you will find private teachers for most pursuits.

Most British expats have at some point taken Spanish classes, and as such it is a very good way to meet people in a similar situation to yourself. You will find Spanish classes advertised in the local expatriate press, on local college notice-boards, and on any web-based notice-boards for the area. Alternatively you could advertise for a language exchange in the local press. The cheapest way to learn Spanish is almost certainly by enrolling at the nearest *Escuela Oficial de Idiomas*. These are government funded language schools that now offer courses in Spanish for foreigners at a range of levels. The price per semester is currently just €88.95 (there are two semesters per year). Further information: www.eoidiomas.com.

University of the Third Age

Those living in the Costa del Sol, the Costa Blanca or the Costa Brava have easy access to free, English-language courses run by the University of the Third Age. The U3A, as it is known, is an educational and social association which began in France in the 1970s. There are now around 1,773 U3As in thirty-nine countries, offering free educational courses to people of any age that are not in full-time employment.

The U3A is quite a unique organisation in that it has no paid teachers. Everybody involved is a volunteer and they teach whatever subject they have gained expertise in during their working life. The U3A in Calpe for example has around 50 different courses ranging from creative writing to computing, gardening to genealogy and Painting to Petanc. According to Mary Anderton, one of the founder members of the Calpe group, history and Spanish have proved to be the most popular, but the range of courses is constantly increasing. Members of the U3A pay a levy of around €12 per year, which entitles them to attend the courses that attract their interest.

The U3A is as much a social institution as it is educational, and runs events and trips within Spain and abroad. For Mary Anderton, the social aspect has been very important to the wide appeal of the organisation:

'Part of the reason we have been so popular amongst expatriates here is the feeling of camaraderie that is gained from joining. Many people have told me that they found it very difficult to make friendships when they first arrived in Spain, but that joining the U3A made them change their minds about returning to the UK. Members work together in small groups, but we also have much larger meetings once a month at which everybody comes together. Three years ago in Calpe we only had 50 members, now we have more than 500.'

Costa Brava: www.u3acostabrava.org
Costa Blanca: http://u3acalpe.org
Costa del Sol: www.u3acostadelsol.org

GARDENING AND HORTICULTURE

Only thirty years ago, Spain was still very much a rural country with an agriculturally-based economy. Whilst economic liberalisation and industrialisation have come on in leaps and bounds, the Spanish still have a special relationship with the land and its produce, which is celebrated in traditional festivals and ferias up and down the country. New arrivals to Spain are often delighted by how well fruit and vegetables flourish in the Mediterranean sunshine, and this was certainly the case for ex-pat Michael Harvey, who now runs a nursery in Andalucia: *'We were amazed at how quickly things grow here, and there's so much variety. It is so much better than gardening in England. Just in our orchard we have mangoes, bananas, lemons, limes, grapefruits and oranges.'*

But the Spanish do not exclusively till the land in order to produce food for the table. A visit to the annual *Festival de los Patios*, held in Córdoba each May, where private patios displaying oases of colour are opened to the public, is proof enough that they take an enormous amount of pride in the aesthetic rewards of gardening. Even in larger cities it is common to see apartment balconies overflowing with brightly coloured blooms.

For many retirees to Spain, the ability to spend so much time in the garden is one of the greatest pleasures of their new life. As expat David Kitching puts it: *'Some of my happiest hours have been spent outside with my trowel!'*

Gardening in Spain – Clodagh and Dick Handscombo

Clodagh and Dick are practical gardeners who have a colourful flower garden and harvest fresh fruit and vegetables 365 days a year. They were recently described in the local press as 'the new Good Life couple'! They have this to say about gardening in Spain:

Gardening is the number one hobby for us and many others who have retired to Spain and for good reasons:

1. *Gardens in Spain are to live in and not to look at through the window. The climate allows them to be enjoyed throughout the year once there is summer shade and shelter from cold winter winds. And the long spells of sunny autumn, winter and spring weather are ideal for developing new gardens from scratch or improving mature gardens.*

2. *There are an amazing number of colourful often perfumed plants of all sizes that can be grown in Spain by the amateur gardener.*
3. *In many areas it is possible to grow and harvest a diversity of healthy fruit and vegetables 365 days a year.*
4. *The design, development and maintenance of a garden with different soils, climate and plants can provide invaluable mental and physical exercise.*
5. *A Spanish garden gives many retired couples the chance to work together on an inspiring and satisfying lifetime project without the constraints of work or family ties.*

We know of retired couples whose only hobby is gardening and who slave away for many hours a day to create an enviable botanical garden. But most also want to follow other interests. It is therefore important to :

- *Clarify the lifestyle you plan to achieve in Spain and the role your garden will play. For most it will be important to provide places to rest, siesta, cook al fresco, eat, exercise and enjoy a sundowner.*
- *Design a garden that will be manageable both in the short term and as you grow older.*
- *Decide whether you will do all the landscaping and planting yourself or employ a gardener or landscaper to help you make faster progress.*
- *Decide whether you will have only a flower garden or include a few fruit trees and even grow your own organic vegetables to be harvested daily when at their best. For example, a 'lunar' lemon that flowers and fruits several times a year will ensure a supply for cooking and G&T's, an orange tree: your daily vitamin C, an olive tree: olives for pickling each winter and an almond tree: spring blossom and a summer harvest of nuts.*

Clodagh and Dick Handscombe have written three books on gardening in Spain: 'Your Garden in Spain – practical ideas for gardens that suit your Spanish lifestyle' and 'How to Grow Your Own Vegetables and Fruit in Spain', both published by Santana Books (www.santanabooks.com), and 'Practical Gardening on the Costa', published by Costa Blanca News s.l. (www.costablanca-news.com).

As the expatriate population grows, new gardening clubs are springing up along the coast and further inland. They advertise their meetings in local English-language newspapers and magazines. There is also a growing network of informative garden centres, some expatriate owned, and local agricultural co-operatives can be helpful. Interesting Botanical gardens exist in Lloret de Mar, Blanes, Valencia, Malaga and Madrid and the gardens of many monastery and palace gardens open to the public, such as the Alhambra in Granada, can be an inspiration.

TRAVELLING AND TOURISM IN SPAIN

Most foreigners retiring to Spain expect to travel widely within their adopted country. Spain has so much to offer in terms of landscapes, coasts and history that you could spend the majority of your time in retirement travelling around and still not see it all. The best place to find information is the Spanish National Tourist Office, which has a huge network of local offices in the towns and cities. It is beyond the scope of this book to explore all of the travelling opportunities in Spain, but listed below are some ideas of how to make the most of your retirement in Spain.

Beach breaks

Whether or not you like to partake in the straw donkey and banana boat tourism that has grown up around the Spanish costas, it was the country's superb beaches that first attracted foreigners to Spain in large numbers, and is still doing so. Spain's beaches offer sugar-white sand, lapped by clear turquoise waters, and the climate allows you to enjoy many of them all year around. If you want a seaside break, complete with nightclubs and entertainment centres, then you have a wealth of resorts on the costas to choose from. However, the tourist centres do get very crowded in the summer and as a resident of Spain you have the time and resources to find more tranquil, unspoiled beaches where the only cause of stress is deciding which bar to watch the sunset from. The Spanish National Tourist Office (www.spain.info) lists each beach by region. Below is a pick of the best beaches mainland Spain has to offer.

Mainland Spain's Best Beaches by Coast

Mediterranean Coast – North East to South West

Costa Brava – L'Estartit. Long beach of fine golden sand joined to the little fishing village of L'Estartit. Just 2km offshore are the Illes Medes, which offer some of Spain's best snorkelling and scuba diving.

Costa Dorada – Platja de San Sebastián, Sitges. Calm waters and fine sand in the shadow of Sitges' steepled church, One of the most scenic beaches on the coast.

Costa del Azahar – Peñiscola. Sandy beach fronting a very pretty town, overlooked by a fourteenth century castle. Offers visitors the perfect seaside break.

Costa Valencia – Playa de la Devesa, Parc Natural de L'Albufera. This beach is situated in the heart of a nature reserve and offers miles of golden sand, backed by dunes and pine groves. Although it feels isolated there are good services and a handful of beach bars. Also good for sailing and windsurfing.

Costa Blanca North – Les Rotes, Parque Natural de Montgó. Series of stunning coves backed by the natural park. The beach offers snorkelling and scuba diving, and secluded bays for those who want to get away from it all.

Costa Blanca South – Isla de Tabarca, off the coast of Elche. The beaches on this 2km long island are only accessible by boat from Alicante, Santa Pola or Torrevieja. It is a perfect day trip to get away from the hoards and discover isolated bays to swim in.

Costa Calida – Playa Cala Bolete Grande, Cabo Tiñoso, Cartagena. Beautiful, unspoiled beach with clear blue sea, only accessible by foot from La Azohía. Also very good for diving if you have your own equipment.

Costa de Almeria – Cala de Monsul, San José, Parque Natural Cabo de Gata-Nijar. Again accessible only by foot or by sturdy car along unpaved roads, this is an extremely beautiful, horseshoe-shaped bay offering tranquillity amongst the dunes.

Costa Tropical – Playa el Muerto, Cotobra beach, Almuñecar. A real treat to find. A path from the crowded Cotobro beach weaves through the jutting rocks to this tranquil haven of sand, shingle and calm water.

Costa del Sol – La Rada Beach, Estepona. Wide swathes of sand, gentle waters and one of the cleanest beaches on the costa. The beach is separated from the town centre by a palm lined promenade. A good place for water sports.

Atlantic Coast – South West to North East

Costa de la Luz – Zahara de los Atunes. Golden beach backed by dunes and the very attractive village of Zahara, which is famous for its tuna. The beach rarely becomes overcrowded and the resort is extremely peaceful.

Rías Baixas – Isla Monte Faro, Islas Cíes, Rias Bajas, Galicia. Just off the coast of Vigo lie the tiny Cíes Islands, accessible only by boat from June to September. The east side of the island offers calm waters for swimming and sandy unspoiled beaches. There is also very good bird-watching here.

Rías Altas – Playa de Covas, Viviero, Rias Altas, Galicia. White sand beach with calm waters and a long promenade. The beach resort is close to the charming seaside town of Viviero.

Costa Verde – Playa de San Lorenzo, Gijón, Asturias. The most popular beach in Asturias, accessible from the city of Gijón. It offers 1.5 km of sand and good facilities.

Costa Vasca – Zarautz, Basque Country. One of the best surfing beaches in Spain with huge waves and equipment rental readily available. Non-surfers will also enjoy the attractive old town centre and the waterfront promenade.

Green Tourism

The traditional beach holiday will always be popular, but for some the crowded resorts, the heavy traffic of the coastal roads and the late-night noise of youthful revellers have lost their appeal. Radically improved transport systems in the interior of the country have allowed the backwaters of Spain to enter the limelight, as increasing numbers of tourists seek areas of natural beauty and tranquillity and an insight into more traditional ways of life. Recognising the appeal of this form of tourism, the Spanish government has ploughed billions of euros into increasing rural facilities, and there is now a comprehensive range of accommodation, as well as exciting activities such as pony trekking, walking, cycling, canoeing etc. on offer.

Casas Rurales. There are more than 6000 official country houses, and many more that have not registered. Accommodation at these varies from bed and breakfast at a farmhouse to half-board or self-catering in a restored manor. Most are in beautiful locations and offer wonderful hiking terrain right on your doorstep. Todo Turismo Rural (☎914-659567; www.todoturismorural.com) is a nationwide organisation offering a variety of accommodation.

National Parks. Large areas of Spain's wild and beautiful terrain have been set aside for the purposes of preservation and for the enjoyment of nature lovers and ramblers. Visits to the national parks should be organised in advance via your local tourist office. Further information on the individual parks is available from www.mma.es or from the Spanish National Tourist Office: www.spain.info

---

Top 5 National Parks in Spain

In a recent survey conducted by the daily Spanish newspaper, *El Pais,* readers voted for their favourite national parks, providing an 'insider's guide' on where to go:

1. Parque Nacional de los Picos de Europa. Provinces: Asturias, Leon and Cantabria. This was the first area of Spain to be declared a national park in 1918. The park is made up of 64,660Ha of territory lying in the highest part of the mountain range, with 200 peaks above 2000m. Guided tours available from July to September. Recommended visiting time: 2 to 4 days. Contact: ☎985-848614; e-mail guias.picos@oapn.mma.es.

2. Parque Nacional Ordesa y Monte Perdido. Province: Huesca. 15,607Ha. Recommended visiting time: 2-4 days. Contact: ☎974-243361.

3. Parque Nacional de Doñana. Provinces: Huelva and Seville. 50,720Ha. Free entrance to the park, but guided visits by car offered for €21. Recommended visiting time: 2 to 3 days. Contact: ☎959-448640.

4. Parque Nacional de Sierra Nevada. Provinces: Granada and Almeria. 86,208Ha. Free access to the park. Guided tours available. Information on possible routes available from the park office. Recommended visiting time: 3 to 5 days. Contact: ☎958-026300; e-mail sierra.nevada@oapn.mma.es.

5. Parque Nacional de Cabañeros. Provinces: Toledo and Ciudad Real. 40,000Ha. Walking tours need to be booked in advance. Guided 4x4 tours available from Conserfo (☎926-775384). Contact: ☎926-783297; e-mail icabaneros@oapn.mma.es.

Specialist Breaks

Activity Breaks. If you fancy a week or two of kayaking, abseiling and caving, no experience required, there are several companies that will offer a package of hotels and activities. Try *The Adventure Company* (www.adventurecompany.co.uk; ☎0845-450 5311). They are a UK company, but offer packages excluding flights, which can be organised from Spain.

Cooking. *Tasting Places* offers 6 night breaks in Seville that allow you to discover the cuisine and wines of Andalucia. Learn how to make the best tapas and regional dishes. Contact: ☎020-74600077; www.tastingplaces.com.

Dancing. *Dance Holidays* offer short breaks all over Spain, combining specialist dance lessons from Flamenco to Salsa with a chance to explore a new city. Contact: ☎0870-286 6000; www.danceholidays.com.

Golfing Holidays. Atlantee Golf Clubs Association operates a voucher system that allows clients to enjoy eight of the best golf clubs in Andalucia. Further information: www.atlantee-golf.com.

Horse Riding. There are many companies in Spain offering guided horse-riding breaks through Spain's countryside. Try *Ride Worldwide* (☎01837-82544; www.rideworldwide.com).

Yoga. *Spain Yoga* offers yoga and tai chi holidays in the tranquil surroundings of the Alpujarras, Andalucia. ☎958-785834; www.spainyoga.com.

Naturist Holidays. One of the many things to flourish after the end of the Franco regime was naturism and around 400,000 Spaniards regularly practice it. Over 220 beaches are designated *'playas naturistas'* and there are naturist resorts such as Eagle Peak (www.eaglepeakspain.com) and naturist second homes (www.selectvillas.org). There is even a nude run held in July each year in protest against Pamplona's Bull Run (www.runningofthenudes.com). It seems that Spain is the place to let it all hang out.

Spa Holidays. If the relaxing lifestyle of the retiree gets too hectic for you, then a visit to one of Spain's many spa complexes may be the answer. Spa holidays are one of the latest trends in short breaks and a range of new complexes have sprung up in recent years. A visit to a spa is all about pampering and relaxation and offers a combination of healthy cuisine, wellness seminars and a range of body treatments:

Hotel Botanica, Tenerife: Contact: ☎922-486000; www.hotelbotanico.com.
Gran Hotel Elba, Estepona: Contact: ☎952-809200; www.slh.com/elba
   estepona.
Ecologic Natural Spa, Palma de Mallorca: Contact ☎971-768587.
Hotel Balneario Alhama, Granada: Contact: ☎958-350011; www.balneario
   alhamadegranada.com
Incosol Hotel and Spa, Marbella. Contact: ☎052 868771; www.incosol.com

Skydiving. UK company *Black Tomato* (☎020-7610 9008; www.blacktomato. co.uk) offers skydiving breaks in the foothills of the Pyrenees, which includes 2 days training and 2 days of skydiving. Their standard package includes flights from the UK, but those already in Spain can order a tailor-made break.

Water Sports Holidays. Spain has a number of *Estaciones Nauticas,* water sports resorts where you can book a package that includes your favourite activities and accommodation. There are currently fifteen such resorts located at popular water sports destinations. Contact: ☎902-361489; www. estacionesnauticas.info.

Wine Tours. Spain has over 50% of the EU's vineyards, producing a range of wines. The most famous are Rioja and Ribera del Duero reds, recognised as some of the finest wines in the world. More and more vineyards are offering tours and tastings, so it is simply a matter of finding the closest to you and enquiring. If you are looking for a longer wine tasting tour, there are many companies offering just that. Try Vintage Spain (www. vintagespain.com).

Accommodation

Accommodation in Spain ranges from the luxury, state-sponsored Paradors to simple Fondas and campsites. The Spanish Tourist Office website has a facility to search for any type of accommodation in any region (www.spain.info). Many hotels offer reductions for pensioners, though there are no official regulations. It is always advisable to book accommodation well in advance, particularly during festivals, fiestas, public holidays and in August when most of the country is on holiday.

- **Campsites.** Camping is a very popular option in Spain and there are over 1000 *campings* or *campamentos turisticos*, which receive around 6 million guests per year. Campsites can be booked directly or via the *Federación Española de Empresarios de Campings* (☎914-481234; www.fed-camping.com). Lists of campsites are available from the Spanish Tourist Office, and in the Camping Federation's annual *Guia de Campings*.
- **Fondas.** Identifiable by a square blue sign with a white F, these are the least expensive of places to stay in Spain and are often positioned above bars.

Fondas are slowly disappearing as Spain upgrades its tourist facilities.

○ **Casas de Huéspedes/Pensiones/Hospedajes.** Simple guesthouses. The distinction between these has blurred over the years, but all three are fairly cheap options for tourists.

○ **Hostales.** These are far more common and although slightly more expensive than the above, they offer good functional rooms, often with a private shower. They are categorised from one to three stars.

○ **Hoteles.** There are more than 10,000 hotels to choose from ranging from the basic to the most luxurious. Spanish hotels are star-graded from one to five, but stars are granted by the regional governments and hence standards vary from region to region.

○ **Casas Rurales.** Country houses in beautiful rural locations.

○ **Paradors.** Spain's state-run five-star hotels are for those looking for a stay with real character and luxury. The paradors are a unique range of converted castles, palaces and historic buildings, all offering comfort and excellent service. There are currently 91 paradors in Spain, with more than half of them in historic buildings. Further information is available from www.parador.es.

Stay in a Cave

For something completely different, try staying in one of the stunningly located caves of inland Andalucia. They have been totally refurbished with luxury modern living facilities and make an interesting alternative to run-of-the-mill accommodation. Temperatures inside are a constant 19°C, even if it is baking hot outside.

Cuevas P.A. de Alarcón: www.cuevaspedroantonio.com; ☎958-664986.

Minotel España S.L.: ☎952-052560.

Promociones Turísticas de Galera: ☎958-739068.

Rail

The Spanish national rail network, RENFE (*Red Nacional de los Ferrocarriles Españoles*) has a length of around 13,000km; it stretches out from the centre point of Madrid where its three principal lines begin, two of which extend to the French frontier crossing the Basque country and Catalonia and the third to Andalucia and Levante. There are three types of train: the local trains: *cercanías*, the regional trains: *regionales*, and the long-distance trains: *grandes líneas*. Long distance trains are graded and priced according to their speed. Talgo 200, TER, AVE, InterCity, Trenhotel and Estrella require the largest supplements. Cercanías run very frequently and cover the surrounding towns and villages. It is possible to buy a season ticket for these trains, which is also valid on the city buses and metro.

The fastest trains are called *Alta Velocidad Española* (*AVE*), and are the Spanish equivalent of the French TGV. AVE routes are currently fairly limited, but the project is ongoing and will eventually cover most of Spain's intercity routes. Those travelling long distances might like to consider the Trenhotel service, which runs overnight and offers compact compartments with bunk beds.

Trains are clean, comfortable and generally reliable. As already mentioned, there are concessions for seniors on train travel with the *Tarjeta Dorada* (see above). It is always advisable to reserve your seats. It is advisable to make reservations in advance since station ticket offices have erratic opening hours. Instead, go to the RENFE office in town or to any travel agent. All train fares and times can be viewed on the website www.renfe.es, which has a booking service in English. Telephone ☎902-240202 (domestic) or ☎934-243402 (international) for information and reservations. From the UK tickets can be bought from Spanish Rail (☎020-7224 0345; www.spanish-rail.co.uk).

Tourist Trains

The following are specially run trains which follow routes of great natural beauty and/or cultural value. Most are seasonal. Bookings must be made in Spain through local travel agents or directly with the operators.

El Transcantabrico: San Sebastian – Santiago de Compostela. March to June. ☎914-533800; www.transcantabrico.feve.es.

Al Andalus Express: Seville – Ronda – Granada – Madrid. April to June, September to October. ☎915-701621; www.alandalusexpreso.com.

Tren de la Fresa (The Strawberry Train): Madrid – Aranjuez. Saturdays and Sundays, May to October. ☎902-228822.

Limon Expres: Benidorm – Gata. Tuesday to Saturday, all year. ☎966-803103; www.limonexpres.com.

Tren Cremallera: Rives de Freser – Nuria (Gerona). All year. ☎972-732020; www.valldenuria.com.

Tren Turistico del Pirineo: Lerida – Pobla de Segur. February to October. ☎973-290795.

Tren Cremallera de Montserrat: Montserrat Monastery. Every day. ☎932-051
515; www.cremallerademontserrat.com.

Tren de Cervantes: Alcala de Henares. March to June; September to December.
☎918-810634; www.alcalaturismo.com/tren.html.

Ferrocarril Turístico Minero: Rio Tinto Mines (Huelva). ☎959-590025.

Coach and Bus Services

Spain has a very comprehensive bus/coach service and many of the smaller
villages are accessible only by bus if you are reliant on public transport.
Prices are very reasonable, and although the quality of the services varies,
buses are usually fairly reliable and comfortable. Local journey times are
often faster than trains, depending on the route, and at around €5 per
100km, they are certainly cheaper.

The only real drawback with coaches is that many different companies
operate different routes, and finding comprehensive travel information
can be difficult. Although the local bus station provides timetables and
sells tickets for all of the coach companies, many towns still have no main
bus station, or they have several, and buses can leave from a number of
different places.

Those reliant on public transport should bear in mind that buses offer a
drastically reduced service on Sundays and holidays.

Generally seat reservations for the long-distance routes can be made
only a day or two in advance from the bus/coach station or departure
point. The relevant local tourist office can supply details of bus services
in the area.

Internal Flights

Internal air travel is a growing market in Spain and a number of new carriers have sprung up to cope with the demand. Some of these, such as *Vueling Airlines*, have adopted the no-frills philosophy that we have become
accustomed to in the UK, making it easier and cheaper to get around the
country. All of the airlines mentioned below have regular special offers
between various Spanish cities. Bear in mind that budget airline companies operate on a very fine margin of profitability and competition is cut-
throat, so companies and routes come and go.

Air Berlin: ☎901-116402; www.airberlin.com. Departing from/flying to: Alicante, Bilbao, Madrid, Málaga, Palma de Mallorca, Sevilla, Valencia.

Air Europa: ☎902-401501; www.aireuropa.com. Departing from/flying to: most airports in Spain, including Mainland Spain, the Balearic and Canary Islands.

Air Madrid: www.airmadrid.com. Main focus is to fly from Spain to Latin America, but has also started offering low-fare internal routes.

Binter Canarias: ☎902-391392; www.bintercanarias.es. Departing from/flying to: El Hierro, Fuerteventura, Gran Canaria, La Gomera, La Palma, Lanzarotes, Tenerife Norte and Sur.

Futura: www.futuradirect.com. Low fare shuttles from Mallorca to Alicante and Malaga.

Iberia Airlines: ☎902-400500; www.Iberia.com. Departing from/flying to: most Spanish airports including Mainland Spain, the Balearic and Canary Islands.

Lagun Air: www.lagunair.com. Low-fair airline based out of León flying to Madrid, Barcelona, Vaelcia, Alicante, Malaga, Seville, Jerez, Mallorca, Menorca, Ibiza.

Spanair: ☎971-745020; www.spanair.com. Departing from/flying to: A Coroña, Alicante, Barcelona, Bilbao, Fuerteventura, Gran Canaria, Ibiza, Lanzarote, Madrid, Málaga, Menorca, Oviedo, Palma de Mallorca, Santiago de Compostela, Sevilla, Tenerife, Valencia, Vigo.

Vueling Airlines: ☎933-787878; www.vueling.com. Departing from/flying to: Barcelona, Valencia, Bilbao, Palma de Mallorca, Sevilla, Madrid.

Ferries to Spain's Islands and Enclaves

If you tire of mainland Spain, then it is just a short hop across the water from the Costa del Sol to the Spanish enclaves of Ceuta and Melilla, and from the Costas Blanca and Brava to the Balearic Islands. Most people choose to fly to the Canary Islands due to the distance, but if you wanted to take the ferry, there is a regular service from Cadiz.

Balearia: ☎902-160180; www.balearia.com. Daily passenger/car services: Denia – Palma; Ibiza – Palma & Formentera; Barcelona – Ibiza, Alcudia & Ciudadela; Alcudia – Cuidadela.

Buquebus: ☎956-652065; www.buquebus.es. Daily ferry services between Algeciras and Ceuta.

Compañia Trasmediterranea: ☎902-454645; www.trasmediterranea.es. Passenger/car service: Barcelona & Valencia – the Balearic Islands; Denia – Ibiza;

Inter-island services. Also Malaga – Melilla; Almeria – Melilla; Algeciras – Tanger – Ceuta. Also from Cadiz – the Canary Islands.

Iscomar Ferries: ☎971-437500; www.iscomarferrys.com. Daily services: Alcudia – Ciudadela. Other services: Palma – Barcelona; Palma – Valencia; Mahón – Valencia; Ibiza – Denia; Ibiza – Formentera (summer only).

Lineas Fred Olsen: ☎902-100107; www.fredolsen.com. Services: Santa Cruz de Tenerife – Agaete (Gran Canaria); Los Cristianos – La Palma; Los Cristianos – Gomera, Los Cristianos – El Hierro; Lanzarote – Fuerteventura.

Mar-Ship: ☎902-100132. Operates mini-cruises from Valencia and Barcelona to Mallorca.

Romeu y Cia S.A.: ☎965-141509; www.algerieferries.com. Services from Alicante to Argel and Oran all year round.

INTERNATIONAL TRAVEL FROM SPAIN

Living in mainland Europe, there is no need to restrict yourself to Spain. As vast and varied as your new homeland is, you are bound to want to travel back and forth to the UK, around Europe and even further. Spain has good connections to its former territories in Latin America. If these are not to your taste, then there are connections all over Europe by train and no-frills charter and scheduled flights. Alternatively you can cruise the Mediterranean, or use the ferries from Spain to visit North Africa.

You can book holidays through travel agents (*agencias de viajes*), which is recommended for long-haul journeys. A useful site for finding your nearest agent in Spain is the website: www.agencias-de-viajes.com, which allows you to search by area or type of holiday. Increasingly the internet is the booking method of choice as it is so versatile, informative and instant.

Senior concessions and no-frills air and train fares are not the only budget travel opportunities available. As in the UK, agents tend to put unsold flights and holidays directly on the market at discounted prices, about two weeks before the departure date. The great thing about being retired is that you are much more flexible about when you can travel. This is the time to take advantage of such last minute offers. Try the following websites: www.atrapalo.com; www.es.lastminute.com; www ofertasparaviajar.com.

By Air – No Frills

If you have become accustomed to low-cost, no-frills flying from the UK, you will be pleased to discover that this method of travel has also caught on in Spain and is transforming the way people travel. Over 40 low cost airlines operate in and out of Spain. Most of these are foreign owned, but homegrown newcomers *Vueling* are forcing Spanish carriers to rethink. Spanair has recently launched four international destinations and there are rumours of a future Iberia low-cost subsidiary, a *Lagun Air* re-launch, and the possibility of an *Air Andalucia*. Obviously the big players *Ryanair* and *easyJet* offer a range of flights in and out of Spain. For a full list of the no-frills carriers with flights from Spanish airports visit www.attitudetravel. com/spain/lowcostairlines/. The Spanish low cost airlines and those that offer a large number of budget routes are detailed below.

No-Frills Carriers from Spain to European Destinations

Air Berlin: www.airberlin.com. Third biggest European low-cost airline. Flies to/ from mainland Spanish airports to/from Germany, Austria, UK, Switzerland, Holland. Also flies from Mallorca to Spain, Portugal and Hungary.

Air Madrid: www.airmadrid.com. Main focus is to fly from Spain to Latin America, but has also started offering low-fare European routes.

easyJet: www.easyjet.com. 2nd largest European low-cost airline, operates routes from Spain to the UK,Switzerland, France and Germany. This is the cheapest airline for flights to France.

Ryanair: www.ryanair.com. Europe's largest low cost airline. Vast number of routes to and from Spain, to/from Belgium, France, Netherlands, Germany, Ireland, Italy, Sweden and the UK.

Spanair: www.spanair.com. Offers low fares from Spain to Dublin (Ireland), Ancona (Italy), Stockholm (Sweden), Copenhagen (Denmark).

Vueling Airlines: www.vueling.com. Low fares to Portugal, Italy, France, Belgium and the Netherlands.

By Train

RENFE, the company that operates the Spanish public railways, offers numerous long-distance services. The discounts offered for pensioners have been detailed above. It is also possible to buy a Eurodomino pass, which entitles the holder to unlimited travel in another European country for three to eight days in one month. Alternatively, the Interrail pass allows bearers to travel in up to 28 European countries. Contrary to common belief, interrail passes are available for all age groups. Enquire at your local train station or tourist office for further information or contact *European Rail Ltd.* (www.europeanrail.com) or *Rail Europe* (www.raileurope.co.uk).

Direct international connections from Spain:		
Madrid – Paris	Barcelona – Paris	Valencia – Montpellier
Madrid – Lisbon	Barcelona – Zurich	
	Barcelona – Milan	
	Barcelona – Montpellier	

PUBLIC HOLIDAYS AND FIESTAS

Throughout Spain there are hundreds of celebrations with ancestral rites that have been preserved for centuries in order to maintain regional identities. If there's one thing the Spanish are good at, it is celebrating, and they do it as regularly and enthusiastically as they possibly can. Indeed the number of fiestas throughout Spain is growing year on year as local people set about energetically recovering customs and ceremonies that had been long forgotten.

Most of these celebrations have a religious origin, others are based on historical events, and other fiestas have origins that have been lost in the mists of time, but in almost all cases the most important aspect is that the entire local community comes together to enjoy themselves. Most towns in Spain have their own festival, usually linked to the patron saint. Some of the fiestas are simply days off, but others are week-long parties, where all work stops and the people take to the streets. Some of these have become famous worldwide, such as San Fermíne (Pamplona's bull-running festival), or the ferias of Seville.

There are ten national public holidays per year, but each region has four more local public holidays. In addition, the various regions and localities have their own festivals and carnivals which may not officially be public holidays but when most facilities will be closed. The national holidays are shown below. If a holiday falls on a Tuesday or Thursday, most people take an extra day's holiday on the Monday or Friday in order to give them a long weekend (known as *puente* – bridge).

NATIONAL PUBLIC HOLIDAYS	
1 January	New Year's Day
6 January	Epiphany
March/April	Good Friday
1 May	Labour Day
15 August	Assumption
12 October	National Day
1 November	All Saints' Day
6 December	Constitution Day
8 December	Conception
25 December	Christmas Day

Local Festivals

There are so many local fairs and festivals in Spain that it would be impossible to cover them all in detail. The most famous, if only for the reports of deaths and injuries every year, is certainly **San Fermin** in Pamplona. Locals, overly enthusiastic tourists and the clinically insane run with the bulls through 825 metres of Pamplona's streets to the Bull Ring and attempt to get away with as few injuries as possible. The bull run takes place every morning from 7-14 July and has become the focus of the festival, although there are also fireworks and festivities which continue well into the night for the entire week.

Another fiesta which has received international infamy is **La Tomatina** in Buñol, essentially an enormous tomato fight between the townsfolk. There are numerous urban legends as to how this bizarre ritual started, but it is commonly held that the festival dates back to 1945 when a carnival of *Gigantes y Cabezudos* (giants and bigheads – traditional characters in Spanish festivals since medieval times) turned into an enormous brawl, as fate should have it, very close to the tomato vendor. The riot was broken up by the police, but the following year, on exactly the same day, the same thing happened. Despite being officially banned by the police at this time, the tomato fight has continued unabated every year since.

One of Spain's most colourful and vibrant festivals takes place in Valencia every year in the week around St Joseph's Day, 19 March. **Las Fallas de San José** consists of a week of endless processions, bullfights, firework displays and most importantly fire. Each *barrio* (neighbourhood) of Valencia produces its own giant papier-mâché representation of popular satirical figures (*las fallas*). The judges choose a winner and the others are ceremoniously burnt at the finale of the festival, the *nit de foc*. At midnight the entire city is ablaze with enormous fires in every street, the sky lights up with fireworks and the smell of gunpowder is everywhere. The people of Valencia then dance and drink in the streets until the early hours.

Spain's biggest annual party however, takes place in Seville two weeks after *Semana Santa*, (also an excuse for carousing and frivolity in Seville). **La Feria de Abril** is an extraordinary spectacle of flamenco dancing, horseback parades and bullfights. Although the *feria* began as a market fair, a means of exchange between the local towns in the Middle Ages, it has blossomed into an extravaganza that lasts all day and all night for a week. During this time the *Real de la Feria* on the far bank of the river fills with rows of *casetas*, tents which bulge with singing and dancing, and the sounds of *Sevillanas* spill out into the night. Virtually all of the women wear traditional costume, which consists of brightly coloured gypsy dresses. Many of the casetas are booked by private groups and associations but there are a number of public tents set up by the town council. During the day the fair moves to the streets of Seville where music plays on every corner and bars serve food and drink in the streets.

FESTIVALS IN SPAIN			
Date	Festival/Where	Brief Description	Further information
January			
1st Sunday	La Vijanera, Silio, Cantabria	Colourful mountain carnival designed to drive out the evil spirits of the old year.	http://turismode cantabria.com ☎901-111112
2nd	Día de la Toma, Granada	Anniversary of the retaking of Granada by the Christian Monarchs.	www.granadatur.com ☎958-247146
2nd or 3rd Sunday	Fiesta de San Antonio Abad, Arona, Tenerife	Procession and dancing through the streets, with games, a beauty pageant and a huge paella feast.	☎922-239592
7th– Feb18th	Festival de Musica, Canary Islands	Classical music festival held mainly in Las Palmas de Gran Canaria and Santa Cruz de Tenerife	www.festivaldecanarias .com

February			
1st-5th	Feria Mundial del Toro (World Bullfighting Fair), Seville	Everything to do with the noisy, colourful world of bullfighting.	☎954-478700 http://www.fibes.es/ v_toro06/index.html
Feb 23rd – Mar 1st (2006)	Carnaval, Sitges	The Sitges *Carnaval* is one of the best known of all the carnivals that take place around Spain. It is a huge glittering party complete with outrageous costumes and flamboyant floats.	☎938-110611 www.sitges.com
24th-Mar 11th	Flamenco festival, Jerez	16 days of flamenco shows and classes.	www.festivaldejerez.es ☎956-327327
March			
1st	Carnaval de Teguise, Teguise, Lanzarote	Villagers dress up in grotesque costumes for the *Danza de los Diabletes* (Dance of the Little Devils) which dates back to the 15th century.	www.teguise.com
7th –April 4th	Terrassa Jazz Festival, Catalonia	Free concerts with some big names in the world of jazz	www.jazzterrassa.org
24th - April 1st (2006)	Festival de Cine (Film Festival), Las Palmas, Gran Canaria	Features and short films aired outside in various locations. Awards presented.	www.festivalcinelas palmas.com
15th-19th	Las Fallas, Valencia	See above	www.fallas.com ☎963-606353
April			
Palm Sunday	Traditional palm procession, Elche, Alicante	Palm procession with origins as far back as 1371.	www.turismedelx.com
9th-16th (2006)	Semana Santa (Holy Week), Seville	Elaborate processions of church brotherhoods complete with floats, costumes, music and street theatre. Very spectacular.	www.turismosevilla.org
25th-30th (2006)	Feria de Abril, Seville	See above	☎954-234465
May			
4th-15th	Fiesta de los patios, Córdoba	Private home-owners all over the city open their flower-filled patios to the public.	www.infocordoba.com

7th-14th	Feria del Caballo (horse fair), Jerez	Incredible displays of horsemanship, a large agricultural show and general celebration.	www.webjerez.com
Last 2 weeks	Festival de Tres Culturas, Murcia	Festival promoting tolerance and celebrating the three religions of Judaism, Islam, Christianity	☎968-277700
June			
23rd- Jul 9th	Festival Internacional de musica y dansa, Granada	Classical music festival packed with concerts and recitals, all performed in the Alhambra palace.	www.granadafestival.org ☎958-221844
24th	St John's Day, Alicante	Bonfires throughout the night signal the start of five days of festivities.	www.alicanteturismo. com
29th	Batalla de vino, Haro, Rioja	An enormous wine fight in Rioja's capital with combatants soaking each other in thousands of litres of the stuff.	www.haro.org ☎941-303366
July			
6th-10th	European Balloon Festival, Igualada, Barcelona	Around 40 hot air balloons from around the world take to the skies, attracting thousands of spectators	www.ultramagic.com
7th-14th	San Fermin, Pamplona	See above	www.sanfermin.com ☎948-420100
2nd Saturday	Festival de la Sidra, Nava, Asturías	A celebration of Spanish cider brewed in the region.	www.ayto-nava.es ☎985-718412
22nd-23rd	Danza de los Zancos (stilt dance), Anguiano, La Rioja	In honour of Mary Magdalene, the men and boys of the town dance on metre-high stilts through the town.	☎941-291260 www.lariojaturismo.com
29th	Fiesta de Santa Marta de Ribarteme (Festival of near-death experience), Las Nieves, Galicia	Those who have had a near-death experience make a pilgrimage to the virgin of the resurrection either carrying a coffin, or being carried in a coffin! Locals dress up as the Grim Reaper.	☎902-200432 www.turgalicia.es
Whole month	Almagro Festival de Teatro Clásico, Castilla la Mancha	One of the biggest theatre festivals in Spain, paying homage to classical theatre.	www.festivaldealmagro. com

August			
First Saturday	Descenso Internacional del Sella, Ribadesella, Asturias	20km annual canoe race that began in 1929. Open to anybody who applies.	www.descensodelsella.com
4th	Festa de Cantir (Water Jug Festival), Argentona, Barcelona	A day's festivities based around water (the town is home to the Santo Domingo springs). Includes strongman and water blowing contests.	www.museucantir.org
2nd Sunday of the month	Festa do pulpo (octopus festival), Carballiño, Galicia	Celebration of the octopus in all its culinary glory. Visitors gather to sample the different dishes available.	☎ 988-530007
2nd and 4th weekends	Carreras de caballos, Sanlucar de Barrameda, Andalucia	International horse racing along a 1,800 km stretch of beach.	www.carrerassanlucar.com
16th	San Roque Festival, Sada, La Coruña	Held in honour of the area's patron saint. Culminates with a huge sardine roasting event on the beach.	☎ 981-221822 www.turismocoruna.com
1st-30th	Festival Internacional, Santander	Features musicians and ballet groups from around the world	www.festivalsantander.com
11th-19th	Feria de Málaga, Málaga	A week of music, dance, traditional costume, bullfighting, and fireworks.	www.ayto-malaga.es
Final wednesday	La Tomatina, Buñol, Valencia	See above	www.turisvalencia.es ☎ 962-500151
Last Saturday	Festa da Istoria, Ribadavia, Galicia	Recreation of an authentic medieval town with a traditional market, theatre, music and a ball.	www.turgalicia.es ☎ 988-471275
September			
16th-25th (2005)	Carthaginians & Romans Festival, Cartagena	10 day festival telling the story of the clash between the Romans and Carthaginians from the founding of the city, to its taking by the Romans.	www.cartaginesesyromanos.com

24th	Fiesta de la Mercé, Barcelona	Festival honouring Barcelona's most popular unofficial patron saint, complete with colouful parades, live music and sporting events.	www.barcelonaturisme.com
4th-27th	Festival de Otoño (Autumn festival), Jerez	Celebrations based around the 3 main passions of Jerez: horses, grapes and flamenco.	www.webjerez.com
Last week	Moors and Christians Festival, Benidorm	One of the town's biggest fiestas with battle re-enactments, street parades and fireworks.	www.benidorm-spotlight.com/fiestas.htm
October			
2nd week	Cava Week, Sant Sadurni d'Anoia, Catalonia	A week long celebration of the region's most famous wine. Includes tastings, dinners, the crowning of the cava queen, and the arrival of 1,000 revellers from Barcelona on the 'Cava train'.	www.barcelonaturisme.com
12th	El Pilar, Zaragoza	Fiesta in honour of Nuestra Señora del Pilar. The 'pillar' is the column on which the Virgin Mary apparently alighted when she appeared to St. James.	http://zaragozaturismo.dpz.es/
25th	Saffron Festival, Consuegra, Toledo	Celebrating the end of the back-breaking saffron harvest. Surrounding villages compete against one another in saffron picking races and cooking competitions.	www.castillalamancha.es
November			
1st	Tosantos, Cadiz	All Saint's Day is one of the biggest religious events in Spain. In Cadiz there are markets, processions and festivities.	☎956-807061 www.cadizturismo.com
1st or 2nd weekend	Kite festival, Corralejo, Fuerteventura	Kite-flyers from around the world meet to perform impressive tricks	☎928-866235 www.sunnyfuerteventura.com/kite-festival/
13th 14th	Fiesta de Aguardiente, Potes, Cantabria	Tastings and brewing demonstrations of the local tipple: Orujo.	☎942-730787

December			
8th	Festival of La Virgen de la Inmaculada, Sevilla	Public holiday throughout Spain but Seville's parades and floral displays are particularly worth seeing.	www.sevilla.org
24th	Noche buena, Luque, Andalucia	The people celebrate Christmas eve by taking to the streets, playing instruments and chanting.	www.ayunluque.org
28th	Verdiales, Málaga	Festival of local mountain flamenco just outside Málaga, complete with musicians in brightly coloured costumes.	www.ayto-malaga.es
31st	Festa de l'Estendard, Palma de Mallorca	Incredible procession commemorating the Christian conquest of the city in 1229.	www.infomallorca.net

KEEPING IN TOUCH

It has never been easier to keep in touch with friends and family. Wherever you live modern technology is making it possible to maintain regular contact without the vast telephone bills that this once generated. The cheapest new way to communicate is almost certainly internet telephone calls or VoIP (Voice over internet protocol). The advantage of this system is that you are not tied to a landline, and the cost of calling another country is the same as calling the house next door. All you need is a broadband internet connection – now widely available in Spain.

Telephone

Telefónica (www.telefonica.es), Spain's equivalent to BT, was privatised in 1998 and although it has lost its monopoly, it still retains a powerful hold on the telephone service, with 87% of the market share. After deregulation, a number of call providers appeared (see box below), which can be considerably cheaper if you are making regular long distance calls. If you use a different provider, you still go via telefónica and pay their standing charges, but call costs are reduced. Some providers offer *tarifas planas,* or flat-rate charges. Others offer a discounted indirect phone service, which involves dialling an access code before every call. As always, it pays to shop around. For a comparison of the rates of the different providers, visit the following website: www.teltarifas.com/particulares.

Telephone Companies	
Aló: www.alo.es	**Jazztel**: www.jazztel.com
Auna: www.auna.es	**Ruta10**: www.ruta10.com
BT Ignite: www.btglobalservices.com	**Soltelecom**: www.soltelecom.es
Capcom: www.capcom.net	**Spantel**: www.spantel.es
Comunitel: www.comunitel.es	**Tele2**: www.tele2.es
Euskaltel: www.euskaltel.es	**Uni2**: www.uni2.es

To get a telephone installed in a new property you will need to go to the local Telefónica office (the address of local offices can be found in the yellow pages – *las Páginas Amarillas*). Take along your *residencia* or passport and the *escritura* (if you are renting a property take along your rental agreement) as well as some form of proof of address. If you are renting a property you may be asked to pay a deposit. Charges are currently around €150 for the initial connection fee and approximately €10 plus VAT at 16% per month's landline rental (the standing charge). You can buy or rent a handset. Connections should not take more than a few days to install, though in more isolated areas this may take longer. Those aged over 65 with a low income are eligible for discounts when using Telefónica services. If you are taking over the account of a previous owner you will need to arrange for the telephone company to close the existing telephone account, and send a final bill to the owners of the property on the day that you take possession (the day you hand over the purchase price to the *notario*).

British handsets need an adapter to work in Spain, so it is best to buy a new one when you arrive.

Mobile Phones. It will be prohibitively expensive to continue using your UK mobile once you have arrived in Spain, so it is best to buy either a new phone or to have the SIM card in your phone replaced with a Spanish one.

The mobile phone arm of Telefónica is MoviStar (www.movistar.com). There are also other operators in Spain including Vodafone (www.vodafone.es), the first company to break Movistar's monopoly, and Amena (www.amena.com). As elsewhere in the world, mobile phone coverage varies from area to area. Some of the more isolated and mountainous areas of the country will have problems with coverage and you should check with the various operators to see which can provide the best coverage for your home area (as well as the best deals).

Mobile phones are very popular in Spain, and phone outlets and agents are not hard to find in the towns and cities. There are two ways of paying for calls: either by setting up an account with a service provider, or by using pre-pay cards bought from *supermercados, estancos,* etc. If you decide on the first option, you will need to provide proof that you are a resident in Spain.

Internet and E-mail

When you install your phone lines, you might want to connect to the internet with the Internet Service Provider owned by the telephone company. This usually allows you a free internet connection with calls at local rates. Free connection software is also available from most computer shops, with companies such as Tiscali. The telephone companies also have discount tariffs for heavy internet usage called *tarifa plana*. These charge a flat rate irrespective of usage, that allows you to be connected to the internet either twenty-four hours a day or only during off peak times, depending on the deal you choose. It costs around €25 a month for an unlimited connection, but shop around for the best deals. The main providers are www. tiscali.com, www.terra.es, www.jazztel.com and www.ya.com.

ADSL broadband is now universal in most urban areas and fairly cheap to install. Offers including free installation are often available, so again it is best to shop around. Line rental works out at around €35 per month for a standard 256k bandwidth. The advantage of broadband is of course that it is considerably faster and hence allows you to listen to the radio or make phone calls via the internet and allows you to be constantly connected, without interfering with your telephone line.

Once you are connected to the net, you will want to send and receive e-mails. Many accounts can be checked anywhere in the world via a webpage, for example hotmail, yahoo, wanadoo, supanet etc. However it is likely that you will have an account set up in the UK that uses Outlook Express rather than the web to receive e-mails. In these circumstances there is a useful service at www.mail2web.com which will check the emails waiting to be downloaded from your UK service provider, without any set up. All you need is your e-mail address and password.

Internet Phone Calls. To make a phone call over the internet you will need broadband, and then it is simply a matter of downloading the relevant software. Internet telephony from pc to pc is completely free (other than the normal cost of broadband) and allows you to make calls for as long as you wish, to anywhere in the world. All you need is a telephone headset, or speakers and a microphone, all of which can be bought cheaply at any computer shop. With the simple addition of a webcam, you can also see the person you are talking to.

This recent marvel of modern technology, known as Voice over the Internet Protocol (VoIP) is striking fear within the traditional telecommunications companies. The technology is constantly evolving, and not only can computers call other computers (peer-to-peer), but they can also make calls to a landline. There are a number of VoIP providers in Spain, offering a range of different packages. Some providers charge a monthly subscription fee, whereby all calls to landlines are free, and others have no standing charges, but there is a minimal call charge.

By far the most popular VoIP provider is Skype (www.skypc.com). As well as peer to peer calls, Skype also offers a service known as SkypeOut, whereby you buy credit that allows you to call landlines and mobiles from your pc at a very reduced rate; and SkypeIn, a service that gives you a standard phone number based anywhere in the world. The advantage of this is that if you live in Spain, but all of your friends and family live in London, you could obtain a London phone number for your friends and family to call cheaply, and you would receive the calls on your computer in Spain.

Having Friends and Family to Stay

It is very likely that as soon as you move to Spain, you will have a flurry of people coming to stay with you. Some people worry about how easy it will be to see their loved ones on a regular basis, but as one retired expat in Calpe explains, you can sometimes have the opposite problem:

The problem is not staying in touch with people, it's getting rid of them! We have had so many people to stay in the last year since we moved out here that there comes a point where you just want to say – 'Right. Time for you to go home now. Let me get on with my life!'

Other expats complain that their guests come over and want to live it up every night, not really taking into account that your life is not a permanent holiday (well, not quite anyway!). Whatever you do, make sure that you buy the house that suits you rather than becoming obsessed with accommodating potential visitors. It is useful to have a spare room for visitors. Indeed John Howell, a solicitor specialising in helping people to move abroad claims that *'The number one feedback we have from people is – If only I'd bought a bigger property. Everybody wants to visit us and we simply don't have space for them'*. Nevertheless there are alternatives to buying a house with more space than you will necessarily need. Your guests can stay in a local guest-house, or alternatively you could consider converting outbuildings that can also be let out when you have no visitors. This is a very popular option for those who have bought in a rural setting. For information on renovating a building see *Your New Home in Spain*.

WORKING, VOLUNTEERING AND STARTING A BUSINESS

As mentioned in the introduction, retirement is no longer a period of total inactivity for many people. Those who spent the last years of their hectic working lives daydreaming of kicking back their heels in the sunshine, may be surprised that this can actually become quite dull. This was certainly Ian Adams's experience, when he retired from his job as a mechanic to move to Spain:

> *It takes a while to adapt to not working. I did no work at all for the first year, and the end of it I was really bored. Then somebody asked me to work on their car and I found that I actually enjoyed it! When I was in the UK, I had been working 70 hours a week and I was so burnt out that I said I'd never touch a car again. Having had a bit of a rest though, I really enjoy it. I've remembered that it's what I do best, and I am not doing it because I have to, but for pleasure, which makes a huge difference.*

Getting a part time job is actually a very good way of meeting new people and establishing a routine for your new life. Bear in mind that paid work may be hard to come by. Spain has comparatively high unemployment and job opportunities in rural areas may be almost non-existent. Nevertheless, if you live by the coast, then there are always seasonal opportunities in tourism and catering. If you have a trade or a skill and can speak some Spanish, then your chances of finding employment are much higher. By law, all employers must register vacancies with the state-run *Instituto Nacional de Empleo (INEM)*, the Spanish equivalent of the Jobcentre. Branch offices are pretty evenly distributed and can be found online at www.inem.es, or in the yellow pages. You should also ask around locally to see what might be on offer.

If you take on any form of paid work, you should make sure that your employer registers you for tax and social security purposes. The black economy (*economia sumergida*) is an enormous feature of the Spanish labour market, but be warned: government inspectors are clamping down hard on both employers and employees who work cash-in-hand.

Starting a Small Business

It is estimated that as many as 51% of the British moving to Spain choose to set up their own businesses or go self-employed. Some of these businesses have become extremely large and successful but the majority are very small affairs designed simply to generate a little extra pocket money. Expat Raymond Fletcher's business falls into the latter category:

I still keep my hand in with a bit of extra work. Every Sunday I go down to the local market and sell CDs on a stall. Music has always been an interest of mine and it also brings in a little bit of extra cash to keep me going. My UK pension is paid into an account in the UK and about once a year I go back and buy up a whole load of stock with that money. Then, when I am over here I can live off the sales that I make at the market. That way I avoid losing money through exchange rates and through the charges on bank transfers.

The fact that there is an enormous community of foreigners in Spain is a tremendous advantage as there will always be a demand for those offering, in English, the kinds of services to be found at home. Many foreigners choose to tread the well-worn and perilous path of opening a bar, restaurant or café. It should be noted however, that some find being on the other side of the bar does not quite meet their expectations, and given the level of competition, many struggle to make a living. The most successful businesses run by foreign entrepreneurs in Spain, are those which fill a necessary gap in the market and cater to both the expatriate market and the Spanish market. The key to success in Spain is an original and creative approach, coupled with an enormous amount of preparation.

Although Spain once presented a maze of complex procedures and formalities to those wishing to start their own business, this situation has improved enormously in recent years, and there is plenty of help available. It is beyond the scope of this book to cover the procedures of starting and running a business, but detailed information can be found in *Starting a Business in Spain* published by Vacation Work Publications (www. vacationwork.co.uk).

Voluntary Work

Volunteering (*ofrecerse voluntario*) opportunities are much more readily available than paid work, and do not usually have the same level of language requirement. Offering your services is a good way to give something back to the society you have joined, of creating more of a structure to your new life, and of making new friends.

Voluntary work can take almost any form, though your good intentions will be restricted if you do not have a grasp of Spanish. Nevertheless, those who are living in expat heavy areas will find that many of the charities that exist in the UK such as the Red Cross, Age Concern etc. have also set up on the costas and are happy to welcome English-speaking volunteers to help out in their charity shops. Once you have got a measure of your new community, you will be able to find such opportunities within the local press, or simply by enquiring amongst your neighbours.

Those who do speak good Spanish will always be in demand to act as an interpreter, either at the police station or at their local health centre or hospital. Failing that, you will almost certainly find something that ties in with your interests such as environmental protection, animals, children, cookery, schools etc. You should not expect payment but travel expenses are usually reimbursed. Your local *ayuntamiento* (town hall) maintains a list of organisations needing helpers so it is worthwhile making enquiries there.

Useful Contacts

International Voluntary Service (IVS Field Office): ☎01206-298215; www.ivs-gb.org.uk.

UNA Exchange: United Nations Association; ☎029-2022 3088; www.una exchange.org.

Dirección General de Cooperación al Desarollo y Voluntariado: ☎900-444 555; www.madrid.org/voluntaries.

Coordinadora de ONG para el Desarollo España, CONGDE: ☎902-454600; www.congde.org.

English Town: ☎915-914840; www.vaughanvillage.com.

Ecoforest: ☎661-079950; www.ecoforest.org.

Sunseed Desert Technology: ☎950-525770; www.sunseed.org.uk.

Personal Finance

CHAPTER SUMMARY

○ It is vital that you only consult regulated advisers in Spain. There are a lot of unregistered financial cowboys out there, against whom you will have no right to seek compensation if things go wrong.

○ **Banking.** It is advisable to maintain a bank account in the UK as well as opening one in Spain, especially if you still have property or income there.

  ○ It is illegal to overdraw your Spanish bank account without prior arrangement. However, overdrafts are available and interest is limited to 2.5 times the current bank rate.

○ **Pensions**. Examine your payment options when receiving your pension from abroad. Your UK bank may charge for making the transfer and the Spanish bank may also apply a commission.

  ○ Those who move to Spain before reaching retirement age should arrange to continue paying national insurance contributions in the UK in order to qualify for a British state pension when they reach 65.

○ **Taxation.** Anyone spending 183 days or more in Spain during the tax year is deemed to be tax resident and will be liable to pay Spanish tax.

  ○ Retired persons will not need to file and income tax return unless their gross income exceeds 7,500 euros.

  ○ Wealth tax is collected every June, but unless you have considerable business interests and valuable property in Spain, it is unlikely that you will be eligible to pay much.

○ It is very important that anybody with assets in Spain makes a Spanish will. This will avoid time-consuming and expensive legal problems in the long run.

○ The rules applying to Succession Tax differ wildly between the different autonomous communities. Always take expert local legal and financial advice on your own particular circumstances.

FINANCIAL ADVICE

Anyone considering retiring to Spain should take specialist financial advice regarding their own situation. Most people in a position to retire overseas have an amount of capital to invest, or will have once they sell their UK home; and it is essential to take good advice on how and where this may best be done. Moreover, those who intend to maintain connections with both the UK and Spain will need advice on how their taxation affairs can be managed to their own advantage. If you are considered tax resident in Spain (for which there are various criteria), all of your income and assets worldwide are potentially liable to Spanish tax. In theory, you may also be liable for UK tax, but in practice, there is a double tax treaty between Spain and the UK, which protects you from paying twice. Siddalls advises that before you buy property, invest capital, arrange pension payments or plan your estate, you should seek professional advice from experts who know the Spanish system.

A financial adviser can offer guidance on property purchase, taxation, insurance, pensions and much more. The difficulty is identifying those advisers that have permission to, and are qualified to, offer cross border advice. In the UK, financial advice, including arranging financial contracts is controlled and regulated by a strict set of 'Conduct of Business' rules laid down by the Financial Services Authority (www.fsa.gov.uk). UK financial advisers are required to maintain Professional Indemnity Insurance to protect clients against poor advice and are required to ensure their businesses are solvent above strict financial limits. In addition, they are required to deal with complaints within specific timescales. If a complaint remains in dispute, they are required to then submit to and abide by a Financial Ombudsman ruling. The Omdudsman, an independent complaints arbitrator, can make compensation awards for a client up to £100,000.

Unfortunately, in Spain, financial advice is not a regulated activity. This should not to be confused with the entirely separate action of a 'middleman' arranging the purchase of financial contracts, this is known as 'intermediation'.

> Intermediation is controlled in Spain, codes of conduct are in force and most intermediators are required to be insured. There are three regulators in Spain. The Bank of Spain (*Banco de España*) for banking activities, The National Securities Commission *(Comisión Nacional del Mercado de Valores – CNMV)* for stocks, shares and collective investment funds, and the Office for Insurance and Pension Funds *(Dirección General de Seguros y Fondos de Pensiones - DGS)* for insurance and pension contracts.

Many so-called financial advisers in Spain hide behind the fact that advice is not regulated and they have no insurance or complaints procedures or rules to abide by yet still arrange contracts. There are many who are not registered in either the UK or Spain and care should be exercised as you have no right of recourse or to seek compensation for poor advice if you use an unregulated adviser. The CNMV has even produced a leaflet in English called *'Financieros Chiringuitos'* (Financial Fly By Nights), to warn investors against rogue advisers as well as publishing warning lists on the internet (www.cnmv.es).

Protected Advice

For financial guidance in the UK, only take advice from an adviser regulated by the Financial Services Authority.

For financial guidance in Spain, take advice only from an adviser registered with one of the three Spanish regulators, or take advice from a UK registered financial adviser that has a special "EU Passport" permission to advise in both the UK and Spain.

Financial Advisers

Bravo Asesoría: Avda. de Condes de San Isidro 23, 1° 29640 Fuengirola; ☎952-473062; fax 952-462006; www.gestoriabravo.es;

John Siddall Financial Services Ltd (Siddalls): Lothian House, 22 High Street, Fareham, Hampshire PO16 7AE; ☎01329-288641; fax 01329-281157; e-mail spain@johnsiddalls.co.uk; www.siddalls.net. Spanish office: C/ Maria Auxiliadora 5, Local 10, 29602 Marbella, Malaga ☎952-903205. Long established independent financial adviser providing investment, retirement and tax planning for those people moving to, or already living in Spain to help people to minimise the effect of Spanish taxes on capital and investments.

Need An Adviser.com: Prosperity House, Water Street, Burntwood, Staffordshire, WS7 1AN; ☎0870-950 7788; fax 0870 051 0015 or Spain ☎918-371323 or 678-044135; e-mail espana@needanadviser.com; www.needanadviser. com. Award winning and family owned Independent Financial Advisers and Chartered Financial Planners. UK FSA 'passport' authorised in Spain for advice on property, mortgages, trusts, investments, pensions, wills, inheritance tax, income tax, residencia and much more.

Conti Financial Services: 204 Church Road, Hove, Sussex BN3 2DJ; ☎01273-772 811; fax 01273-321 269; www.mortgagesoverseas.com.
Spain Accountants: ☎952-791113; www.spainaccountants.com.

BANKING

All banking activity in Spain is controlled by the *Banco de España*, which has branches in all provincial capitals. Banks in Spain are divided into clearing banks and savings banks and there are also a number of foreign banks operating throughout the country.

To open an account in Spain you will be required to present your passport or some other means of proof of identification, proof of address, and sometimes an NIE number (see *Basics*). It is advisable to open an account in person rather than rely on a *gestor* to do it for you. It is also advisable to open an account with one of the major banks as they are likely to have far more branches.

The two banking giants in Spain at present are the BSCH (*Banco de Santander Central Hispano*), which in 2004 negotiated a takeover of Abbey National to create the world's eighth largest bank, and the BBVA (*Banco Bilbao Vizcaya Argentaria*). Other banks in Spain include *Sabadell Atlántico* (owners of *Banco Sabadell, Banco Atlántico, Banco Herrero and Solbank* – a specialist expatriate bank) and *Banco de Andalucía*. Barclays, Britain's third largest bank also has a very large presence in Spain having bought out *Banco Zaragozano* in 2003. Most large towns will have at least one branch of these banks and in the cities there will often be several branches, offering all the usual banking facilities, including mortgages and internet and telephone banking facilities. Standard bank opening times are from 9am to 2pm on weekdays and from 9am to 1pm on Saturdays, although these may vary from bank to bank.

It is best to open a bank account in Spain immediately on arrival – or even before leaving home. This will enable you to settle any bills that you may get for any professional advice and for day-to-day costs taken while on, for example, a reconnaissance trip to Spain.

When choosing a bank, it is a good idea to ask friends and acquaintances for recommendations. Banks in resort areas and cities usually have at least one member of staff who speaks English, however, those in rural areas generally don't. Service in small local branches is often more personalised than in larger branches and the staff less harried. However, smaller branches may not offer such a choice of banking services and are less likely to have English-speaking staff.

ATMs

There are now ATMs (automated teller machines) all over Spain and you can usually even find them in the larger villages. Three ATM networks operate in Spain – 4B (the most common), ServiRed and 6000 and you can generally use any ATM to draw money from your account, although there may be a fee charged. As well as cash withdrawals, paying cash into your account and consulting your balance, some ATMs now allow you to carry out other transactions such as renewing your mobile phone card or making theatre seat reservations. Spanish ATMs offer you a choice of language.

Bank Accounts

Those who are resident in Spain for tax purposes may open the type of current account (*cuenta corriente*) and savings account available to all Spanish citizens. Non-residents may only open the current and savings accounts available to foreigners, which will still allow you to set up direct debits to pay utility bills while you are away from your property and keep a steady amount of money in the country. Note that current accounts pay very little interest on the balance. Sometimes it is as low as 0.1%. It is therefore sensible to keep as little as possible in a current account and deposit the rest in a savings account.

The *Cajas de Ahorro* saving banks are similar to British building societies. They usually offer a more personalised and friendly service than the clearing banks. They have branches throughout Spain, which, apart from the *Catalan La Caixa* and *Caja Madrid*, tend to be regional. Many of the savings banks actually started out as agricultural co-operatives and some still act as charitable institutions – investing part of their profits each year in social and cultural causes. The savings banks all issue a bankcard enabling the holder to withdraw money from the ATMs that they operate.

For a short term savings account you can open a deposit account (*libreta de ahorro*), from which withdrawals can be made at any time. Interest will also be added twice yearly to the average credit balance, but this is likely to be negligible unless the account balance is €1,500 or more. For larger amounts of money, long-term savings accounts (*cuentas de plazo*) and investment accounts are also available and will earn more interest, as the money has to be left in the account for an agreed period of time. The longer the set period that the money remains untouched, the better the interest earned. Interest rates vary and the best rates are obtained from accounts linked to stocks and shares although, of course, there are associated risks of losing some or all of your investment.

Spanish bank charges cover just about every banking transaction imaginable and are notoriously high. Particularly high are charges made for the payment of cheques into your account and for transferring money between accounts and/or banks. Before opening an account be sure to ask for a breakdown of any charges that may be forthcoming, including annual fees. If you plan to make a lot of transfers between banks and accounts you may be able to negotiate more favourable terms.

Internet Banking

Over recent years the use of internet banking in Spain has flourished. Spanish banks offer some of the most sophisticated home banking software in the world. This is largely because Spain was a fairly late developer, so when they finally decided to establish internet banking facilities, they were able to do so with the most up-to-date technology on the market. Almost all banks offer internet banking and once you have set up an account with a username and password, it is possible to carry out most banking transactions online. There are also a number of internet/telephone only banks operating in Spain, such as *ING Direct* (☎901-020901; www.ingdirect.es); *Patagon* (☎902-365366; www.patagon.es); *Evolvebank* (☎902-157213; www.evolvebank.es); *Uno-e* (☎901-111113; www.uno-e.es).

Internet banks often offer relatively high-interest current accounts and internet banking is obviously very useful for checking on your account and carrying out banking transactions while abroad.

Banking Procedures

Bank statements are usually sent out to all customers every month and are available on request at any time. Overdrafts and loans are available on request and all the usual services, such as standing orders and direct debit are available from the banks in Spain.

Most Spanish banks will provide cash on presentation of an international credit card (e.g. Mastercard, Access, Visa, American Express). Cardholders are able to withdraw up to their credit limit, which only takes a few minutes, but it is an expensive way of buying euros and it is cheaper, although not as quick, to pay in a sterling cheque to the Spanish bank where commission charges will usually be less. Even if you are moving permanently to Spain it is a good idea to keep your bank account at home open. This will allow you to transfer money (from a pension, or income accrued from property rentals or business) between accounts if you wish and will be useful when visiting friends and family in 'the old country'.

Overdrafts, known as *giros en descubierto*, have a peculiar non-legal status in Spain as officially all debts must be documented so that a bank can take legal action against a customer who defaults on payments. However, overdrafts are readily available and the interest on them is limited to 2.5 times the current bank rate. Note that it is illegal to overdraw your Spanish bank account without prior agreement.

If you plan to keep most of your money outside Spain and to periodically transfer money from your account back home to your account in Spain, you will need to enquire how long it will take to clear before you can access it and what the bank charges are for this service. Banks tend to take their time transferring money as the longer it swills around in their system the more profit they make. Specialist currency exchange companies can make regular payments for mortgages, salaries and pensions faster and more cheaply than banks.

Opening a Spanish Bank Account from the UK

Although some people may be more confident opening an account with a Spanish branch of a UK bank, they will find that these banks function in just the same way as the Spanish national banks. Barclays Bank is the most widely represented of the British banks in Spain with branches throughout the country. Halifax Hispania is also becoming more widespread. Those who wish to open an account with one of either Barclays or Halifax's branches in Spain should contact their local branch in the UK, which will provide the relevant forms to complete. Alternatively, the London offices of the largest Spanish banks are also able to provide the forms necessary to open an account with their Spanish branches. The banks that will provide such a service include Banco De Santander Central Hispano, Solbank, and Banco Bilbao Vizcaya Argentaria (see *Useful Contacts* below).

If you are a resident for tax purposes in Spain remember that 15% of any interest earned on your account will be retained and paid to the Spanish tax office on your behalf. However, this tax can be deducted from tax payable on the next year's income tax return.

Offshore Banking

From a retired person's point of view, if he or she has a sum of money which they wish to invest or put into a long-term deposit account (for a minimum of 90 days) it is well worth looking at the tax-saving options like cash ISAs (Individual Savings Account), which the high street banks and building societies all offer in Britain in addition to the offshore account. Banks, building societies and merchant banks all offer accounts through offshore banking centres in tax havens such as Gibraltar, the Isle of Man and the Channel Islands. The basic difference from an onshore account is that these investments pay income gross of tax which of course is ultimately taxable but they do offer legal ways of paying less tax.

These ways of paying less tax are mainly through roll-up funds, an investment vehicle in which you buy shares; and offshore life insurance, which practitioners like to stress is really an integral part of Britain's tax planning industry. For how much and when to sell you certainly need the advice of a financial planning expert, or a company to administer the fund for you. You can also defer paying tax to a time of your own choosing, perhaps when you anticipate you will need the money or when you enter a lower tax bracket income-wise. Offshore life insurance policies offer similar tax savings.

For these offshore accounts, the year-long deposits tend to demand a minimum sum of £10,000. As with all deposit accounts, interest rates work on the basis that the more inaccessible one's money, the higher the rate of interest paid. Interest can be paid monthly or annually and although the account holder will receive much the same gross amount of interest either way (although slightly less on the monthly payments because of the number of transaction charges involved) the monthly payments which bring with them a steady income flow seem invariably more popular with retired account holders. Most of the high street banks and building societies offer useful explanatory leaflets.

A disadvantage of offshore accounts is that many offshore 'tax havens' such as the Isle of Man and Jersey are 'blacklisted' tax haven territories within Spanish law and certain types of investment may face higher tax penalties rendering the gross tax roll-up ineffective. The advice of a specialist financial adviser should be sought.

Offshore Trusts

One important tool for the investor moving to Spain is offshore trusts. Shares, bonds, funds, bank deposits etc. can all become free from Spanish income tax, wealth tax, inheritance tax and capital gains tax, simply by putting them into trust. Trusts, although complicated, are possibly the most effective tool for individuals wishing to minimise their tax liability. Put simply, setting up a trust involves giving assets to 'trustees' – usually a trust company located in a low tax regime. The way in which trustees manage your assets will be stipulated when the trust is set up. Some people hand all control over their assets to the trustees and others prefer to play more of an integral role in the management of their assets.

The trustees hold the assets for you in trust, and as a result those assets are no longer treated as yours for tax purposes. This allows you to only receive the income you need from the assets (on which you will be taxed in Spain), rather than the total income generated by those assets (the rest of the income will not be taxed as it will be located in a low-tax regime). Trusts also help your heirs to avoid inheritance tax. Trusts can therefore be immensely beneficial, even to those of modest means. However, they must be set up to comply precisely with Spanish tax law and this is a very complicated matter as Ashley Clark, Director of *Need an Adviser.com* explains:

> *Spain is a 'Civil Law' country with a written constitution, unlike the UK (and its offshore dependencies) that has developed its 'Common Law' over the last one thousand years or so. From medieval times where monks placed ownership of their monasteries 'in the trust of others' under a vow of poverty, to present day onshore and offshore tax planning, trusts are known and popular with the British for asset protection. Technically, Spain does not recognise the use of a trust although it may do so under certain circumstances for residents who are not Spanish Nationals. This*

complex area of tax planning is best dealt with by an experienced financial adviser. It is also necessary to take advice on this type of investment vehicle months in advance of your move to Spain.

Useful Contacts

Banco de España: ☎915-385 000; www.bde.es.

Banco Santander Central Hispano: ☎020-7332 7766; www.bsch.es.

Banco Bilbao Vizcaya Argentaria: ☎020-7623 3060.

Bank of Scotland International (Jersey) Ltd: ☎01534-613500; www.bankof scotland-international.com.

Bank of Scotland International (Isle of Man) Ltd: ☎01534-613500; www.bank ofscotland-international.com.

Barclays Bank España: ☎901-101610; www.barclays.es.

Bradford and Bingley International Ltd: ☎01624-695000; www.bbi.co.im.

Ex-Pat Tax Consultants Ltd: ☎0191-230 3141; www.expattax.co.uk.

Lloyds TSB – Isle of Man Offshore Centre: ☎08705-301641; www.lloydstsb-offshore.com.

Need an Adviser.com: UK☎0870-950 7788; Spain ☎918-371323; www.need anadviser.com.

Solbank: ☎902-343999; www.solbank.com.

UK PENSIONS AND BENEFITS

Receiving Your UK State Pension in Spain

As already described in the *Basics* chapter, if you are already receiving a UK pension, you should make arrangements to have it paid directly into your Spanish account before you leave the UK. To do this you need to contact the pensions service in the UK (www.thepensionservice.gov.uk; ☎0845-6060265) and search/ask for details of Overseas Direct Payment in local currency. For occupational and private pensions, contact your provider. The UK State Pension is payable in full anywhere in the European Economic Area. Note that Pension Credit is not payable outside the UK.

Pensions are not frozen at the level they reached on arrival in Spain; instead the pension will rise in accordance with any increases which take effect in the UK. The DWP Overseas Benefits Directorate office in Newcastle publishes Leaflet SA29, which provides details on EU pension

and social security legislation. This leaflet can be downloaded from http://
www.dwp.gov.uk/international/sa29/index.asp. Further help and advice
is available from the International Pension Service (☎0191-218 7777).

UK Government (Public Sector and Civil Service) pensions are normally
paid into UK accounts only after basic rate income tax has been deducted.
The tax paid cannot be reclaimed even if you are non-resident. This does
form part of the UK's Taxation Treaty with Spain and you should not
declare this income in any Spanish tax return as untaxed income. It has
already been taxed.

Private UK company pensions are paid as per the rules of the individual
company. They may say that your company pension may only be paid into
a UK account, in which case it will be necessary to set up a standing order
from your UK account to your Spanish account.

It is important to examine your payment options when receiving a
pension from abroad as the bank may charge for making the transfer, and
your bank in Spain may also apply a commission. It therefore pays to shop
around. Those living on the Costa del Sol often use the banks in Gibraltar
to avoid the charges that Spanish banks make on sterling payments. It
may also be more sensible to have the money transferred in quarterly
instalments rather than monthly, as the charge is often less. Alternatively
a currency dealer, such as Currencies Direct (☎0845 389 0906; www.
currenciesdirect.com) will transfer your money on a monthly basis free of
charge and at a more competitive rate than the banks.

Those who move to Spain before reaching retirement age, but do not
intend to work, should arrange to continue paying national insurance
contributions in the UK in order to qualify for a British state pension
when they reach 65. Failure to do so may result in not being eligible for a
UK pension upon reaching retirement age. Seek advice on this issue from
the Inland Revenue National Insurance Contributions Office (☎0845
302 1479; www.hmrc.gov.uk/nic/).

Those planning to start receiving their pension in Spain should request a
Retirement Pension Forecast, which will tell you the amount of state pension
you have already earned, and the amount you can expect to receive at state
pension age. This should help you to plan exactly how far your pension will
go in Spain. To receive a forecast, complete form BR19, available from any
Jobcentre Plus or online at www.thepensionservice.gov.uk/resourcecentre/
br19/home.asp, and return it to HM Revenue and Customs.

Exportable UK Benefits

On top of your UK pension, once you have received Spanish residence, you are still entitled to some UK benefits such as any Bereavement Allowance (payable for up to one year), and Widowed Parent's Allowance. However, there are a number of benefits that you can no longer receive once living abroad. These include Disability Living Allowance, Income Support, Pension Credit, Attendance Allowance, and Carer's Allowance. Some pensioners therefore find their income substantially reduced upon moving to Spain.

Winter Fuel Payments abroad have caused some confusion, but the situation currently is that anyone who received a Winter Fuel Payment in the UK before moving to Spain may continue to receive the payments (£200 per year, per household for people over 60, with an extra £100 for people over 80). If you left the UK before January 1998, you will not be able to receive this benefit outside the UK. For further information contact the Winter Fuel Payment Centre (see below).

Further information is available in two leaflets; '*Going Abroad and Social Security Benefits*' (GL29), available from your local social security office, and the DWP's leaflet SA 29, mentioned above. A useful source of advice and information on any of the above issues is the International Pension Centre (see address below).

Useful Addresses

Winter Fuel Payment Centre: Southgate House, Cardiff Central, Royal Mail, Cardiff, CF911 1ZH; ☎029-2042 8635; help line 08459-151515; fax 029-2042 8676; www.thepensionservice.gov.uk.

International Pension Centre: DWP, Tyneview Park, Benton, Newcastle-upon-Tyne NE98 1BA; ☎0191-218 7777; fax 0191-218 3836; www.dwp.gov.uk.

Private Pensions

It is possible to continue contributing to a personal pension plan abroad and many of the European private pension companies have offices in Spain. You may also consider continuing to contribute to a UK personal pension after you leave the UK. Tax relief on contributions to a UK personal pension will cease after you have utilised any unused tax allowances left behind. Thereafter, you can still contribute but without the additional tax relief credit. Alternatively, those who retire to Spain early may consider taking out a Spanish pension plan. Spanish pensions usually require a small minimum monthly payment, sometimes as low as €30. Lump sum contributions can be made whenever you like, although they must usually be more than around €600. Pensions should be index-linked so that they keep pace with inflation. Index-linked policies ensure that capital is tax free after contributions have been made for fifteen years, but there is an increasing scale of tax penalties for early surrender. Some of the main Spanish pension providers are listed below.

Private Pension Plan Providers in Spain

Axa Seguros y Reaseguros: www.axa-seguros.es.

Caser Seguros: ☎902-222747; www.caser.es.

Direct Seguros: ☎902-404025; www.directseguros.es.

La Estrella Seguros: ☎902-333433; www.laestrella.es.

Seguros El Corte Ingles: ☎901-122122; http://seguroeseci.elcorteingles.es.

Winterthur: ☎902-303012; www.winterthur.es.

PERSONAL TAXATION

Currently, foreigners resident in Spain will find that they pay approximately the same amount of tax as they would elsewhere in the EU. There is no special tax relief for foreigners residing in Spain; capital gains and disposable assets are included as part of income and are taxed accordingly; residents are liable to pay Spanish tax on their worldwide income. This means that all income is taxable, be it from a pension, private investments, dividends, or interest.

Non-residents as well as residents of Spain need a tax reference number – *Número de Identificación Extranjero (NIE)* –a tax identification number for foreign residents and property owning non-residents. You will need this not only for matters concerning tax but also for other matters like opening a bank account; it is also required when registering an *escritura*. See *Basics* for details of how to obtain an NIE.

Most taxes are based on self-assessment whereby the individual is responsible for reporting and calculating any taxes due. Depending on how complicated your affairs are, you will be able to complete the self-assessment forms yourself or use the services of an accountant versed in the tax laws of both Spain and your country of residence. A cheaper option is to use a *gestor* (see *Basics*).

The Spanish Tax Agency (*Agencia Estatal de Administración Tributaria* commonly referred to as the *Hacienda*) has a website at www.aeat.es with information on Spanish taxes in general and some pages translated into English. For more information on the Spanish tax system, contact your nearest Spanish embassy or consulate, the *Ministerio de Hacienda*, (☎901-335533) or your local tax office.

Taxation Status

The Spanish tax authorities work on a residence-based system of taxation. Anyone spending 183 days or more in Spain during the Spanish tax year (ending 31 December) is deemed to be a resident and will be liable to pay Spanish tax. This holds true whether or not one is in possession of a formal residence permit; faking tourist status will not, therefore, exclude unwilling contributors from paying their share of taxes.

In 1998 the *Ley del Impuesto Sobre la Renta de No Residentes* (Non-residents Income Tax Act) was passed by the Spanish government to tackle the problem of wresting some taxable income from the one million or more non-resident property owners in Spain. Under this ruling, anyone who is not resident in Spain, i.e. who spends less than 183 days in the country each year, is still liable for Spanish tax on income *arising* in Spain. Owning property is considered to produce a taxable income of between 1.1% and 2% of the value of the property based on the *Valor Catastral* (the rateable value of the property). To cover this, non-residents pay a small amount of tax known as *Patrimonio*. There are no deductions or allowance on this tax against expenses.

Double Taxation Agreements

Spain has reciprocal tax agreements with a number of countries around the world, including the UK, which avoids the possibility of someone being taxed twice on their income from renting property, pensions, gifts, inheritance, etc. – once by the Spanish and once by the tax authorities in their home country.

However, there may be a slight hitch during the initial period of Spanish residence because, for instance, the UK and Spanish tax years run from April to April and from January to January respectively and therefore UK nationals in Spain may be taxed by both the Spanish and UK authorities in the overlapping months of their first year in the new country. In this case, you would be able to claim a refund of UK tax by applying to the Inland Revenue through your local UK tax office. They will supply you with an SPA/Individual form (which offers relief at source for tax refunds concerning interest, royalties and pensions) or with the SPA/Individual/Credit form (which provides repayment on dividend income for anyone who has suffered double taxation on moving to Spain). Once the form has been filled out, take it to the *hacienda* (tax office) in Spain. They will stamp it and then you can return it to the British tax authorities as proof that you have paid Spanish tax and are therefore no longer liable for British tax. It is a procedure that should be carried out while you are in Spain and not after your return to the UK. It is important to keep accounts of your income, expenditure etc. while in Spain in order to meet any problems that may arise.

Income Tax (IRPF)

Income tax is known in Spain as IRPF (*Impuesto Sobre la Renta de las Personas Físicas*). Residents are taxable on all sources of worldwide income, both earned and unearned at a rate which varies between 15% and 45%. This includes pensions. In most cases, UK state and private pensions received in Spain by a tax resident will be subject to Spanish income tax. However, retired persons need not file a tax return unless their gross income exceeds €7,500 - (the *minimo vital*). Before you become liable for income tax you deduct the minimum from your gross income and also deduct various other allowances depending on your circumstances. Up-to-date information about the minimum earnings before tax is liable can be obtained from the Spanish Tax Office website (www.aeat.es). It is a good idea to consult a tax adviser if you are over this limit, at least for the first few years. Tax advisers in Spain are usually quite cheap, and a *gestor* (see Basics) will offer even cheaper rates.

Tax Returns. Those whose financial situation is relatively uncomplicated can draw up their own tax return and advice on how to do this is available from the local *hacienda*. Tax return forms can be purchased from the tobacconists (*estanco*) for around €0.30 or from your local *agencia tributaria* office. There are three kinds of tax return form. Form 103 is the abbreviated declaration, form 101 is the simple declaration and form 100 is the ordinary declaration. Business and professional activities must be recorded on the last, the *declaración ordinaria*, which is the longest and most complex of the three and will usually require the help of an accountant to complete. For those with complex tax returns or those for whom the word 'tax' succeeds only in producing blind panic and a feeling of deep nausea, the *asesor fiscal* offers invaluable assistance. For fees beginning at around €60 for relatively straightforward tax returns, this god-sent official will complete the form on your behalf and frequently save you a lot of money by virtue of his or her wisdom and general expertise.

○ The Spanish tax year runs from 1 January to 31 December. Returns should be made between 1 May and 20 June. Late filing of a tax return leads to a surcharge on the tax due.

○ Returns should be submitted to the district tax office where you are resident for tax purposes. Alternatively you can file the return and pay at designated banks in the area, which allows you to transfer the cash to the tax authorities straight from your account.

○ To file your tax return you will need to have your most recent receipt for the payment of your *Contribucion Urbana (IBI)* – if you are a property owner – as a percentage of the official value of your property is calculated as if it were income and then added to your income tax total. You will also need your end-of-year bank statement, which will show any interest you have been paid and your average balance over the tax year.

○ You must also take documents pertaining to any other property you own, or any other shares, stocks, investments, insurance policies or bonds you have, as well as copies of your passport and residence permit. Any other major assets in Spain will also need to be declared as well as any tax paid in another country.

○ You will always need to state your NIE reference when dealing with the tax agency.

Wealth Tax (Impuesto Extraordinario Sobre El Patrimonio)

Wealth Tax is calculated on the value of an individual's assets in Spain on 31 December every year and is imposed on those who are non-resident or resident in Spain for ordinary tax purposes. A non-resident pays Wealth Tax at the same rate as a resident and must declare the value of the property owned in Spain (calculated on the *valor catastral* and declared on the *escritura*), vehicles and investments (if applicable) and the average cleared balance of a Spanish bank account over the previous year. Deductions are available against debts on a property or mortgage.

While a non-resident need only declare assets and property in Spain, residents must declare their worldwide assets when assessing their payment of Wealth Tax (though a resident pays nothing on the first €150,253 of the valuation). Because the tax is on the individual, unless you are a resident and you have considerable business interests and valuable property in Spain it is unlikely that you will be eligible to pay much. Wealth Tax is collected every June; the rate beginning at 0.2% for assets valuing €167,129 or over held in Spain. The upper bracket of tax payable is 2.5% on assets over €10,695,996.

VAT (Impuesto Sobre el Valor Añadido – IVA)

The rate of VAT in Spain is normally 16%, though commodities such as food products used for human or animal consumption, water, veterinary products or products to be used in the production of food, seeds and fertilisers carry a rate of 7%. There is a super-reduced IVA of 4% on standard bread, flours and cereals used for the production of bread, milk (in different forms), cheese, eggs, fruit and vegetables, books, periodicals, pharmaceutical products, vehicles for handicapped people and prosthesis (artificial arms, teeth, etc.) Health, education, insurance and financial services are all exempt from VAT as is the transfer of any business, providing the buyer continues the existing business concern, rental of private property etc. IVA does not apply in the Canary Islands, Ceuta or Melilla. In the Canaries a regional tax (Canarian Indirect General Tax – IGIC) is charged instead at a rate of 5%.

WILLS AND INHERITANCE

Making a Will

It is very important that anyone who buys property in Spain should make a Spanish will in order to avoid the time-consuming and expensive legal problems which will otherwise result from Spanish inheritance laws and taxes, as one expat from the Valencia region warns: '*When my husband died recently, the fact that he had a Spanish will was a real help as everything was sorted out in 2-3 weeks. With an English will it could have taken months and months*'. Having a Spanish will for Spanish assets also avoids the hassle of waiting for the granting of probate from your country of origin, and allows the will to be dealt with immediately under local laws, thereby speeding up the will's execution. It is therefore advisable to make two wills, one which disposes of Spanish assets and another which deals with any UK assets, rather than trying to combine the two. However, it is vital that these two wills do not conflict with one another.

Problems arise when people die intestate, i.e. without a will. Usually Spanish law will be applied to the Spanish assets of the deceased, although this could give rise to legal wrangling as there may be a case for applying the rules of the home country to the estate. The cost of these arguments between lawyers and tax officials will be borne by your heirs, so it is always best to make a will. If a person dies intestate then the Spanish law of succession determines who shall inherit. According to the law of 'compulsory heirs' (*herederos forzosos*) in Spain, two-thirds of the deceased's estate must be left to his or her children. Spanish inheritance rules are far more restrictive than those that apply under British law. Only one third of the estate can be disposed of freely.

However, if a foreigner makes a will in Spain, then they are not subject to these restrictions and may dispose of their assets as they please. The only consideration to bear in mind however is that non-relatives may be liable for larger amounts of succession tax. A Spanish will does not exempt the inheritors from succession tax (see below), although this will only effect those who have inherited a sum which exceeds the current non-taxable tax threshold; and even then inheritance tax rates are only really very high in the case of property being left to non-relatives. The closer the relationship between the deceased and the heir, the lower the rate of inheritance tax. Indeed unmarried couples are treated as complete strangers in the eyes of the Spanish legal system. It is for this reason that executors and trustees are unusual in Spain.

It is always advisable to use a Spanish lawyer to draft your will and to advise as to its contents. The cost of drafting a simple will is around €150, plus the cost of the notary. All Spanish wills can be made out in two columns, one in Spanish and one in English, as long as this is approved by an official translator.

Types of Spanish Will

The most common form of will in Spain is the **open will** (*testamento abierto*). This type of will is made before a notary, who keeps the original document in his files. The notary will also send a notification of the will to the Central Registry of Spanish Wills (*Registro Central de Última Voluntad*). The notary may require the presence of two witnesses, who must also sign the will. Once drawn up, you will be presented with a copy (*copia autorizada*). It is also possible to draw up a **closed will** (*testamento cerrado*), the contents of which will remain secret until your death. Unlike an open will, this *must* be drawn up by a Spanish lawyer. This will is presented before the notary in an envelope. You must then declare before the notary that the provisions are contained within the envelope, whereupon the notary will seal the envelope in the presence of witnesses. The notary then files the will and sends a notification of it to the Central Registry in Madrid.

There is a third type of will in Spain, although it is not recommended as the processes for its execution are more complicated. The **holographic will** (*testamento ológrafo*) is written entirely in the handwriting of the testator, who must also sign and date it. No witnesses or other formalities are required, although it is sensible to voluntarily register the will in Madrid. Upon the death of the testator, the will must be verified as genuine before a judge, who will require the closest relatives of the deceased to authenticate the handwriting.

Having made the will it should ideally be kept in a safe place along with bank accounts and insurance policies. Another copy should be held by the executor of your estate, or by your lawyer although it is fairly uncommon to appoint an executor in Spain. If at any point you decide to change your will then it is possible to revoke provisions made in a will, even if you had previously declared your intention not to revoke them.

Spanish Succession Tax (Impuesto Sobre Sucesiones y Donaciones)

Gifts on the death of an individual can still bring high rates of taxation in Spain – sometimes at a rate as high as 82% on inherited wealth. Spanish Succession Tax is paid by the persons inheriting, and not on the value of the estate of the deceased. If the deceased was resident in Spain for tax purposes then all of his or her assets worldwide will be subject to succession tax; if the deceased was a non-tax resident then only the property in Spain will be subject to tax – the rest of the assets being subject to the tax in the country of residence. If the beneficiary is a resident of a country that has a double taxation agreement with Spain then he or she will not be taxed twice.

Property is valued by the Tax Agency at the market rate, or the *valor catastral* depending on which is the higher. Furnishings etc. are usually valued at 3% of the value of the property. Outstanding debts are deducted from the value of the assets, and stocks and shares and bank balances are valued at the date of death. Another point to recognise is that under Spanish law, life insurance policies written in trust in the UK are not binding should the policyholder die whilst a resident of Spain. The policy proceeds will be taxable.

> The Spanish tax authorities impose penalties if matters are not cleared up quickly.
> For example, there is a window of six months in which to pay taxes on the Spanish
> estate after death. If taxes are not paid within this time limit, a surcharge of 20% will
> be applied, and further, additional interest on the original demand will be charged.

If a joint owner of a property in Spain dies, there is no automatic inheritance by the other owners of the property. Even if the property is left to a beneficiary in the owner's will, there will be a transfer tax payable. Because the tax is based on the size of the gift, the more you inherit the more you will be taxed. However, the nearer the relative is to the deceased, the less tax is payable on inherited gifts. Near relatives are also entitled to receive a proportion tax-free. One way of making sure that a beneficiary of a will is not liable for crippling taxes is to register a newly purchased property in the name of the person/s who will eventually inherit. Because the property will stay in the name of the original named owner on the death of the buyer of the property, the taxes and fees usually incurred on transference of title deeds will be minimal.

The tax payment is calculated on the degree of kinship between the deceased and the person inheriting. Allowances (at differing rates) are given to direct descendants less than 21 years of age, direct descendants (spouse, parents, children, siblings) over 21 years of age and other relatives (uncles/aunts, cousins, nieces/nephews). The rate of tax payable after the allowances on kinship is then multiplied by a rate ranging from 1%-1.4% dependent on the existing wealth in Spain of the person inheriting.

However, if the recipient is not resident then they will pay no added tax as long as they have no wealth in Spain. There is also tax relief available on family homes and businesses and 95% of the net value of such properties if the recipients are either the children or spouse of the deceased. However, the property will need to remain in the hands of such recipients for ten years – and continue to be used as a family home or business – if inheritance tax is to be avoided.

> Note that the inheritance tax rules can differ wildly between the different autonomous communities. For example, the tax authorities in the Basque country, Navarre and Cantabria have all but abolished succession tax for inheriting spouses and children, reducing it to about 1%. Some other regions (including Valencia, Murcia, Madrid and the Balearic islands) accepted proposals made by the previous government for a phased reduction of succession tax (down to 1%) by 2007 for spouses and children. The first phase of these changes was implemented in 2004, but in many of the regions the second phase has not happened. It is always best therefore to take expert legal and financial advice on your own particular circumstances.

Bereavement

In the unfortunate event that a relative, partner or close friend should die while in Spain there are a few essential formalities which you will have to deal with. If this person dies in hospital then the hospital authorities will take care of the administrative details. However, should they die at home, then the first step is to inform the municipal police *(Policía Municipal)* who in turn will advise the forensic judge *(Juez Forense)* who will have to come to the home to authorise the removal of the body. Should the deceased have been receiving medical care, you should also contact his or her doctor. As in the UK, an autopsy is not necessary unless the forensic judge or the doctor is in any doubt as to the cause of death.

You will need to contact a funeral director *(pompas fúnebres)* who will often deal with a lot of the paperwork on your behalf. For example, it is quite common for a funeral director to obtain the consulate death certificate on behalf of the deceased's relatives. He or she will frequently also ensure that the necessary official certificates are delivered to the family and contact a British pastor to perform the burial service.

Funerals in Spain are usually held within 24 hours of death, but they can be delayed in order to allow for friends and family to arrive. In these circumstances the body will be kept in a morgue at additional cost. It is possible to have the body repatriated for cremation in the country of origin, but such procedures are expensive as the body must be embalmed and transported in a lead lined coffin.

A foreigner can be buried in most Spanish cemeteries, whether or not he or she was a Catholic. However, other options include a British cemetery in Málaga, an international one in Benalmadena and crematoriums in Madrid, Seville and Málaga. You will find that the British and international cemeteries have the familiar subterranean burial plots to which we are accustomed, while Spanish cemeteries consist of raised graves with the bodies placed in niches. A funeral service will cost a basic rate of around €1,000 although this can rise quickly with transport costs and other fees. Most Spanish cemeteries rent out burial plots for varying time periods and, while you will find that municipal cemetery rates are quite inexpensive, purchasing a plot can be very pricey; so it's worth enquiring at the town hall for details.

The death certificate is issued by the Civil Registry (*Registro Civil*) or at the offices of the local Justice of the Peace (*Juzgado de Paz*) depending on the locality. The certificate is usually available for collection within 2-3 days. It is a good idea to get a number of original copies of the death certificate as many authorities may require them. These may include the British consular office in your location, Department of Work and Pensions in Newcastle, Paymaster General, Inland Revenue, probate office, banks, insurance companies etc. It is also a good idea to keep a copy for your own records.

Executing the Will

In order to start the procedures involved in the execution of a Spanish will, it is first necessary to apply to the *Registro Central de Última Voluntad* in Madrid for the *Certificado de Últimas Voluntades* (literally – certificate of last wishes). Most people use a gestor for this process, who will send an original copy of the death certificate with full details of the deceased. However, those with sufficient Spanish can find the official form which needs to be completed in any *estanco* (tobacconists). The death certificate will be returned, along with the required document within 2-3 weeks. If you do not know whether the deceased had made a will, the Registro Central will be able to tell you as every will is kept on file here. If the will exists then the registry will be able to supply you with the document's certificate number and the name of the notary who authorised it. If there is more than one will, only the last one made is legally valid.

Once received, the certificate must be taken to a notary who will prepare the inheritance deed (*Escritura de Aceptación de Herencia*). This deed must be signed simultaneously by all heirs, or a representative who has been issued power of attorney. The notary will require full details of all assets plus a number of other documents such as deeds, receipts for property tax, details of bank accounts, shares etc. Once the *escritura* has been signed, a copy must be taken to the tax office in order to pay the death duties. This should be done within six months of the death, otherwise surcharges will be applied. If the assets include property, then the inheritance deed must also be presented at the Property Registry (*Registro de Propiedad*) so that the names of the new owners of the property may be registered. Another copy of the deed should then be presented at the local town hall and the *Plusvalía* tax paid (this must also be done within six months of the death). Succession tax must be paid before the assets in Spain can be released. It may therefore be necessary to take out a loan in order to pay the taxes and ensure the release of the assets.

Healthcare

CHAPTER SUMMARY

○ The Spanish system of public healthcare was recently voted one of the top five in the world, and is free to all foreign pensioners with a residence card.

○ Once in Spain it is advisable to register with the health services as soon as possible. At the social security office you will be issued with a health card which must be produced whenever medical treatment is required.

○ Pensioners should bear in mind that once they have become resident in Spain and qualified for state healthcare, they are no longer entitled to free NHS treatment in the UK.

○ All dental practices in Spain are private. The cost of treatment is generally lower than in the UK and many practices offer membership schemes with an annual fee.

○ **Hospitals.** Waiting lists for hospitals are shorter in Spain than in the UK and those who have been waiting for too long for an operation under the state system are often referred to private hospitals free of charge.

　○ Spanish nurses have a slightly different role to UK nurses in that they are only there for their professional medical skills. The patient's family is expected to deal with welfare issues.

　○ Aftercare is an area that is lacking in comparison to the UK. Spanish hospitals do not have health care visitors.

○ The Spanish have a long tradition of looking after the elderly in the family home and as a result, state and private residential care centres are thin on the ground. People should make provisions long in advance for the point when they will no longer be able to look after themselves.

○ Home care is often provided by social services but the quality of this service varies dramatically between regions.

THE SPANISH HEALTHCARE SYSTEM

It is generally agreed that the Spanish system of public healthcare, available free to all pensioners with a residence card, is very efficient and the quality of care of an extremely high standard. Indeed it was recently voted one of the top five healthcare systems in the world. Many British expats living in Spain claim that the system is more advanced than the NHS and that waiting lists for operations are far shorter. Many doctors and nurses speak English and most hospitals and clinics in the main tourist areas provide interpreters.

However, the Spanish healthcare system is not perfect. Bear in mind that the availability of certain services does vary from locality to locality and if facilities are not available to meet your specific needs, you may have to travel to another area for treatment. As some hospitals only treat private patients, it is as well to know which hospitals in your area provide national health treatment. A list of national health centres and hospitals may be found in your local office of the *Instituto Nacional de la Seguridad Social (INSS)*, or indeed in the local Yellow Pages (*las páginas amarillas*).

Those who fear a shortfall in services in their area could consider taking out private insurance (see below). For those who do not qualify for public healthcare, it is essential to take out private health insurance, and you will not be eligible for a residence card without it.

A list of English-speaking doctors will be available from the local British Consulate. You may choose your own general practitioner, provided that the GP's number of patients does not exceed the limits established within that particular area. Pensioners in Spain are entitled both to free medical care and free prescription medicine. However, Spanish social security does not cover dental treatment, dentures or spectacles.

Remember to take copies of medical records with you to present to your new doctor. It is also a good idea to find out the generic name for any prescribed medication that you are taking, as this can vary from country to country.

The E121 and E106

The first step for retired UK citizens, before moving to Spain, is to obtain the form E121 from the Pension Service. This form gives access to the Spanish health system for British state retirement pensioners, their spouses and dependent children, and for anyone receiving the UK Incapacity Benefit. Without it, you will be charged for treatment. Your form must be registered at the local social security office (*Instituto Nacional de Seguridad Social*), for which you will need your residence permit. If you are submitting the E121 for registration before the application for residencia has been approved, you should submit a copy of the residencia application form.

Those who move to Spain before UK state retirement age are able to obtain temporary cover for healthcare by filling in form E106. This form is also available from the Department of Work and Pensions (☎0191-218 7777), or the Inland Revenue.

The European Health Insurance Card (EHIC – formerly E111)

Reciprocal medical arrangements which exist between the UK and Spain under EU regulations make it possible to obtain mainly free medical treatment for shorter-term visitors to Spain for no more than three months at one time. This arrangement may well be helpful for those going on a house-hunting trip to Spain or those who already have holiday homes there. However, this agreement only covers temporary residence, not the first three months of permanent residence in the new country and applies only to emergency medical treatment.

To qualify for such treatment you need a European Health Insurance Card (EHIC). It is possible to apply online (www.dh.gov.uk/travellers) or at the Post Office. Cards applied for online arrive within seven days.

An EHIC normally expires after a three-month period and is not valid once you have left the UK permanently. Until recently the authorities did not really bother to control this, and the EHIC was sufficient. These days the rules are far more likely to be enforced, and patients may well be asked for flight tickets as proof of when they arrived in Spain. Once a residence permit has been applied for (i.e. after three months) permanent arrangements should have been made. Explanatory leaflet SA29 gives details of social security, healthcare and pension rights within the EU and is obtainable from main post offices and also from the DWP Overseas Directorate, Tyneview Park, Whitely Road, Benton, Newcastle-upon-Tyne NE98 1BA.

Registering with the Health Service

The importance of registering with the health service is something that the majority of expatriates underestimate. First and foremost you will want to ensure that if you fall ill you will not run into problems. British consulates are registering a rise in the number of people seeking advice on healthcare.

Although 225,000 Britons are registered to vote in municipal elections in Spain, only 49,436 have completed the E121 form and registered with Spanish health authorities. Not only are expatriates putting themselves at risk, but they are also placing a huge strain on the Spanish system. If patients are registered under the E121 scheme, governments in the EU can reclaim a share of healthcare costs from the patients' home countries. By not registering, many expatriates are still receiving treatment but it is costing the Spanish government millions of euros. Increasingly local authorities are displaying a hardening stance towards expats who demand treatment without having registered. It is rare that they would refuse treatment in serious cases, but they could feasibly send people back to Britain. The only way to avoid this drain on an overstretched health system is by taking your E121 and registering with the health authorities as soon as you arrive in Spain.

How to Register

It is essential that all British nationals intending to move to Spain register their change of address with the Overseas Division (Medical Benefits) of the Department for Work and Pensions Benefits Agency before leaving the UK. Once in Spain it is advisable to register with the health services as early as possible. Pensioners should take form E-121 (see above) to their nearest social security office (*Instituto Nacional de Seguridad Social – INSS*. Your nearest office can be found as www.seg-social. es or in the Yellow Pages). However, it is possible that before registering with social security, you will need to be registered as resident at the town hall (*ayuntamiento*) – this is not the same as obtaining the *residencia*. Always visit the town hall first to ask for guidance about medical registration, as the procedures differ in different parts of Spain. It will save time if you take your NIE number, copies of your passport, and proof of where you live (any utility bill addressed to you should suffice).

At the INSS you should apply for a Spanish health card (*Tarjeta Sanitaria*) sometimes referred to as a SIP card. Often you will be issued with a temporary card, and the official card will be posted to you at a later date. Take this card to your nearest health centre (*Ambulatorio*) and ask to register with a doctor.

The health card, or a photocopy of it, must be produced whenever medical treatment is required and will cover the holder for medical treatment and most prescription charges.

In Spain, further information about social security can be obtained from the INSS (☎ 915 688 300; www.seg-social.es).

Visiting the Doctor

Whatever you may have heard about the poor time-keeping of Spaniards, and their mañana attitude, this tends not to be the case with doctor's appointments which are very punctual. Nevertheless, they may over-run as Spanish doctors are particularly good about giving each patient as much individual attention as they need and doctors' surgeries often display a sign stating that the duration of the consultation cannot be precise. As in the UK, appointments are usually made a few days in advance, but there is always a doctor available for urgent matters. Where necessary doctors do make home calls.

Healthcare is an area where the language barrier becomes enormously important. You are putting yourself in a potentially dangerous situation if you cannot convey exactly what the problem is to your doctor, and even if you have found a doctor with a good level of English, he or she may not be able to pick up on the subtleties of your problem. Maurice Hamlin of www.practicalspain. com advises that *'If you are coming to live in Spain, it is sensible to have a resumé of your medical history translated into Spanish, in particular detailing any specific illnesses, drugs required or allergies'.* If you have any particular medical concerns, it may also be a good idea to invest in one of the comprehensive English-Spanish medical dictionaries available from bookshops.

If you are concerned about visiting the doctor then you should take an interpreter with you. They can be found in the *paginas amarillas* (yellow pages), or Age Concern España (www.acespana.org) keeps a list of them. As expat Sarah Moore explains, making yourself understood is not just for your own peace of mind, but also for that of the doctor:

Sometimes the language barrier can be a real problem and the doctors usually prefer that an interpreter go with the patient, at least if it's a first visit to a GP, in order to explain any pre-existing health problems. Although many doctors do speak English they prefer to have an interpreter just in case there are any misunderstandings and to really make sure they fully understand.

Prescriptions. Having successfully conveyed your concerns to the doctor, he may well give you a prescription which can then be collected from the *farmacia*. The majority of prescriptions for pensioners are free. If for some reason you are not covered under the Spanish state healthcare system, then you will find that most medications are far cheaper than in the UK.

Prescriptions received from hospitals must be paid for up front at the pharmacy, but it is then possible to obtain a note from your GP allowing the pharmacist to make a full refund.

Other Medical Services

Dental Care. All dental practices (*Clinicas Dentales*) in Spain are private. If you have private health insurance then you can opt to have a comprehensive dental policy included. Otherwise you should pay the dentist directly.

Generally the price of dental treatment is lower than in the UK, although it is worth shopping around before registering as fees can vary. On the costas, it is very easy to find an English-speaking dentist, or even English-run practices, although these tend to be more expensive than the Spanish practices. The level of competition is high in these areas and many surgeries offer a free consultation and an estimate for any work required. Many practices also offer membership schemes, whereby you pay an annual fee that includes consultations and regular check-ups. Always take recommendations from locals before registering with a dentist.

Smaller practices, and those located in rural areas and small towns do not always offer the range of services that you might be accustomed to in the UK, and you may have to visit a specialist for anything other than a check-up or a filling. Orthodontic, corrective and cosmetic treatment are all available in Spain, but may involve a visit to the nearest large town.

Opticians. English-speaking opticians are widespread on the costas and in the big cities. In smaller towns and rural areas you may have to practise your Spanish. The majority provide free eye tests for new customers. Find you nearest optician in the Yellow Pages under '*Opticas*'.

Pharmacies. Pharmacists in Spain are extremely well trained and can recommend treatments over the counter. As a result many people visit pharmacies (*farmacias*) rather than go to the doctor for minor ailments. If the pharmacist cannot help then they will usually recommend a doctor or specialist who can.

Pharmacists have the same opening hours as shops, but they work a rotation system for nights and public holidays. The chemists that are open out-of-hours are known as *farmacias de guardia,* details of which are posted in local newspapers and in the windows of chemists. It is usually necessary to ring a bell and be served through a hatch at the out-of-hours chemists.

Remember that all forms of medicine are sold exclusively at pharmacists, and the supermarkets are only allowed to stock basic first aid equipment.

LOCAL HEALTH ISSUES

The health benefits of living in Spain are enthusiastically expounded by expatriates. The warm climate and Mediterranean diet are certainly factors that help explain the longevity of Spain's people and there are very few health concerns that are specific to Spain. Expat Margaret Hales warns that heatstroke can sometimes be a problem for newcomers to Spain, but she says '*You soon learn to follow the example of the Spanish: to stay out of the midday sun, and to take a siesta during the hottest part of the day*'.

Creepy Crawlies

It pays to be aware of the following irritations, especially for those who enjoy countryside rambles:

Processional Pine Caterpillars: The most common irritation. Found in all areas of Spain, and especially where there are pine trees, these caterpillars can be recognised by the way they travel nose to tail in a 'procession'. Do not touch them as their hairs are poisonous, causing a rash and irritation. If you live in an area where these creatures are common, it is a good idea to keep anti-histamine tablets to hand.

Scorpions: The Mediterranean Scorpion is found all over Spain and the European Black Scorpion is found in the northern regions. A sting from either type is unpleasant but not dangerous. Check your shoes in the morning if you are staying in a particularly arid area of the country.

Mosquitoes: Common in areas with stagnant pools of water. Mosquitoes are mostly an irritation, but they can also pass on diseases. Malaria was eradicated in Spain in 1964, but they can carry other diseases. For example, in 2005 the West Nile virus was bought into the Barcelona area by mosquitoes. Always use repellent.

Spiders. The most dangerous spider in Spain is the Black Widow, which gives a nasty (but not fatal) bite. They are quite rare, but are most likely to be found in arid parts of Almeria and Aragon. They are sometimes spotted in Valencia and Andalucia as well. Tarantulas are common in Toledo, but their venom is weak and does not affect humans. Brown Recluse Spiders are also found in parts of Spain. Their bites are painful and cause blistering. All spider bites should receive medical attention as soon as possible.

Community sanitation is generally very good, and health concerns related to foods and beverages are minimal. You should take the same common sense precautions, such as thoroughly washing fruit and vegetables, as you would in the UK. Diseases transmitted by insects are not a concern in Spain. Nevertheless insects and bugs that can cause irritation and are best avoided are discussed in the box below.

PRIVATE MEDICAL INSURANCE

Although the level of convenience, comfort and attention offered through private insurance schemes is superior to that received by public health patients, the treatment itself will not necessarily be of a higher quality. Nevertheless a growing number of foreign residents in Spain are opting to remove themselves from the Spanish National Health Service to take out private health insurance. One of the advantages of UK health insurance schemes is that their policies cover the claimants for treatment incurred anywhere in Europe, not just in Spain itself.

Spanish insurance policies are widely available and have a distinct advantage over those offered in the UK in that payment for medical treatment is made in the form of vouchers. This means that you can use them to pay for services at the time of treatment, rather than having to pay for treatment up front and then claim back costs from an insurance company after the event. However, although the premiums on Spanish insurance policies may appear cheaper and more attractive than those offered by British companies you may well find that a policy is limited to specific local hospitals – not too helpful if you are in urgent need of treatment but nowhere near a hospital on the policy list. Additionally, the small print needs to be read very carefully (perhaps treatment is only refunded if surgery is performed, or outpatient treatment is not included in the policy). Other policies may offer limited cover on surgery, medicines and hospital accommodation. If you do decide to get a Spanish policy make sure that you have read the small print in an English translation.

Sanitas (☎952-774450; www.isanitas.com) is the leading private healthcare provider in Spain with more than 1.2 million members. Their Health Plan is specifically aimed at foreigners living in Spain. The cost of private health insurance varies according to age.

Useful Contacts – Private Medical Insurance

AXA PPP Healthcare: ☎01892-612080; www.axappphealthcare.co.uk.

British United Provident Association (BUPA): ☎0800-001010; www.bupa.co.uk.

Exeter Friendly Society: ☎01392-353535; www.exeterfriendly.co.uk.

Expacare Insurance Services: ☎01344-381650; www.expacare.net.

Goodhealth: ☎020-7423 4300; www.goodhealthworldwide.com.

Healthcare International: ☎020-7665 1627; www.healthcareinternational.com.

Sanitas: ☎902-102400; www.sanitas.es.

EMERGENCIES AND HOSPITALISATION

Emergencies

The emergency services in Spain are extremely good. Public ambulances are contacted on ☎061. The Red Cross (Cruz Roja) also have an emergency ambulance service (☎952-443545). Failing this there are 24 hour private ambulance services, listed in the yellow pages. Most clinics and private hospitals also operate their own ambulance services. All ambulances are equipped with emergency equipment and drivers and staff are trained to provide first-aid.

All public hospitals provide 24-hour casualty and emergency treatment (*urgencies*) and there are also 24 hour private medical centres, which tend to offer bilingual staff along the Mediterranean coast. The telephone numbers of first aid stations are listed at the front of telephone directories. In an emergency, a hospital must treat you, regardless of your ability to pay.

Hospitalisation

Whilst the Spanish healthcare system is first rate, there are not enough hospitals, especially in the poorer areas. This is not to say that waiting lists are horrendously long in Spain. Most expats agree that they are shorter than in the UK. However, waiting lists are getting longer, especially in the coastal areas where hospitals have been overburdened by the massive influx of older foreign residents. Patricia Webb of Age Concern España explains how the Spanish are dealing with the problem:

I've been taking people to the hospitals here in Torrevieja for five or six years now, and the service used to be incredibly quick but these days people are having to wait longer and longer to have an operation. The Spanish recognise this and are building new hospitals, which will ease the problem in time. Another good policy is that if you have been waiting for a long time for an operation in a state hospital, then you are often referred to a private hospital free of charge. These hospitals have an obligation to take a number of state operations every year in order to ease the pressure.

The majority of expatriates talk favourably of their experiences in Spanish hospitals and the level of care that they receive. Although the language barrier can create problems, many doctors speak at least some English and as one expat points out: *'Hospital doctors are very good about explaining exactly what's going on to the families – they have a lot of patience'.*

You should be aware however that the role of nurses in Spanish hospitals is different to that which we are accustomed to in the UK. Generally they are only available for their professional medical skills, and not for welfare issues such as serving food or dealing with bedpans. Patricia Webb explains:

As Spain is so family orientated the hospitals expect families to go in and help look after the patients. They like the families to be there and they feel that it is better for the patient to have somebody they know there. It's a different attitude. Of course, if there is nobody that can go in then the nurses will do everything.

As the family is expected to frequently attend to the patient, hospitals offer excellent facilities for visitors, such as reclining armchairs for those who wish to spend the night. The majority of hospitals offer rooms with just two beds, rather than large wards. Sharing with a Spaniard is quite an experience, as the 'two visitors at a time' rule is unheard of, and more often than not the entire extended family will bustle in and out, fussing over the patient. Those who have no visitors themselves often find that the extended family of their Spanish neighbour will lend a hand. Alternatively in many of the cities and coastal areas it is possible to ask for a visit from an English-speaking hospital visitor.

One thing to bear in mind, according to Age Concern España, is that aftercare is not so well provided for in Spain. Spanish hospitals do not have healthcare visitors in the same way that they would in the UK.

RETURNING TO THE UK FOR TREATMENT

The advantages of being officially resident in Spain, and therefore entitled to health care, can also be a disadvantage for people who still spend long periods of time in the UK. Under the current Department of Health regulations **anyone who spends more than three consecutive months living outside the UK, with the intention of permanently living abroad, is no longer entitled to free NHS hospital treatment in England**, except in the case of an emergency. This includes people in receipt of UK state retirement pensions.

Those who are not permanently resident in Spain (i.e. spend less than six months a year there and have not applied for a *residencia*) and spend more than six months a year in the UK may still receive NHS treatment free of charge. However, residents of Spain, who have activated their E121 (or E106) and receive free healthcare in Spain may not. They may only be exempt from charges if NHS treatment is needed urgently upon their return to the UK for a condition that arose after leaving Spain. Equally, emergency treatment is provided free of charge, regardless of nationality.

Returning to the UK permanently. The moment that you take up permanent residence in the UK, you are once again entitled to the full range of free NHS treatment. This is discussed further in the final chapter, *Returning Home*.

CARE IN THE HOME AND RESIDENTIAL CARE

Spain has a long tradition of looking after its old people in the family home and this has presented a major problem for many retired expatriates who have reached the stage where they can no longer care for themselves. In most areas of Spain the infrastructure for caring for the elderly is simply not yet in place. The provision of social care can vary enormously from one local authority to another. According to Judy Arnold-Boakes of *Age Concern España* in a recent article in the *Observer*, '*In some areas the authorities don't pick up the bill when a person runs out of money and in some areas they do. Some areas provide the full range of social services help. Others don't. And what is the policy today may not be the policy in 15 years*'. It is therefore recommended by British consular officials that people should make provisions long in advance for the point when they will no longer be able to look after themselves.

The Spanish home-care and residential care system is not equipped to deal with the influx of elderly patients to Spain - Martine de Volder, nurse in Tenerife.

The influx of retirees to Spain has created quite a problem. I have seen too many people in a terrible state because they could not afford proper nursing. If the elderly are healthy then there is no problem, but issues arise when one or both partners need some help. Many people are forced to return to their country of origin in order to receive full-time care. There are very few public nursing homes and even the private homes have enormous waiting lists. Home care can be provided by social services in the town where you live, but this is a minimal service.

Further problems arise when people are living illegally in Spain. Many are forced to pay for people, who are not professionals, to visit them in their own homes, as they are not eligible for support from social services. Often these people have no training and are simply earning extra money by offering caring services. This is potentially disastrous as the patients may be very vulnerable.

Retirement Homes

It is only in the last few years that long-term care homes have sprung up in any number. Each region has a different number available and different criteria to access them. Generally, there are very few council-run care homes, and the demand is certainly greater than the supply. However, as Patricia Webb of Age Concern España explains, the situation is improving.

They are certainly building a lot more retirement homes here – it's become something of a boom business. I have taken a few people to have a look around them. They are very pleasant, but it's a big decision to make, especially if you are quite independent. At the moment most retirement homes are intended primarily for Spaniards and it is rare for them to have English-speaking staff. That can be a problem – if an older person doesn't speak Spanish then they can become very lonely.

Those that cater solely for expatriates are extremely few and far between. However, there are a number of retirement complexes on the costas that offer 24-hour medical facilities. Further details of these can be found in the chapter *Your New Home in Spain*.

The vast majority of Spanish retirement homes are privately run and

they are usually expensive. A recent survey by the Spanish website www.
inforesidencias.com found that the cheapest retirement homes cost around
€1,000 per month, and the most expensive (in Cataluña) cost as much
as €2,300. The price also depends on the kind of services on offer. As in
the UK, you can find anything from simple sheltered accommodation,
through to nursing homes with 24-hour care. Those who have been
surviving happily on a UK state pension will find that it is no longer
sufficient and most people are forced to sell their homes in order to pay
the ongoing fees. Of course there will come a point when the proceeds
from the sale of a house runs out, at which point you may find yourself in
trouble. In some areas of Spain, the local authorities will accept foreigners
into their care homes and help to subsidise the costs, but this is far from
universal. Some countries have responded to the problems faced by their
older citizens living in Spain by establishing their own nursing homes,
but the British government does not accept that it has a responsibility to
provide care for citizens resident outside the UK.

Finding a Retirement Home

A full list of public and private retirement homes in Spain can be found by
geographical region at the following web address: **http://www.imsersomayores.
csic.es/senires/mapaprovincias.jsp**
Click on your region and then select *visualizar el listado de los resultados.*

Care in the Home

As Martine de Volder mentions above, home care is available from social
services. Indeed, it is a legal requirement that town councils (in communities
with a population of more than 20,000) provide home-help for those who
are unfit to look after themselves properly. The council sends a carer to
provide assistance with, for example, cooking, cleaning and shopping.
However these services can vary dramatically in quality from one area
to another and often carers can only come in for fifteen minutes a day,
with no services provided in the evenings, at weekends, or during public
holidays. In order to qualify for this kind of assistance, the expatriate must
have a residence card, and also be registered at the local town hall.

Those concerned for their own vulnerability may like to consider the
Red Cross Tele-Alarm system, which is operated in several areas of Spain.

This allows the elderly to be in contact with someone who can help them 24 hours a day. Subscribers wear a button, either on a pendant or wrist band, which if pressed sends a signal down the telephone line to the Control Centre. The centre can see the person's details immediately and ask them the nature of the problem or, if they are unable to speak, contact the emergency services. Subscribers to this potentially life-saving facility pay a one-off installation charge and monthly rental and service charge. Further details can be obtained from *Age Concern España* (www.acespana. org). IMSERSO (*Instituto de Mayores y Servicios Sociales*), the government run agency for pensioners also runs a tele-alarm service (*Teleasistencia Domiciliaria*), that has far greater coverage of the country. However, these services are run only in Spanish. For further details visit http://www.seg-social.es/imserso/mayores/may_tas.html.

Also of interest to the increasingly immobile is the burgeoning availability of the types of mobility aids we are used to in the UK, such as stair and bath lifts, mobility scooters, wheelchairs etc. These are becoming much easier to locate in Spain, especially in areas with a high concentration of expatriates. Prices tend to be much lower than in the UK. One company with a number of shops in Spain is Mobility Abroad (☎01375-377246; www.mobilityabroad.com).

MENTAL HEALTH

Problems with mental well-being can affect anyone during the course of their lives. However, expatriates with high expectations of retirement can find themselves overwhelmed by feelings of isolation once they have moved away from loved ones and their usual support network. Additionally, life-changing events such as bereavement or a marriage break-up are very hard to cope with on your own and may be even harder in an alien environment. Often feelings of isolation or loneliness can be fairly easily countered by finding ways to meet new people and become part of a new community (see below).

However, if the situation becomes more serious, there is no need to despair. Help is available in Spain. In areas where there is a high concentration of expats, you are likely to find English (or at least English-speaking) counsellors that specialise in all kinds of problems, including relationship and bereavement counselling, advertised in the yellow pages and the expatriate press. A list of mental health associations in Spain can be found at www.enusp.org/groups/s/pai.htm.

Avoiding Feelings of Isolation and Loneliness

According to Age Concern España: *'Nobody need be lonely out here. For those who want it, there are plenty of clubs and associations, and there is a huge amount to do. All you have to do is make the first step'.* Below are some suggestions for expanding your social network:

Contact your local expat group. Search the internet for specialist support groups in your area, or just social groups, and arrange to go to a gathering.

Visit your local hogar de pensionistas. Most towns in Spain are well served by a pensioners club, a place for older people to meet and enjoy subsidised club facilities. If you have reached pensionable age, visit your local branch and at the very least find out what activities are available in your area.

Join a Spanish class. If your Spanish is not up to scratch, joining a local class is a great way to make new friends, and improve your chances of integrating into the Spanish community. Ideas for learning Spanish are covered in *Basics.*

Volunteer work. Many of the major UK charities have set up in expat areas, and outside of these areas, the Spanish voluntary sector is strong. Ideas for voluntary work are covered in *Quality of Life.*

Develop a new interest. All sorts of activities are discussed in *Quality of Life.* Find out what goes on locally and think about broadening your horizons.

In extremis remember that you can call the Samaritans from Spain ☎+44 8457-909090.

Depression. Although Spain once had a reputation within the medical profession for not taking mental health issues seriously, over the last twenty years this attitude has been completely overhauled and there are plenty of highly qualified counsellors and psychologists available. Reforms have led to mental health centres being set up across the country and your local GP will be able to refer you to a specialist. The independent Spanish Alliance for Depression (*Alianza para la Depresión*) may be worth contacting if your Spanish is up to it. They organise self-help meetings in various areas of Spain (www.alianzadepresion.com).

Relationship Counselling. Retirement itself is a big adjustment for any relationship, as one expat couple in Javea point out: '*The wife is used to the* *husband going out to work every day, and having her own space. Suddenly he's there getting under her feet all the time, and you get a One Foot in the Grave scenario!'.* These strains on a relationship are compounded by moving abroad, as they go on to explain:

'You find that you are thrown together a lot more – you do a lot more as husband and wife than you would in the UK, especially when you first move here and don't really know anyone else. That can be a problem as you don't always want to do the same things as your partner, and you can't always expect them to want to do the same things as you.'

Usually these minor troubles are surmountable, but real problems can arise if one partner adapts to the new life better than the other, or if one partner always had reservations about the move. Feelings of isolation may turn to resentment and without an outlet, such as a strong social network, the new life could become a catalyst for relationship breakdown.

Again, if you live in an area where there are large numbers of expats, you are likely to find counsellors and therapists that speak English. An alternative is to use *Relate Direct*, a UK telephone counselling service that allows for three way therapy sessions (☎01788-563818).

Alcoholism. Drinking alcohol is an enormous part of the culture in Spain. 52% of the adult population drink regularly and during fiesta time young and old alike will enjoy the local alcoholic speciality. Wine is served with most evening meals and children may drink it (watered down) from a very early age. The Spanish take an enormous amount of pride in their local wines and like to extol the virtues of wine's health properties when drunk in moderation. The Spanish also drink a fair amount of spirits and it is not uncommon to see men enjoying a brandy or anis before lunchtime. Despite all of this, drunkenness is frowned upon in Spain. The Spanish like to drink, but not so much that they lose control, and they are often quite shocked by the binge excesses of tourists on the costas.

Over-indulgence over a two-week period is one thing, but it is not a lifestyle that can be maintained. Unfortunately, there is a well-known tendency for those living an expatriate lifestyle of constant socialising to slide into alcohol dependence. An AA member on the Costa del Sol explains:

One of the biggest problems of the expat lifestyle is alcoholism. Drink is a lot cheaper out here and people drink more because that is a part of what they came here for. It is part of the holiday lifestyle that they expect to have. But holidays can't last for ever and sometimes the drinking becomes a habit. What people need to realise is that there is so much more to life in Spain than sitting in the sunshine and drinking.

Those who think they may have developed a problem should get in touch with Alcoholics Anonymous. In the coastal areas and in the major cities, there are huge numbers of English speaking meetings. To find your nearest one, simply look in the local paper, or on the AA website (see below). The Spanish version of AA is *Alcohólicos Anónimos,* which has 488 branches in Spain, with around 10,000 members.

Contacts for Dealing with Alcohol Dependency	
Alcoholics Anonymous (UK)	☎0845-769 7555;www.alcoholics-anonymous. org.uk. Website lists English-Speaking groups in Spain.
Alcoholics Anonymous (Continental Europe)	www.aa-europe.net.
Alcohólicos Anónimos	☎985-566345; www.alcoholicos-anonimos.org.

Crime, Security and the Police

CHAPTER SUMMARY

○ Crime rates are considerably lower in Spain than in the UK, although they have been steadily rising over the last 30 years. The most likely annoyance is petty street crime, although it is unlikely to be violent.
○ Tourists are the main focus of petty criminals who favour pick-pocketing and thefts from vehicles.
  ○ Petty crimes can be reported via a dedicated telephone number/website.
  ○ Those who live outside the tourist saturated areas will probably enjoy a blissfully crime-free existence.
○ The image and reputation of the Spanish police has improved markedly in the last few decades.
  ○ You are most likely to deal with the *Policía Municipal,* found in every small town.
○ Expatriate developments and *urbanizaciónes* have been a target for burglars in the past as many of the properties are left empty for long periods of time. It pays to be extra vigilant in such areas.
○ These days most *urbanizaciónes* make security a top priority and many have security gates and neighbourhood watches. Some even have their own 24-hour security guards.
○ There are a number of scams that unsuspecting newcomers to Spain should look out for, such as the fake gas inspectors and fraudulent financial advisers.

CRIME

The Spanish have always displayed a great respect for law and order, (whilst at the same time complying only with those minor laws that suit them, especially those relating to noise pollution, parking and driving in general!) Sadly, democracy in Spain has appeared to come hand-in-hand with a crime rate that has been rising steadily over the last thirty years. However, the Spanish figures for car crime and burglary are still significantly lower than Europe's most crime-ridden country in this respect: Britain. The use of firearms in street crime is still uncommon, and sexual assaults are very rare. Obviously the big cities have their dangerous areas, where there is a great deal of street crime, but even in the cities most areas feel safe at night, due to the Spaniards' tendency to stay out late and move in large groups. The only real concern for most people living in Spain is petty crime: pick-pocketing, muggings, scams and other forms of robbery.

One focus for crime is, unsurprisingly, tourism, with much petty theft located along the costas and directed at the thousands of tourists who visit them each year. The varieties of crime indulged in range from purse snatching and car break-ins to theft of property left on the beach to armed burglary. Vehicles are rarely stolen, but their contents, especially if left on display, are a staple target for thieves. A classic form of robbery in Spain is bag-snatching carried out by the passenger of a moving motorbike, or even from a car; so be wary of carrying bags over your shoulder when walking along the road. The problem appears to be getting worse, especially on the coast, as one expat living in Torrevieja noted: *'Most women don't carry handbags in this area now because in the last few years there has been a spate of bag-snatching. It is incredibly frustrating, especially if you are carrying your residencia at the time, which is difficult to replace'.* However, in pleasant contrast to this rather bleak picture, those who live away from the tourist-saturated coastal areas will most probably enjoy a blissfully crime-free existence.

Avoiding Pickpockets and Car Thieves

There is little you can do after the event; and it is best to prevent such traumas by taking sensible precautions.

- The British Foreign Office recommends that whilst travelling in Spain you should keep your passport, credit cards, travel documents and money separately. And you should ensure that you have a good insurance policy. It is better to 'travel light', preferably without a large, inviting-looking hand or carrier bag. These precautions apply equally to residents (thieves do not tend to distinguish between residents and holiday makers).
- Never carry large amounts of cash. Most insurance companies will only pay out up to €100.
- Pickpockets are at their most comfortable in a crowd, so be careful in places like the metro.
- Don't allow yourself to get distracted, many thieves operate in pairs – one of whom gains your attention, whilst the other relieves you of your wallet
- Never leave valuables in your car, especially if you are driving a car with foreign number plates or a hire car.
- Lock your car when paying at petrol stations.
- Make sure your car is fitted with an alarm and/or steering lock.

Reporting a Crime

All persons involved in a crime or accident should report it to the police. This is called making a *denuncia*, and is required by law for all cases, ranging from bag snatching to more serious crimes and incidents. In most towns you should report a crime to the *Policia Municipal*. However, in larger towns you will be directed to the *Policia Nacional*, and in the countryside you may have to report to the *Guardia Civil* (the differences are explained below).

Petty crimes, such as burglary or pickpocketing can be reported by telephone or via the internet. This is a useful alternative to queuing at the police station, although it should only be considered in the cases of burglary and non-violent thefts, where you have no additional information that may be of use to the police. All insurance companies will demand a police report to back up the claim, and this is an easy way to get the ball rolling. Once you have reported the crime you are given a reference number which you should then take to the police station within 72 hours. Because you only have to sign the report, you are able to bypass the queues.

Telephone: ☎902-102112. There are a number of officers on hand who speak English, although you may have to wait for some time until one is available.

Internet: www.policia.es. Crime report forms are available in several languages.

POLICE

Whilst Spain may no longer be as crime-free as it was thirty years ago, the Spanish police have improved markedly. Spain has three different types of police (described below), which may intitially be confusing for the new resident. On top of this, the Basques and Catalans both have their own police forces; a result of the Spanish experiment with devolution in which both these Communities were granted home policing. Those who live on a large urbanización will also come across *vigilancias*, who are essentially private security guards, although they work closely with the local police.

The *Policía Municipal* is the least intimidating and most sympathetic force; and can be found in every small town. These are definitely the people to approach in cases of minor disaster; if you are hopelessly lost; or need to ask the time. They are mainly concerned with minor infractions and disputes between neighbours and can be recognised by their dark blue uniforms with either white or light blue shirts. Each local force deals solely with their area and the quality of service varies enormously from region to region.

The *Guardia Civil* is a 60,000 man force which patrols the rural areas of Spain. They also act as customs officers and frontier guards. The Guardia Civil are less approachable and many people advise that you avoid them unless you have had a road accident, in which case you must report it to them and just grin and bear it. Established in 1844 to combat banditry in the countryside, the Guardia Civil is a predominantly military force which has failed to lose its reputation as a reactionary and somewhat hostile militia, called out to combat riots or strikes as well as more peaceful demonstrations. However, in recent years they have been partially demilitarised and their reputation is slowly improving. These days their role is to protect the rights of civilians, and they are on-hand to tackle the terrorist threat, and tackle the country's growing drug problem. These are the most readily identifiable police force, wearing a green military-style uniform.

The *Policía Nacional*, was much hated for the violence and repression for which it was responsible in the Franco years. However, in what was a largely successful effort to clean up their image, the government renamed and redressed the Policía Nacional in 1978 (they were previously known as the *Policía Armada*). They can be found mounting zealous vigil over embassies, stations, post offices and barracks in most cities. Serious crime, such as theft, rape or mugging should be reported to the nearest Policía Nacional station. The Policía Nacional also devotes resources and manpower to the *policía de proximidad*, who are old-fashioned beat police. They are also responsible for the documentation of foreign residents, such as *residencias*.

Police Telephone Numbers			
EMERGENCY NUMBER ☎112		National Police	☎091
Local Police	☎092	Guardia Civil	☎062

SECURITY

The last thing anyone wants is to leave home for a week or a month only to return to find that their house has been the target of a burglar's grand night out. Apart from buying an adequate insurance policy, fitting quality locks (it may be a good idea to change all the external locks on a property before moving in) and security grills (ironwork bars – *rejas*) over doors and windows (especially on the ground and first floors) and an alarm system, how else can you make sure than your property will remain secure? CCTV, automated gates and a couple of Dobermans may turn your property into a fortress but will also turn it into a potential target for any thieves that may live locally – they will be watching and waiting for when the house is left unoccupied when you and the rest of the family go away on holiday.

While theft from properties in a small village is likely to be rare (everyone will know everyone else's business and it won't be hard to trace the culprits), in some of the areas populated by well-heeled foreigners, as well as in urban and resort areas, theft is likely to be far more of a common occurrence. In such areas of relatively high crime, insurance premiums will also be higher and there will be stipulations in insurance contracts regarding the provision of adequate home security. One of the benefits of buying into an *urbanización* is that security is often regarded as being of a high importance and there are likely to be neighbours milling around at all times as expatriate Sam Jones points out:

A huge number of new urbanizaciónes have been built in recent years. These places have become a target for burglars because very often people only live there for a few months a year, and the houses are left empty. Nevertheless, security is good - many of the urbanizaciónes have security gates and people tend to look out for one another. There are even neighbourhood watches that operate in many of the British areas.

A burglar alarm placed in a prominent position at the front of a house is a very effective deterrent and should be linked to a 24-hour monitoring centre, especially if the property is in an isolated location. Another good deterrent is the installation of external security lights that use sensors to switch themselves on for a timed period if they sense movement.

A determined thief will be able to break into a property whatever deterrents an owner may devise. All you can do is put as many obstacles in his way as possible. Your insurance company will be able to put you in touch with household security experts who will look over your property and advise on the best options. Remember to get at least two different quotes from two independent companies.

SCAMS AND ANNOYANCES

Spain is not without its shady characters and dodgy dealers. Most of the time they will only serve to irritate you, as with the fake watch, fake sunglasses and fake DVD salesmen that swarm around the bars and cafes of the coastal resorts. Any foreigner living on the costas should also be prepared to be pestered by time-share touts on a fairly regular basis, and with a surprising degree of persistence. More alarming however are the downright con-artists who practise their art on unsuspecting foreigners – those who have recently moved to the area and are still coming to grips with the country and its customs. It pays to keep your wits about you, and some of the more common scams are detailed below.

Gas Inspection Scam. A warning from Age Concern España:

Everybody should be on the look out for people claiming to be from the gas company. It is true that all gas fittings must by law be inspected fairly regularly by the gas company. However, if Repsol, or whoever your supplier is, are going to do a safety inspection, then they will first of all send you a letter advising you of their intention, and then make an appointment. Bogus gasmen will always find a fault with your fittings and charge an exorbitant fee to replace them. Either that or they will be casing the place for a future robbery. You should NEVER let anyone into your house on the spur of the moment. Always check with the gas company first.

Car Hire Scam. After hiring a car at the airport you find you have a flat tire after just a few miles. When you stop two or three men appear from nowhere to help you with the repair, and then proceed to relieve you of handbags and suitcases whilst you are distracted. This scam occurs most frequently in Ibiza and the British Embassy in Spain advises all those hiring cars at airports to check the vehicle before driving off. They also urge caution to travellers in cars who are flagged down by individuals claiming there is a problem with the car.

Investment Scams. Spain has its fair share of fraudulent operations (*financieros chiringuitos*) offering investment opportunities with a guaranteed high return, so you should always be on your guard. If you have any suspicions whatsoever about a company, then you should contact the National Securities Market Commission – *Comisión Nacional del Mercado de Valores* (☎902-149200; www.cnmv.es) before parting with any money at all.

Telephone Scams: Moving to Spain does not mean escaping from the irritations of unsolicited telephone calls. Whilst the majority will be trying to sell you something (often in English if you are a resident of the costas), others are more sinister (i.e. claiming you have won something, or asking you to renew an advertisement that you never placed). Treat them with the same caution and contempt that you would in the UK.

Returning Home

CHAPTER SUMMARY

- Retiring to Spain may not be for everybody and many do return home eventually.
- Retiring abroad is not cheap. Many of those who return home do so because they had not fully planned their finances before leaving and have over-spent on their property or renovations.
- When you return to the UK, contact HM Revenue and Customs and request form P86, which allows you to re-enter the UK tax system after time spent abroad.
- Pensioners who have returned to the UK through financial hardship may be able to claim UK benefits such as Pension Credit aimed at pensioners on low incomes.
- If you return to the UK with the intention of taking up permanent residence again, you will be entitled to receive free NHS hospital treatment from the moment you return.
- **Letting your Spanish Property.** You must decide if you want to offer holiday rentals or you are looking for a long-term tenant. Long-term contracts are for a minimum period of five years.
  - It is a legal requirement for those letting out property to holiday-makers to be registered with the tourist authorities who will issue you with a permit.
  - If you have returned to the UK full-time you will be deemed as non-resident for tax purposes and pay 25% on rental income.
- **Selling your Spanish Property.** Make sure that if you paid the *plus valia* tax on the property when you bought it, it is paid by the purchaser when you come to sell.
  - Capital Gains Tax is charged on the profit from the sale of the property. The amount you have to pay depends on how long you have owned the property.

REASONS TO RETURN

When asked under what circumstances they would consider returning to the UK, most of the interviewees for this book looked aghast and gave an answer similar to that of expat Valerie Mash: '*I would NEVER consider going back! This is my home now and I have adapted to this kind of life. I think I would find it very difficult to return – everybody in England is too busy; always rushing around*'. Nevertheless, for a minority of people, life in Spain simply does not work out. Some find that they are beset by unforeseeable problems and others simply find that life in Spain does not match up to their expectations. For some, living in Spain was just a phase of their retirement, and having got it out of their system, they are ready to try new things.

Younger people tend to return because they find it difficult to make a living in Spain, but for the older generation the major factor is a change in personal circumstances, such as the onset of ill health. Not only can this cause financial strain, but it can also make people pine for the familiarity and the people that they have left behind. Some other common reasons for return are discussed below.

False Expectations. Many people rush into retirement abroad, without having fully considered all of the implications. Having enjoyed a memorable holiday in Spain with wonderful food, scenery and weather, they suddenly decide that they would like to live like that permanently. Sadly it is fairly difficult to live the holiday lifestyle on a permanent basis, as expats Mac and Meryl Macdonald describe:

> *When we have visitors they often complain that we don't want to go out for meals, and to visit bars every night. Because they are on holiday, that is what they expect, but living here full time is really quite different. When you're working full-time, you really need the rest and relaxation that a holiday provides, but you soon get tired of that if it becomes your life. People who don't find new interests here often find that they are floundering to find a shape to their weeks.*

Others convince themselves that moving abroad will be a universal panacea for all of the worries and problems that they faced at home. If your expectations of the new life are too high, then you cannot fail to be disap pointed. Once the honeymoon period is over and the rose-tinted spectacles start to slip, many find that the vision does not match up to the reality and they start to romanticise the things they miss about the UK.

Lack of Preparation. Before moving to Spain you should fully research what the day-to-day reality of retiring to Spain will entail. Without sufficient preparation the practicalities of retiring to Spain could come as something of a shock, as Patricia Webb of Age Concern España explains:

> *People get the idea into their heads that everything is going to be wonderful here, and they tend not to prepare themselves at all. I am always surprised to find that even those who have had a holiday apartment here for years have made little effort to find out what they have to do to move permanently.*

Missing Family and Friends. Although advances such as the budget flight revolution, e-mails, text messages, and internet telephone calls have made the world an even smaller place, many still find that they can become isolated in their new life. The pull of family ties, especially when there are problems at home, or when grandchildren come onto the scene, can be immense. Some never fully adapt to their new way of life, or never feel part of the community in the same way that they had in the UK. Often the language barrier can be insurmountable and only serves to exacerbate feelings of isolation. These feelings tend to come to the fore during times of minor crisis. Dealing with an accident, a theft, or even a small financial problem can be extremely uncomfortable in an unfamiliar environment, without the support of loved ones.

Financial Pressures. Retiring abroad is not cheap: property purchase, renovations, transporting personal effects, buying a car, trips back and forth to the UK etc. mean that the initial stages of retirement can be very costly. Many expats get caught up in the excitement of their new life and fail to make sufficient financial provisions. It is essential to have planned your finances extremely carefully and to have an emergency budget to cover any unexpected crises that may arise.

Bereavement. Expats who suffer bereavement of a partner make up a large proportion of those who return to the UK. Age Concern España explain:

If one partner dies, then the other faces a difficult decision about what to do. Quite often if it's just the woman left, then she will decide to return home, but it really depends. If they have a made a good life for themselves here, then there is no need for them to become isolated, and they decide to stay. I always advise people not to do anything in a hurry, but to sit tight for six months to a year and see how it works out.

However, the death of a partner can considerably reduce the income, and on top of this the remaining partner may be faced with a transfer tax bill in order to transfer the deceased's half of the home into their name. Braving it out on your own is not an option available to everybody.

TAX, SOCIAL SECURITY AND HEALTHCARE

Whatever your reasons for moving back to the UK, there will be practical and financial implications. Before you return to the UK you should go through all of your financial affairs including bank accounts, pension schemes and other income and consider the effect the return to the UK will have on your financial situation.

Tax Considerations

It pays to be very careful regarding your taxation position when returning to the UK. It is just possible, for example, that you may be forced to pay tax arrears for the time that you were out of the country. This can happen If you return within three years of your departure from the UK, and in the eyes of HM Revenue & Customs (the new name of the Inland Revenue, which merged with HM Customs in 2005), you have only had provisional non-residential status. Check with a financial adviser before returning home to ensure that you are not liable for any unexpected taxes.

You should also ensure that your Spanish taxation affairs are in order before you leave. It may be wise to appoint a fiscal representative who will assume responsibility for any final payments that are due. Once you have sold your Spanish property, for example, you will be liable for Spanish capital gains tax on any profit.

When you arrive back in the UK you should request HM Revenue and Customs/Inland Revenue form P86 or download it from their website (www.

hmrc.gov.uk). After you have completed the tax form you should return it to the local tax office (consult HMRC if you do not know which this is).

Pensions and Social Security

It is sensible to contact the Department of Work and Pensions (www.dwp.gov.uk) well in advance of your arrival back in the UK in order to switch payment of your pension to a UK bank account. Follow up any telephone calls to the DWP with written confirmation.

Pensioners on low incomes and with limited savings may qualify for income-related state financial assistance on their return to the UK. Benefits include Pension Credit (towards weekly income) and Housing Benefit (help towards rent). You can enquire about these from the DWP on your return. They are not usually payable outside the UK.

Useful Contacts for Pensioners	
Benefit Enquiries	☎0800 88 22 00
Age Concern	www.ageconcern.org.uk
Pension Assessment	☎0845 3000 168
Pension Credits	☎0800 99 1234
NHS Direct	☎0845 4647 (www.nhsdirect.nhs.uk)
Winter Fuel Payments	☎08459 15 15 15 (www.thepensionservice.gov.uk/winterfuel)

Healthcare

According to *Age Concern España*: '*Ill health is one of the main reasons for people getting into terrible difficulties and having to return home*'. Worsening health combined with financial pressures can make it difficult for retirees to cope in a foreign environment. There is also the fact that as the health of one partner worsens, the other one often finds the strain easier to handle by returning to where there is a family support network. As health worsens, there may also be a wish to see the UK again.

As mentioned in the *Healthcare* chapter, those who are resident in Spain cannot return to the UK simply to receive treatment. However, if you return to the UK with the intention of taking up permanent residence again, you will be entitled to receive free NHS hospital treatment from the moment you return. According to the Department of Health, you should expect to be asked to prove your intention to remain in the UK permanently. You may need to furnish the hospital with evidence, such as documents showing the sale of property overseas etc.

Once resident again in the UK you should register with your nearest GP or health centre and you will be issued with a new medical card. If you can remember your old NHS number, this process is much quicker.

Healthcare Useful Contacts

Care Homes	www.nursing-home-directory.co.uk (by areas)
Retirement Homes	www.bettercaring.co.uk
NHS Direct	☎0845 4647 (www.nhsdirect.nhs.uk)

LETTING YOUR SPANISH PROPERTY

Holiday Lets. Rental returns on short-term holiday lets are high and this kind of contract is probably the best option if you wish to continue using the property as a holiday home. However, it may also mean that during the low season your property will remain empty and you are receiving no income from it. Short-term lets also require a lot of management time as tenants may be coming and going every week or fortnight, especially during the high season. Many foreign property owners employ the services of a property management company to take care of these complications.

Long-term Lets. Long-term rentals are really only a good idea if you do not intend to make personal use of your property. Think very carefully before going into long-term lets and seek legal advice before committing yourself. Ready-printed rental contracts can be bought from tobacconists (*estancos*). Make sure you understand all the clauses in the rental agreement, have the contract checked by a lawyer, and ensure that you are totally happy with any contract you sign with a tenant. Any contract should state who is responsible for the payment of rates, the property tax (IBI) and community charges (imposed by the *comunidad de propietarios*). Usual practice is for the landlord to pay the rates and for the tenant to pay the community charges. Long-term tenants should pay utility bills.

Long-term rentals, regardless of what the contract may state, are for a minimum period of five years. Tenants are expected to pay the rent on time, maintain the property in a good state of repair and may not sublet the property without the permission of the landlord or use the premises for immoral purposes. Failure to fulfil any of these obligations can lead to eviction. As a landlord you will have the right to inspect the property at any time providing you inform the tenant in good time of your proposed visit. The landlord is obliged to carry out any necessary repair work and general maintenance to the property, and replace any fixtures and fittings that have broken or worn out through general wear and tear.

Holiday Vs. Long-Term Lets		
	Advantages	Disadvantages
Short-term (holiday) rentals	Rental returns are up to four times higher than for long-term lets.	Require far more management – tenants come and go every week.
	Your property can be available for personal use during the year – saving on your holiday costs.	Wear and tear on the property will be greater as holidaymakers tend to take less care of the property.
	It is far less difficult to evict problematic tenants.	You may have trouble renting your property in the low season.
	Rent can be altered to reflect demand and income can be maximised at peak periods.	You will probably need to rely on a property management company who may charge a commission of 15%-35%.
Long-term rentals	Rental income is guaranteed throughout the year, not just at peak periods. However, rent will not be as high as for holiday lets.	Long term tenants have far more rights. They cannot be evicted for 5 years, can annul any proposed sale of the property and have the right to pass the tenancy on to their spouse or child.
	You may not require a property management company as far less upkeep will be required.	Evicting tenants can be costly and can involve lengthy legal wrangling.

Taxes and Legal Requirements

It is perfectly legal for owners of private houses, villas or flats to rent out their property without paying any advance taxes or making any business declarations. However, it is a legal requirement for those letting out property on short-term lets to be registered with the tourist authorities. Subject to the property being deemed suitable for letting by the tourist authorities you will be issued with a permit. Although many owners are not registered there are fines imposed for non-registration.

> **Holiday Lets can be Subject to the Whims of Local Bureaucrats**
>
> Before deciding to go down the holiday let route, you should check what the local regulations are. In the Ciutat Vella (Old Town) of Barcelona for example, the local authorities have restricted the number of licences available and closed all new applications. Draconian measures have also been put in place for those who continue to let their unregistered apartment.

It is also vitally important that you register for tax. There is an enormous amount of black market rental accommodation available in Spain. Indeed, a recent investigation discovered that up to 80% of the 400,000 beds on the Costa del Sol were unregistered for income tax. However, in June 2005, Madrid announced new legislation to crack down on the unregulated rental of holiday apartments. Last year alone, inspectors recovered £600 million by cross-referencing 45,000 properties advertised on the internet with local tax records, and then swooping on individuals and agencies along the costas. Property owners are threatened with seizure of their houses if the back taxes are not paid in full.

Those who have returned to the UK full-time will be classed as non-resident and are liable for income tax at the rate of 25% from the very first euro of rental income. It is advisable to keep records of all income generated through renting.

VAT (at 16%) for short-term lets will have to be paid on earnings from rental. Those offering holiday lets should register at the tax office for VAT before beginning operations.

For more information about tax matters you can contact one of the Spanish consulates or the local tax office (*hacienda*) when in Spain. You can also write to the *Ministerio de Hacienda* about tax matters (c/ Alcalá 9, 28014 Madrid; ☎901-335533); or to the *Direccion General de Tributos* (c/ Alcalá 5, 28014 Madrid; ☎915-221000).

SELLING YOUR SPANISH PROPERTY

There is a thriving market for resale properties in Spain and the procedure is quite simple. It may be carried out privately or by engaging the services of a registered property agent who deals with all matters including advertising the property, accompanying prospective buyers and dealing with the legal technicalities of the sale (contracts, signing before the notary, paying necessary taxes on the property etc.). This ensures the smooth progress of the sale and relieves the client of much of the usual worry and concern relating to the sale of a property. As was the case when you bought the property, the vendor (you in this case) does not necessarily need to hire a lawyer, though the purchaser should. Make sure that if you have paid the *plus valia* tax on the property when you bought it, it is paid by the purchaser when you come to sell, otherwise you will have paid the tax twice.

> Note that Capital Gains Tax is charged on the profit from the sale of property and depending on how long you have owned a property before selling on, this tax could be as high as 35% for non-residents and 15% for residents, though there are exceptions to the rules. It is better to hang on to a property as Capital Gains Tax lessens the longer you own a property, and your property should increase in value the longer you own it. If you can afford to, it is often better to hold on to property and rent it out, rather than go for a quick sale.

You can advertise your property for sale through several estate agencies, and negotiate your own contract with them individually – commission rates charged vary, but according to Mark Stucklin of www.spanishpropertyinsight.com vendors should refuse to deal with any agency that charges more than 5%: '*There are well-run, professional, mid-sized and small agencies that charge 5% or less*'. If you bought the property though local estate agents it could be useful to ask them to deal with the vending process.

> Alternatively, it is possible to cut out the middle-man by placing *Se Vende* (for sale) signs on balconies or in the classified ads. The internet is another alternative. Vender Direct (www.venderdirect.com) allows sellers to advertise properties directly to buyers at a flat rate (starting at £137).

There are a number of documents that you will need to gather together when it comes to selling on your property. These are:

o The *escritura*: You will have received a copy of the title deeds to your property after the original was filed with the *Registro de la Propiedad* (the property registry office) by the notary when you originally bought the property. This details any charges, mortgages etc. that there are listed as being against the property.

o Receipt of payment of the *Impuesto sobre Bienes Inmeubles – IBI*: This indicates that the real estate tax has been paid on the property to date and that the property is registered with the local authorities for taxes. The IBI receipt will also show the *valor catastral* – the value of the property as assessed by the local authorities (though this may well be lower than the market rate).

o The *Referencia Catastral*: This is the file number of the property as kept by the *Catastro* (Land Registry). The Catastro has a record of the physical characteristics of the property – boundaries, size of plot, out-houses, pools, etc.

o Copies of all utility bills – preferably going back over a period of five years to give the purchaser an idea of what to expect bills-wise.

o Copies of community charges imposed by the *comunidad*, should your property be part of an *urbanización* or apartment block.

o Copies of the transfer tax, stamp duty and *plus valia* tax that you paid on the property when you originally bought it.

o Declaration of income tax: Depending on whether you are resident or non-resident in Spain your tax liabilities through the sale of property will differ. If you are a non-resident the purchaser will retain a 5% tax deposit from the purchase price and pay it on your behalf to the tax authorities. If you are a resident you will want to make sure that your tax status is known by the notary and purchaser.

ARRIVAL BACK IN THE UK

Moving back to familiar shores should be fairly simple. However, moving anywhere can be fairly traumatic, especially if you have been forced into the move and feel that you may miss the sunshine and relaxed lifestyle of previous years. It will certainly feel unsettling for the first few months as you re-adapt to the life you once knew so well. Below is a list of tasks that will help to ease the transition:

- Visit your financial adviser in order to keep up-to-date with your changing tax liabilities.
- Contact HMRC for a P86 form, or download it from their website, in order to reinstate yourself into the UK tax system.
- Keep proper financial records from the time you arrive back in the UK. These will be essential for your self-assessment tax form.
- Open a UK bank account (if you haven't kept one open) so that you have access to funds for daily expenses, without paying unnecessary charges.
- Review all of your insurance policies.
- Alter your will to reflect the fact that you are back in the UK.
- Contact the Department of Work and Pensions (if you have not done so in advance) to ensure that your pension payments are not interrupted and are sent to the correct place.
- Register with your local GP so that you are able to use the NHS free of charge.

Case Histories

IAN ADAMS

Ian had worked as a mechanic in Surrey ever since leaving school and when he reached his forties decided it was time to re-evaluate his priorities. He now lives on Spain's Costa del Azahar, where he divides his time between tinkering with cars and boats, restoring his idyllic villa amongst the orange groves and walking in the surrounding hills. As he argues: *'I know that I will never get rich out here, but the rewards are in the actual quality of life'.* We asked him:

You are only 44. That's very early to retire isn't it?
I retired early because I was fed up with the rat race. I just got tired of worrying about overheads, and dealing with whinging customers. I could quite easily have come out here to become a mechanic – there's actually a big call for it. But I'm in a position where I don't really need to.

It takes a while to adapt to not working. I did no work at all for the first year, and at the end of it I was really bored. Then somebody asked me to work on their car and I found that I actually enjoyed it! When I was in the UK, I had been working 70 hours a week and I was so burnt out that I said I'd never touch a car again. Having had a bit of a rest though I can take pleasure in it. I've remembered that it's what I do best, and I am not doing it because I have to, but for pleasure, which makes a huge difference. I still do some work for friends and acquaintances but I certainly have no intention of going back to full time work. I repaired a boat yesterday and the guy wants to pay me to go and race it! So you just think, well if I can make money messing about on the Mediterranean, why on earth would I go back and stick my head under a bonnet for 6 or 7 days a week in the rain.

Have you completely cut your ties with the UK?
I've still got a house in England, but its not home anymore. It's a business. I rent it out and that helps to keep us out here as it gives us a monthly

income. We have a letting agent that deals with it and they take a commission but pay me the rent and deal with all the hassles.

Most people do sell up in the UK, but I would recommend that you should hang on to your UK property if you can afford to. There are a number of reasons for this. Firstly, in the last four years that we have hung on to our property it has shot up in value by 30%. Secondly, it gives us security. If anything did go wrong over here, I would still have a property to return to or sell. The people that we know who have returned to the UK are struggling because their money is tied up in Spain and they can't release it. They are finding it very difficult to get back into the housing market in the UK.

And thirdly the UK property should keep giving me a pension when I get old and grey because, the way things are going, I don't think there's going to be a state pension for me by the time I get to 65.

How did you decide where in Spain to live?
We used the internet to research where we wanted to be while we were in the UK but there is no substitute for experience, so we came out here and spent 17 weeks in a caravan looking for the right place to settle. We started off in Barcelona and gradually worked our way down the coast, ending up at Gibraltar. We settled here in Oliva because it seemed more real. Although it's nice to have some English people around you, we like to involve ourselves in Spanish culture as much as we can, which is something that's just not possible in places like Malaga, which are overrun with Brits.

How difficult was it to set up home?
We got a British estate agent, but I really wouldn't advise it. If we did it again we would find a Spanish agent. as you tend not to get ripped off, especially if you have a good interpreter, or someone with a lot of local knowledge. Having been out here a while now, we know people that you can trust and that are well-respected, so it is really better to go through an agent that you get via recommendation. Then you know that you are getting what you pay for.

I would also advise people to get a completely independent lawyer. If your lawyer is recommended by the estate agent, then they could well be on a back-hander and you simply don't know who to trust.

I bought our property cheap and I have done a lot of renovation to the place. You do have to have a great deal of knowledge to do the renovations yourself – Spanish materials are very different from British materials, but I have the time and also I am suspicious of tradesmen here. British tradesmen will try to charge British prices, and Spanish tradesmen, when they realise you are British, will assume you have money and will put the price up accordingly.

I have done most of the work myself. I've learnt how to lay bricks, plaster, do the electrics and the plumbing. It's all fairly straightforward and building materials are so cheap here. We basically knocked all of the internal walls out and started again. We've restructured the inside, built an extension, put a covered terrace out the back, put in another bathroom, another laundry room and a barbecue area. It has been a very satisfying experience.

How well have you settled into your new surroundings?
Very well. We specifically chose to immerse ourselves in Spanish culture and I think the locals are starting to accept us. What I find really lovely now is that when I'm driving down the road lots of Spanish people wave to me because I know them, and I really feel like a part of the community. Recently we got invited to the Moors and Christians celebratory evening. There were 2000 people celebrating in the town, and in the party in our street we were the only two Brits out of about 300 people. Because we try to speak the language they have accepted us. A lot of British people miss out because they don't try to integrate, they don't learn the language or eat Spanish food. But we like to spend our time exploring little out-of-the-way places. Once you get off the beaten track, only then can you start to see the real attraction of Spain.

VALERIE MASH

Valerie's love affair with Spain began when she was just thirteen years old, and at that time she made herself a promise that she would one day live there. It finally happened four years ago when her daughter volunteered to take over the family business. Valerie jumped at the opportunity to retire early and pursue a life-long dream. As she puts it *'I finally felt that I was able to get on with my life'*.

So why Spain?
It all started when I came on holiday here as a child. I went to San Antonio in Ibiza, which at that time was just a little fishing village with 2 hotels and I just fell in love with it. Forever more I thought, when I get a bit more

mature there's no way I will live in England with the cold weather. I will spend my old age out in the sun.

I adore absolutely everything about Spain. I love the weather, the food, the people, the way of life, the fiestas, I just love waking up to a blue sky every morning!

How did you decide where in Spain to live?

I have always lived near the sea and I love swimming, so that was a major consideration for moving to the coast. I have had another property on the Costa del Sol for the last 20 years, but over the years it has got less like Spain down there – it's very touristy and I knew I did not want to move there. I wanted something more tranquil.

For many years I searched for the right area, then one day when I was doing some research in the library, I found two sentences in a book which made up my mind – *'Oliva is one of Spain's best kept secrets known only by Madrileños who visit the area for their holidays. It is a very wealthy area, so it doesn't need any more tourism'.* That was enough for me. I phoned up immediately. There were 2 hotels here then and in neither of them did they speak any English. In a hotel on the costa! So I got on a plane and when I arrived I fell in love with it straight away.

Was it difficult to leave your family behind?

Family is very important to me and I didn't contemplate the move while my mother was still alive. I certainly would not have left her alone in her old age. I still have family at home including my daughter and two grandchildren, but it is not difficult to see them, and I am always on the phone to them. I actually see my brother more often now. When I was in the UK I was in business and very busy all the time, but now he comes over here four or five times a year.

How is your retirement in Spain different to how it might have been in the UK?

One of the main differences here is that I am always outside. If I were in the UK I'd probably be sitting around freezing to death, but here I spend many pleasurable hours on my roof terrace in the sun, blissfully happy. I am delighted not to be stuck indoors. I never watch television – in fact I threw my aerial away the first day I moved here. I swim in the sea, I walk in the mountains and I visit the many new friends I have made here.

Also, my diet is far more healthy here and I feel so much better. I have always loved Spanish cuisine, and I love cooking, so I am really in my seventh heaven here. I get all of my ingredients from the market, it's just so fresh and it tastes wonderful. Living on the coast I eat lots of fresh fish, often cooked outside on the barbecue, and served with a glass of wine.

Another change is that I have abandoned my car now. I simply walk everywhere because it's difficult to park and walking is good for you and much more pleasant. If I am going further afield then I always take the train because public transport is very good here. I've also just got a special pensioner's card that gets me a reduction on the trains – it's great!

MAC AND MERYL MACDONALD

Before moving to Spain, Mac and Meryl Macdonald ran their own business in Norwich organising working holidays for foreign students. At the age of 53, they decided that it was time to put themselves first and head for the sun. They passed the business on to their children and now spend most of the year at their villa just outside Javea. We asked them:

Why did you decide to retire early and move to Spain?
Mac: I retired early because I thought it was time for me to get out. I had worked pretty hard for most of my life and I thought – *'Right. Time to enjoy myself now.'* It had always been our dream to live somewhere warmer than England and to enjoy our lives while we've still got the energy to do it.
Meryl: We chose Spain because we wanted to be somewhere warmer and because we have children and grandchildren in the UK. We wanted to be close enough that we can go home fairly regularly to see them. We thought about Australia and Italy, but it was the convenience of flights from Spain that swung it. We can get flights directly to Norwich.

It was quite a bold move, were you worried that you would come to regret your decision?
Mac: I think we have the best of both worlds because we retained our house in England, so we still have a base, and all of our friends there, so we haven't really given up a lot. We thought that if we sold up completely and then in five years time found that we didn't like it here, it would be

far more difficult to reassemble our lives in the UK and get back into the housing market. So we've kept the option open; a foot in both camps, at least while we can financially. The day will come when we have to make a permanent decision.

Did it take you long to settle into your new life in Spain?
Mac: The first year we just took our holidays out here, while we were tying up loose ends in the UK, and helping the kids with the business. But as soon as that was all done, we moved out here permanently. We do go home occasionally. Every year that we are here, the time that we spend in the UK is shrinking.
Meryl: It has been fairly easy to settle in because we chose to live in Javea at least partly for the reason that there is a large expatriate community, which makes it easy to meet people. It was never our intention to completely immerse ourselves in a different culture, if we had wanted that then we would have moved inland. Having said that, I have thrown myself into learning the language.

How is your Spanish coming along?
Meryl: I started learning Spanish before I left the UK, and I have continued it here. When we first arrived I joined a school in Javea and it was a great way to meet new people, but I have since changed to one-on-one classes and that has really spurred me on.

I suppose one of the downsides of living within such a large expat community is that it is actually quite rare that you are able to use your Spanish. Most people speak English, and then living in this area, there is also Valenciano to contend with. We recently had a lawyer from Madrid staying with us to improve her English – a real live Spanish person – but we had to import her from Madrid! So we still feel very much like foreigners to the Spanish and it is quite hard to integrate.

What effect has living in Spain had on your quality of life?
Meryl: There are so many things that we are able to do here that we couldn't have done in the UK. We always liked to eat out in the garden in England, but with the British summer, you only get about a dozen days a year when you can do that. Here we are able to eat outside right through to December. The weather also affects other things. For example, we

both love to play sport – I play tennis and Mac plays golf and in England games are often rained off.

Mac: We are also able to spend quite a lot of time travelling around visiting new bits of Spain. We recently went away to Xativa – it was a recommendation from friends and there is a wonderful castle on the mountain. We have also done some golfing weekends in various parts of the country.

Meryl: Many people think that living here full-time is like being on permanent holiday, but it is really quite different. I think you need a purpose. When you come out on holiday, it's a chill-out time to do nothing, sunbathe, read and go out every night. When you're working you need that rest and relaxation time. But when you are living here, you're running a home and running your life, which is quite different.

Is there anything you miss about living in the UK?

Mac: No, not really. I sometimes miss things like going to the pub with my mates, but the pros of living here far outweigh the cons.

Meryl: It is also very easy to keep up with developments back home. We have broadband internet, and satellite TV with 7 or 8 news channels, so we probably know more about what's going on than most people at home! We catch up with family news via phone, text messages and e-mail. We have also just set up a web-cam so that when we talk to people on MSN Messenger we can actually see them as well. And there's no cost! Modern technology really does mean that you are never too far away from people.

What advice would you give to people who hope to follow in your footsteps?

I think the most important piece of advice would be that people sort out what their criteria are for their new life. If you move somewhere inland, you will of course find cheaper property, but you may also find yourself ferrying in and out because there is so much going on in the coastal towns. We bullet-pointed about 10 priorities and very quickly realised that we would have to compromise on some of them. We wanted to buy a place where we could walk into town to buy a newspaper and have a coffee, but here we always have to drive. On the other hand, if we had bought a townhouse then we wouldn't have any of the privacy and tranquillity that we have here.

DAVID AND LIZ AUSTEN

David and Liz Austen have lived in Spain for the past four years. They have made the popular resort of Playa Miramar on the Costa del Azahar their home, and although it gets very busy in the summer, they have found that for nine months of the year they virtually have the place to themselves. They advise that anyone thinking of retiring to Spain should simply go for it as, after all, *'life is what you make it'*. We asked them:

What spurred you on to retire early and move to Spain?
I had been working as a lift engineer in the West End for 24 years, and I'd had enough of the rat race in London and of the commute from Kent every day. So when I had the opportunity to retire early, I took it. The company decided that they wanted to get rid of a few of the engineers and I was just waiting for the opportunity really. I did very well with the redundancy and the pension as well, so financially it wasn't a problem. We had an old cottage in Kent but it had become too big for us since our two daughters had flown the nest. It all just made sense.

How long did it take to move your life from the UK to Spain?
We didn't want to burn our bridges straightaway so we put our cottage on the market and bought an apartment down in Eastbourne where Liz's mum lives and lived there for 2 or 3 months. Then we came out to Spain and found an apartment and that was it. We have been in Spain ever since. We eventually sold the apartment in Eastbourne, rather than have the worry of renting it out. We also sold the apartment here in Spain and with the proceeds we were able to buy a villa as a more permanent home.

Why didn't you buy the villa straightaway?
We thought it would be a good idea to have a look around first and see if we liked living in Spain. We lived here for a year before we bought the villa and we still had the apartment in Eastbourne, so that if anything went wrong, we had the option to return to England.

We found an area that we really liked and waited for the right property to become available. You have to know what you are looking for and be in the right place at the right time, especially if you are looking for something in a popular location.

Has the lifestyle in Spain met up to your expectations?
Life is what you make it out here. A lot of people said that we would be bored, but in fact, the opposite is true. There is so much going on if you want to join in. And we like the beach as well. We joined a social club for expats as soon as we arrived and have used that as a base to meet people and find out what the area has to offer. We have found that it's the best way to make friends. Our club offers a lot of activities including organised walks, petanca, social evenings, outings and practical help if you need it. We have also adopted a little Spanish dog who keeps us fit walking him along the beach every day.

We have met a lot of Spanish people on the urbanización where we live. Every Monday Liz visits the local doctor's wife for conversational Spanish. The doctor's wife is learning English so it's a sort of exchange. Liz also attends lessons twice a week, but it's not easy learning a foreign language at our age.

We enjoy travelling around Spain during the winter months when it's not too hot and take the opportunity to explore all that the country has to offer. So we are very busy and life here brings new adventures every day.

ANDREW AND MARGARET SLEPYAN

The Slepyans retired and moved to Spain when they were just 45 years old, but as they put it 'We didn't see it so much as retirement, more a decision to spend more time doing the things that we wanted to do'. Fed up with a hectic working life in the UK, leaving the house at 7am and not getting home until late in the evening, they took the sensible decision to place quality of life at the head of their priorities. They bought a holiday home in Spain six years ago with the intention of one day moving their lives there permanently. That day came sooner than they had expected and within a year and a half they had settled in the Valencia region of Spain. We asked them:

So, why Spain?
We had become a bit disillusioned with England. We are both outside sort of people and we were noticing that the barbecue was getting very rusty, so it seemed more sensible to live in a climate that suited the way we wanted to live.

We liked the idea of living in Spain. When we came out here it was still fairly basic and that was a great relief from living in England where there's too much traffic and you're working all the time. We also came out here for the *vino,* for the food, for the sun and the standard of life.

The economic climate here also played a part. Because of the difference in living costs, we worked out that we could sell the UK house, buy something here and have enough money left over to live off. We don't have any children which has made it easier for us to make decisions that perhaps other people wouldn't have made – we are more financially secure and we don't need to provide stability, so we've been able to take risks.

What made you decide to retire at such a young age?
Before we came out we had been working in IT for about 10 years. We had gone through all sorts of career changes, but for the most part we were fairly self-employed. When we moved to Spain we actually started a computer business in our village and ran that for 2 or 3 years – but we looked upon that as part of our retirement, even though we were actually working quite hard. We have since sold it on and we are now fully retired. We have actually found it quite difficult to adapt to not doing anything. When we had the shop we were always very busy and stressed – so when we gave it up I felt like I'd been abandoned!

It is quite possible that at some point we will go back into work, we are only in our late 40s now, so we're comparatively young. Margaret is always looking for the right job, but I'm a little bit more laid back about it. We have another house here that we rent out and there is plenty to do between the two houses. Being retired there is still a lot to do, and I never feel that I have a lot of time to sit and do nothing. You organise your life around being retired, so you walk down into town every day to get your exercise and your Spanish practice – it all takes up time.

How are you getting on with the language?
Spanish culture is important to us and we are trying very hard to learn the language. We always make a point of talking to the locals and trying to immerse ourselves in the Spanish way of life. We are getting there, slowly. In another 20 or 30 years we should have it sussed!

Do you intend to stay in Spain?
I can categorically say that I can't ever see us moving back to England. We don't miss England at all, but we might not necessarily stay where we are.

We came here for the Spanish culture, but we didn't really realise the sort of culture we were buying into on the coast. It has worked out well. If we had gone straight to the interior, we'd have been completely lost; we wouldn't have known the language or understood anything. Now, although we still like it here, we are looking for more of the real culture of Spain, so we are looking for something away from the coast. The costas have been a stepping stone for us. It will mean moving down in price again, which is what we did when we came from England, so that will be helpful.

RAYMOND FLETCHER

In the UK, Ray worked in the CD distribution business in Cornwall. At the age of 61 he decided it was time to pack it in, and having parted ways with his partner came to the conclusion that it was time for a complete life change. He decided on Spain because he had friends there and had visited the country on numerous holidays. Now, 10 years on, he maintains that it is the best decision he ever made. We asked him:

How has living in Spain improved your quality of life?
Most people move out to Spain for the weather, but I think that it is what the weather enables you to do that is the most important thing. In the UK it's impossible to plan anything in advance because even in August it can be ruined by the weather. Here my plans are hardly ever rained off.

One of my greatest passions is walking, and here in Spain I am able to indulge that passion to my heart's delight. When I first moved to Spain I joined a group in Benidorm that went on long walks twice a week. It was a fantastic way of meeting people. Walking is a very social hobby, and we would always go out for a meal and a few drinks afterwards.

So when I moved up the coast to Gandia I joined another group and again found it to be a great way to make friends. As long as you have an interest like walking there are plenty of like-minded Brits to share that interest with. We walk twice a week. On Wednesdays there is a large group of about 30-40 people, and we do a short walk of around 10 km. Then on Saturdays I take a much smaller group on a longer, harder walk and we decide the route amongst ourselves. There are some really great walks around here and the views are fantastic.

Moving to Spain was a big financial commitment. Have you been able to survive comfortably on your retired income?

The cost of living in Spain is certainly much lower, although it's nothing like it was ten years ago. I have been quite fortunate with the property boom that Spain has been experiencing in recent years. I initially bought a property close to Benidorm but after only a few years, property prices in that area had rocketed and I decided to cash in. I sold my apartment there and moved further up towards Gandia where prices were much cheaper. I was able to find something at half the price, which gave me a bit more money to live off, and now of course, prices here are starting to catch up.

I also still keep my hand in with a bit of work. Every Sunday I go down to the market in Pedreguer and sell CDs on a stall. It's an interest and it brings in a little bit of extra cash. I have my UK pension paid into a UK account and about once a year I go back and buy up a whole load of stock with that money. Then when I am over here I can live off the money that I make at the market, so I avoid losing money through exchange rates and through the charges on bank transfers.

Do you have any advice for people who are thinking about retiring to Spain?

I think my advice would be, rather than to jump in with both feet, to rent somewhere for a year and have a look around to make sure that you have got the right place, that you like the area and that you are going to enjoy it. A minority of people do end up going back to the UK because they miss their families or their home, but I think that can be avoided with a bit of research and a trial period.

Do you ever miss the UK, or think that you might have made a mistake leaving that life behind?

I have absolutely no regrets about having left the UK. In fact, I've said it many times: this is the only good decision I've ever made in my life. Every major step in my life I've usually taken the wrong route, but this is definitely the right one, and I hope to continue enjoying it for many more years.